SECRETS OF THE HIMALAYAN MOUNTAIN MASTERS AND LADDER TO COSMIC CONSCIOUSNESS

(1927)

Yogi Wassan

ISBN 0-7661-0135-5

Kessinger Publishing's Rare Reprints
Thousands of Scarce and Hard-to-Find Books!

We kindly invite you to view our extensive catalog list at:
http://www.kessinger.net

Secrets of the Himalaya Mountain Masters and Ladder to Cosmic Consciousness

By YOGI WASSAN

PUNJAB, INDIA

Copyrighted 1927 by Yogi Wassan
All rights reserved

*Dedicated
to my
Parents and Relatives*

PHOTO OF YOGI WASSAN, 1926

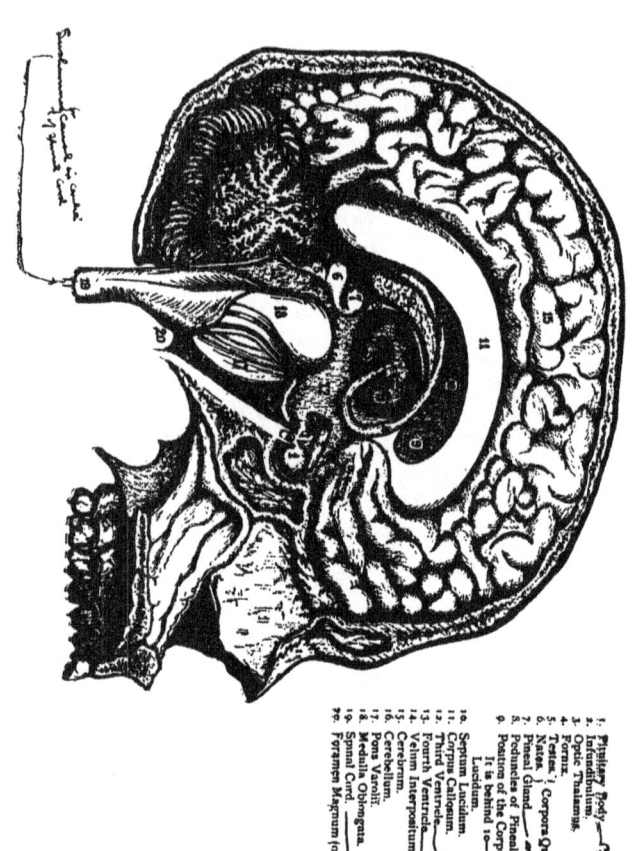

1. Pituitary Body.
2. Infundibulum.
3. Optic Thalamus.
4. Fornix.
5. Testes. } Corpora Quadrigemina.
6. Nates. }
7. Pineal Gland.
8. Peduncles of Pineal Gland.
9. Position of the Corpus Striatum. It is behind 10—the Septum Lucidum.
10. Septum Lucidum.
11. Corpus Callosum.
12. Third Ventricle.
13. Fourth Ventricle.
14. Velum Interpositum.
15. Cerebrum.
16. Cerebellum.
17. Pons Varolii.
18. Medulla Oblongata.
19. Spinal Cord.
20. Foramen Magnum (of the Skull).

CHART OF THE "HOLY MOUNTAIN"

"Universal Brain," "Mysterious Kundalini," "Spiritual Lake," "Holy Water," "Sea of Soul" and "Round Eye." Pineal Gland and Pituitary Body "Kala Kundalini," "Kala Chakra," "Himalaya Mountain," "Spiritual Nourishment" and "Adam and Eve."

Western people say: "Jesus went to the 'Holy Mountain.'". Hindus say: "Buddha went to Himalaya Mountain." According to Sanscrist and Raja Yoya Technicque the "Holy Mountain," "Himalaya Mountain" and Brahm Munda are all within the skull.

The key will be given in the advanced classes for climbing into the "Holy Mountain" and "Himalaya Mountain."

Nos. 1 and 2—Pituitary Body and Gland.

Nos. 12 and 13—Spiritual Lake.

Holy water, spiritual nourishment, known in the Christian Bible as the "Cup of Honey." Greek philosophers call it the "Nectar of Life."

Hindus call it "Amrat." Will be taught more deeply and fully explained in the classes.

Nos. 5, 6 and 7—Pineal Gland.

No. 3—"Round Eye," "Seat of Soul," "Holy Eggs," "Sacred Seal," "Hidden Door," "Hidden Lock" or "Holy Temple."

No. 4—"Door of Brahm" and "Road to Cosmic."

Nos. 9 and 16—Head of the mysterious "Kundalini" or "Sacred Kundalini" and "Serpent." which is lying on the "Holy Eggs."

No. 11—"River of Life."

No. 15—"Holy Mountain," according to the Christian Bible, known in Sanscrit as the "Himalaya Mountain" and Universal Brain.

No. 16—Physical Brain. Directly in under Physical Brain, No. 16, is located what is known in Sanscrit as "Akasha Record" and in the Christian Bible as the "Etheric Record," which lies close to the hollow of the skull.

Between Nos. 1 and 20 is the white hollow or little snake, which is known to the people as "Jacobs Ladder," known in Sanscrit as the "10th Door." Tircotee, "Sirstee, Kalee Calcutee Walee," means "Inner Tongue," "Sacred Tongue" or in other words "Spiritual Tongue," known in Raja Yoya as Ruska Jeeba and "Kechree Mundra."

Which is the valve for irrigating the physical body with "Holy Water" from the "Spiritual Lake."

The physical body is known as the "Village" or "Pinda" in Sanscrit.

This little "Kundalini" or "Kala" is used by "Raja Yoga" for vibrating and exercising all the brain cells and tissues. Making them follow their functions and duties.

Pineal gland brings all seeing power.
Pituitary Body brings all hearing power.
"Holy Eggs" bring all knowing power.

All these three powers create success physically, mentally and spiritually.

Giving you freedom from Sin and Sickness and all disturbing actions surrounding you in your daily life. Bringing you into the "Life Immortal."

Raja Yoga calls it "Pad Nirvana." Lock both your eardrums with your forefingers, tip your tongue backward to the roof of the mouth and rub against it. Always trying to reach the root of the palate and the tail of the little snake.

Humming: Hoon, Yang, Yang, Yang—Hoon, swallowing all the saliva that is produced by the humming and rubbing.

More further keys will be given by Yogi in the advanced classes.

No. 17—Pingala.
No. 19—Sushmuna.
No. 13—Ida.
No. 18—Medulla Oblangata.

All these meanings are translated from Sanscrit by Raja Yoga, Wassan's grandfather.

This is called in India the family secret. I feel sorry that such a wonderful secret should be kept in the dark. It belongs to everyone and should be understood and used by everyone.

So I am doing the best I can for you. I want you to be serious, use it, and give appreciation to the God.

Many other teachers or Philosophers try to translate this mysterious chart. You can look into this matter for an understanding and an explanation.

Many philosophers think that the Kundalini is at the base of the Spine. Many others think it is all over the Spinal column. Others think it is in front of the body, or what is known as the sympathetic nerve center.

This is the first time that this chart has been really and truly authentically translated and given to the western people.

It was translated by Yogi Wassan's grandfather and Yogi Wassan himself.

Many more mysterious secrets about this chart will be given in the Superior Course.

(Copyrighted, 1915, by Yogi Wassan. All rights reserved.)

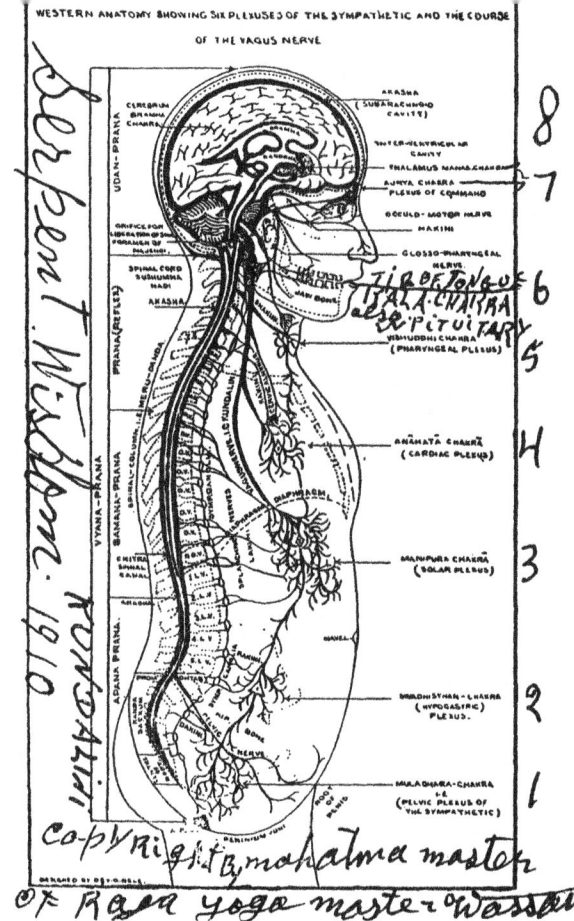

LANDS, PLEXUSES AND PANCHO PRANA
INVISIBLE NO. 1   INVISIBLE NO. 2

This chart shows the outline of the human body. Raja Yoga es it for spiritual development for making the technique of undernding the human body. Bringing seeing, hearing, knowing power ysically.

Making the physical body powerful and vitalizing it. So that u can climb with this body into the "Holy Mountain" or "Himalan Mountain," known as "Brahm Munda."

The knowledge of this chart makes a strong step ladder and a ong Pinda. Makes a strong foundation for building the "Holy mple" on top of it.

Plexus or Gland exercise will be given in the regular classes. present you can use "Cotton Cross-Breathing" and "Blood Irrigan Button Breathing," also "Humming Breathing."

(Copyrighted, 1920, by Yogi Wassan. All rights reserved.)

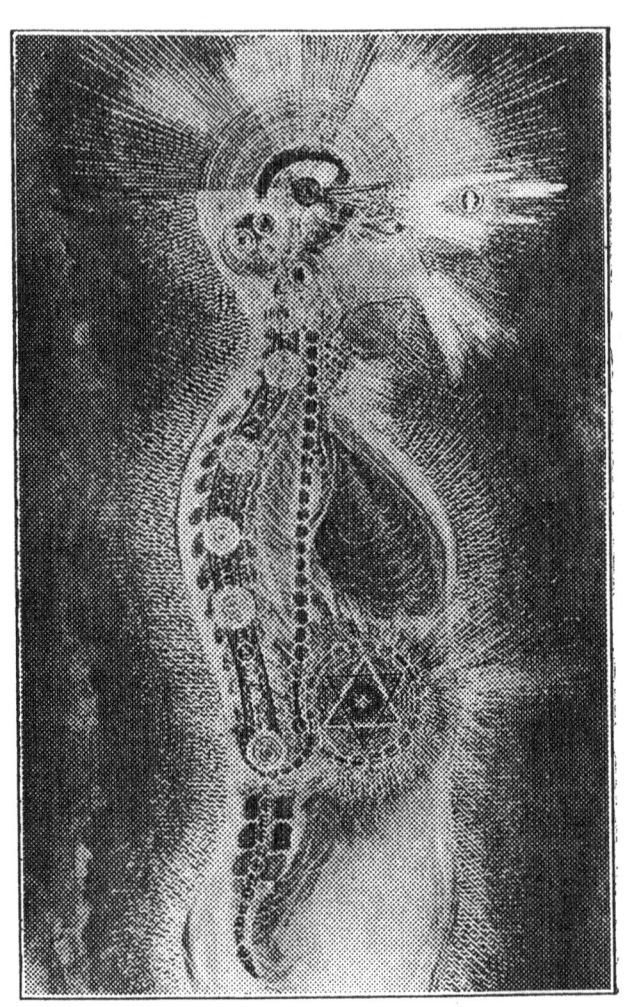

OPANA YAMA HEALTH AND BEAUTY CHART

VISIBLE NO. 1   VISIBLE NO. 2

By knowing, knowledge of this chart, 960,000,000 pores of the body are open, recharging the cells and tissues, magnetizing and vibrating them.

This will create power of Physical magnetism, Mental magnetism and Spiritual magnetism. It will beautify body, mind and soul, bringing super-personality, success and happiness.

Use this chart with the health and beauty, blood irrigation button, for removing all sickness of the body and preventing future sickness and bring super-health.

MORE WONDERS ABOUT THIS CHART:

It opens the fountain of Cosmic Vibration and Cosmic Ray, which brings freedom from disturbing actions surrounding you.

Irrigate the blood to all cells, tissues and internal organs in the body. Rejuvenating them and bring them conscious under the will, packing upward those that are dropping down causing an enlarged abdomen.

There is self healing power in this chart, by irrigating blood upon the dead germs that are forming clots all over the body. Flooding them and dissolving them. Making pure blood and circulating it from the tip of the toes to the top of the head. Keeping new life in the body and giving you an abundance of Pep.

This is one of the keys: hum, Hoon, Yang, Yang, Yang—Hoon. over and over all you like forever. This exercise brings the "Nectar of Life," for eternal youth, giving you seeing, hearing and knowing power physically.

Bring the body like a light, making the ray flow from within, outward, as shown in the chart. The more you practice the more you prolong the ray of life around the body.

That brings occult power and mental power so that you are able to use "Mental Telepathy, thought transference," become a Master Healer, Teacher, Writer, Scientist or Musician. Also bring you daily success.

Your body will become a radio, automatically broadcasting all your desires. So that you do not have to do any special exercise, chanting, meditating and concentrating, which householders have not the time to do. You can do this while engaged in business.

Many more lessons on this chart will be given in the regular and superior courses.

By the study of this chart you will get this six-fold knowledge:

Visible (1)	Visible (2)
Invisible (1)	Invisible (2)
Unseen (1)	Unseen (2)

From this six-fold knowledge you will get these (9) nine powers:

1. Physical Seeing.
2. Mental Seeing.
3. Spiritual Seeing.
4. Physical Hearing.
5. Mental Hearing.
6. Spiritual Hearing.
7. Physical Knowing.
8. Mental Knowing.
9. Spiritual Knowing.

(Copyrighted, 1922, by Yogi Wassan. All rights reserved.)

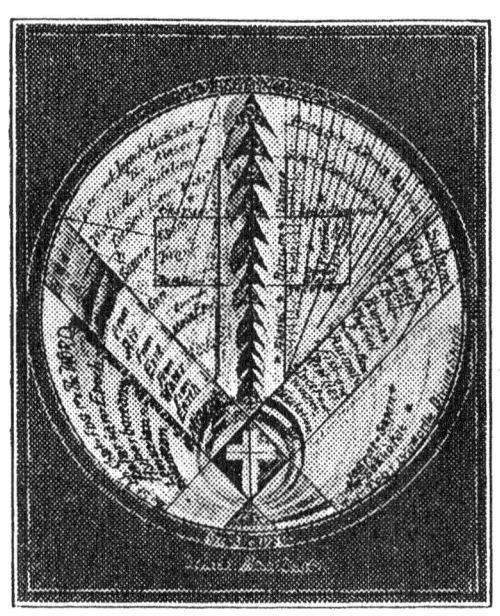

YOGI WASSAN'S EVOLUTION CHART
OF THE UNIVERSE

The secret of this chart will be given mouth to ear.

Beauty of this chart by Raja Yoga. Secret is the giving of freedom from past life Karman and Kukarma.

For it burns up past life Kukarma, by lighting the matches of knowledge.

That will be given in Raja Yoga Maha Atma study.

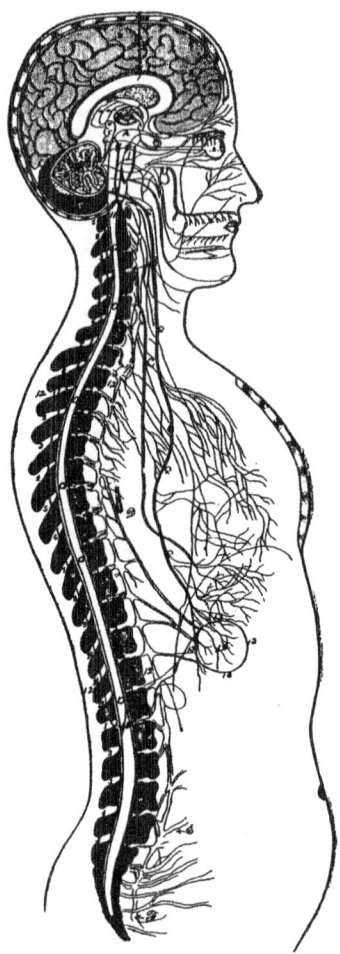

DR. CARY'S CHART

Dr. Cary has been in India for many years. He tried to translate the Hindu Spiritual Anatomy into the Christian Spiritual Anatomy.

Read what he has to say about it in his chart. Think about it and see what is in it.

1. *The "Door of Brahm."* The suture where the bones of the skull meet; a passage-way leading from the optic thalamus outward through the Internal Capsule, the Lentiform Nucleus, the External Capsule and the Island of Reil, the latter being directly under the suture. It is through this passage-way that all vibrations from without impinge upon the organs of special sense, through the nerves. It is the "chimney of Santa Claus" and the doorway by means of which the Ego leaves the body in sleep and at death.

2. *Atma.* The Divine Monad, the cerebrum; corresponds to Aries, and is the Tribe of Gad, or God; the Most High; the Kingdom of Heaven and God; the heaved-up place; the Holy Mountain; the Almighty; the Father, made from the Mother Substance (Mary, Virgin Mare, pure sea or water). In physiological terms this substance is called "pia mater"—tender mother. It consists of the most finely attenuated, the most highly differentiated substance in the body, and when living and vibrating it is more like gas or steam than anything else. The new Jerusalem; "the City of Peace"; the Lotus petals.

3. *The Optic Thalamus.* The Heart of the Lotus; the eye within the chamber; the "All-Seeing Eye"; the Lamb or lamp which (when lit) gives light to all within the house, the Eye "single"; Buddhi.

4. *The Pineal Gland.* The male organ of spirituality and fecundity; corresponds to Joseph; the tomb; corresponds also to the Sun and the sign Leo; it is the 7th Chakra; it is the "First Thief"; electric; Sanscrit name Sahasrara; is the church of Laodikeia mentioned in Revelation; connects with the right sympathetic system.

5. *Corpora Quadrigemina.* "Four fold body"; two nates (buttocks) and two testes (testicles).

A. The top of the Medulla Oblongata.

6. *The Valve of Vieussens.*

7. *The Pituitary Body.* The sixth Chakra; Isis; the "Second Thief"; connects with the left sympathetic system; Manas; corresponds to Mary and is the female organ of spirituality. Note that it is located in a lower position than the male organ; Sanscrit name Ajna; in Revelation it is the Church Philadelphia; sign Cancer, under the Moon; Magnetic body.

8. *Pingala.* Male, electric current; right sympathetic system; connects with solar plexus; the Nadis or nerve currents on right side of spine; connects with pineal gland.

9. *Ida.* Magnetic current; female, Isis; connected with left sympathetic system; semilunar ganglion; connects with pituitary body; Eve; Nadis on left side of spine; Io of the Greeks; Aditi and Vach of the Hindus.

These two currents cross at the base of the skull (Golgotha), the place of the second crucifixion.

10. *Cerebellum.* The home of Man who never dies, the Ego; the Head of the Tree of Life; corresponds to Taurus; the chauffeur of the human automobile.

11. *Gethsemane.* The place of olives (Garden of Olives).

12. *The Twelve Dorsal Vertebrae.* The twelve stones set up ("which are there to this day"), where the Ark of the Most High God entered the Jordan; the Priests are the twelve nerves of forces connected with the solar plexus; for they, having become controlled, serve the Most High God.

13. *The Solar Plexus,* Jacob; containing the seven "breaths"—pneumata, the lunar forces, and the five solar forces, pranas or vital airs; they are the twelve children of Jacob, or Israel.

O. *The Jordan.* The spinal canal; the passage-way for the Kundalini; the Euphrates, the river of crystal "flowing forth from the throne of God."

14. *The Manger,* or cave, in the solar plexus, in which the child Jesus, the fish, seed or fruit is born. In Bible terminology it is the 13th child of Jacob and Rachael. Benjamin, the only one born in the Holy Land. It is Bethlehem, "House of bread." "I am the bread of life"—directly under the house or place of *material* bread. "And they did *eat* thereon."

15. *Sodom and Egypt.* 'Where our Lord was also crucified." The first crucifixion; the descent of the Ego into matter.

B. *The Pharyngeal Plexus.* In Sanscript, Vishuddhi; corresponds to Virgo; ruled by Mercury; Church of Sardis in Revelation. The fifth plexus.

C. *The Cardiac Plexus.* Corresponds to Libra and is ruled by Venus; Sanscrit name Anahata; the fourth plexus; Church of Thiateria.

D. *Epigastric Plexus.* Manipuraka in Sanscrit; Church of Pergamos in Revelation; Scorpio and Mars; third plexus of Chakra.

E. *The Prostatic Plexus.* The second Chakra; Adhishthana in Sanscrit; Church of Smyrna in Revelation; the Home of Sushumna.

F. *The Sacral Plexus.* Muladhara in Sanscrit; corresponds to Capricorn and Saturn; Church of Ephesus in Revelation; the home of Kundalini and Lot's wife; the Bride of the Lotus.

G. *The Pneumogastric or Vagus Nerve.* The channel of the Holy Ghost or Breath. Has six different physical functions.

CHART OF IDA, PINGALA, SUSHMUNA OR WATER SHUMADI

The technique for this chart will be given in the school, mouth to ear. It will be practiced thru demonstration.

Water Shumadi means meditation in water—in a tank. This practice is a short cut and a very powerful one. More technical than any other chart. The teacher must be present, when the student is practicing.

Knowledge of this chart conquers the Universal Power, Universal Chakra and the Universal Devta.

Who practice this will come to Devta. The practice will be given in the "Temple of Cosmic". *Copyrighted by Yogi Wassan,* 1907

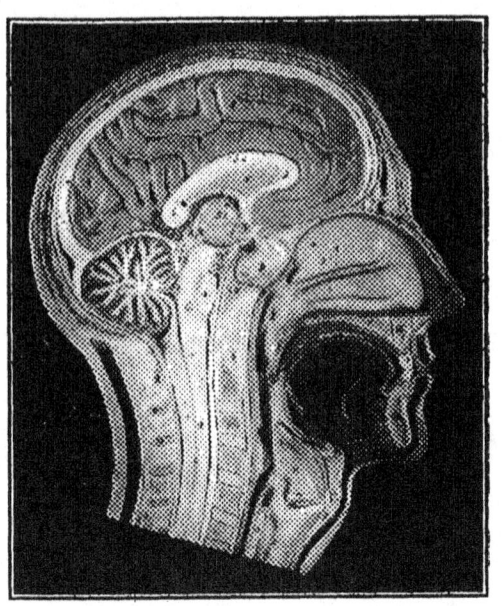

CHART OF THE ADENOIDS
The technique of this chart will be given in the regular courses.

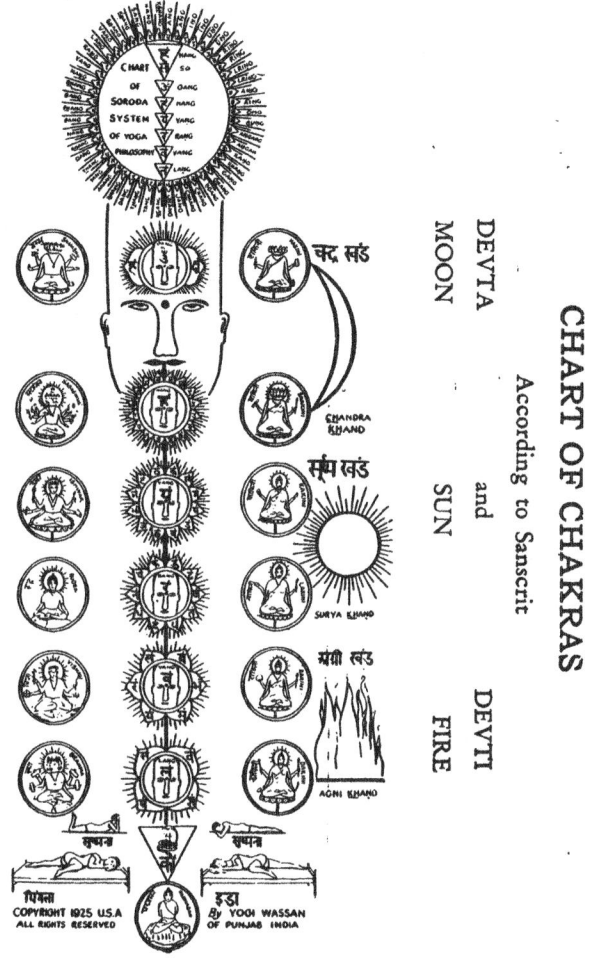

Chakra's Petals and Rays

Automatic sleeping Shumadi, for opening the Chakras which are in the region of the seven nerve centers of the sympathetic nerve system. This is better explained in the chart of No. 2 of glands and plexuses.

Raja Yoga philosophy calls this chart "Pancho Mundra". By the development in this chart you bring seven lighted candles into the body, seven fountains of cosmic ray, making the seven stars in your body sparkle. Seven sparkled light means seven stars in the body.

Which is wonderful development for the householder awakening the latent power within.

More further technique about this chart will be given in the advanced classes.

Copyrighted by Maha Atma Master Wassan, 1926

TABLE FOR EXPLANATION OF CHART NO. 8

Day of Week	Color	Planet	Element	Mantram	Name of Chakra
Sunday	Gold	Sun		So Hang	Sahans Rara
Monday	Orange	Moon		O Ang	Ajuna
Tuesday	Blue	Mars	Ether	Hang	Washooda
Wednesday	Green	Mercury	Air	Yang	Anahata
Thursday	Red	Jupiter	Fire	Rang	Manipura
Friday	White	Venus	Water	Vang	Swadas Astana
Saturday	Yellow	Saturn	Earth	Hang	Muladhara

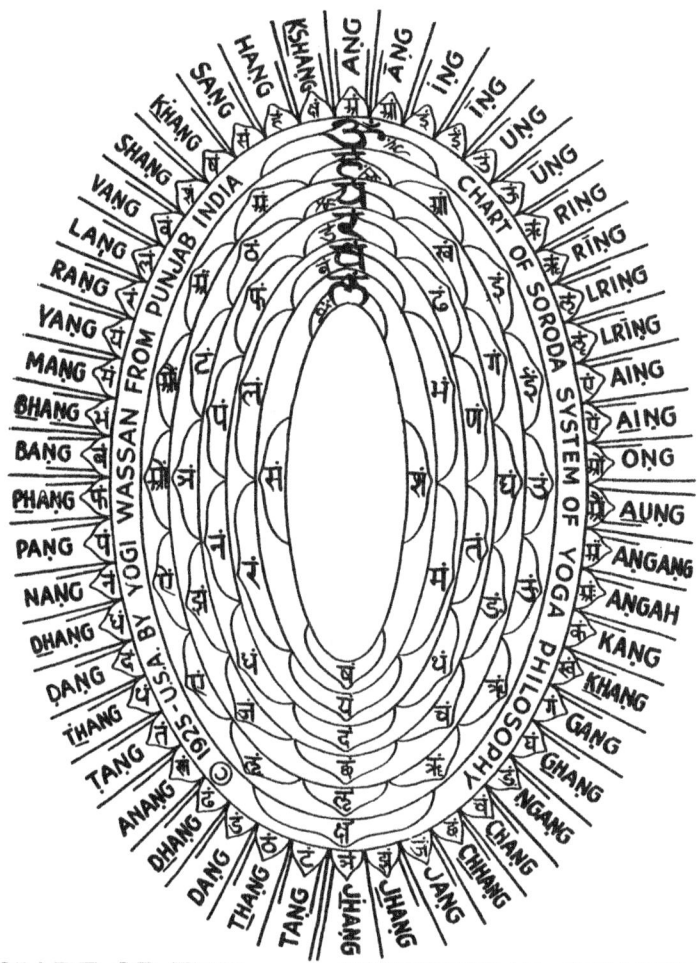

CHART OF THE— UNIVERSAL CHAKRA
UNIVERSAL AURA
UNIVERSAL COLOR

When you have opened the 7 Chakras, according to chart No. 8. Then you will practice chart No. 9, for conquering the Universal Chakra.

There are 2 different sections of Chakras. Seven Chakras in chart No. 8, called by Raja Yoga; Spiritual No. 1 and Spiritual No. 2. In chart No. 9, it is called by Raja Yoga and Maha Atma Philosophy; Unseen No. 1 and Unseen No. 2.

The practice will be given in the superior course. How to conquer the Universal Chakra and Devta. Also see the 7 colored Universal Aura, which is within, all over the universe.

This means to conquer the Universal Chakra and see the Unseen, by becoming unseen yourself.

Max Muller, in His "India, What Can It Teach Us?" Says:

"If I were to look over the whole world to find out the country most richly endowed with all the wealth, power and beauty that nature can bestow—in some facts a very paradise on earth—I should point to India. If I were asked under what sky the human mind has most fully developed some of its choicest gifts, has most deeply pondered on the greatest problems of life, and has found solutions of some of them which well deserve the attention even of those who have studied Plato and Kant—I should point to India.

"And if I were to ask myself from what literature we, here in Europe, we who have been nurtured almost exclusively on the thoughts of the Greeks and Romans, and of one Semitic race, the Jewish, may draw that corrective which is most wanted in order to make our inner life more perfect, more comprehensive, more universal, in fact, more truly human, a life not for this life only, but a transfigured and external life—again I should point to India."

SUPER AKASHA YOGI WASSAN, THE MASTER OF ALL ANCIENT MYSTERY, SAYS:

"You Have Five Solar Plexus"

In Sanskrit the Five Solar Plexus are called "Poncho Mundra." PONCHO MUNDRA means the FIVE NERVE CENTRES of MAGNETIC CURRENT IN THIS BODY. Get the SECRET KEYS to OPEN and DEVELOP

>THE PHYSICAL SOLAR PLEXUS
>MENTAL SOLAR PLEXUS
>SPIRITUAL SOLAR PLEXUS

These three Mundra or Solar Plexus can be opened very easily, with very little practice, and in very little time. In order to open the other two plexus successfully, it is necessary to enter a Shrine, and to live the life of a Renunciation Yogi.

The First Step in Yoga Philosophy

It is very necessary to open the Physical Solar Plexus as soon as possible in order to keep the body young and healthy, in order to recharge and rejuvenate the body. All Oriental and Ancient people learn how to open the Physical Solar Plexus in childhood. It is imperative to do so in order to develop and LIVE in this body.

The following is a list of a few of the POWERS attained when the PHYSICAL SOLAR PLEXUS is opened:

- Power of Eternal Youth and Beauty
- Power of Super Health
- Power of Physical Body
- Power of Physical Magnetism
- Power of Recharging the Body Battery
- Power of Rejuvenation
- Power of Prolonging Life
- Power of Reducing Weight
- Power of Gaining Weight
- Power of Curing All Diseases
- Power of Restoring Eyesight
- Power of Singing
- Power of Vibration
- Power of Self-Healing
- Power of Healer
- Power of Business Success
- Power of Levitation
- Power of Suspension of Animation
- Power of Physical Clairvoyance
- Power of Physical Clairaudience
- Power of Meditation
- Power of Concentration
- Power of Steadiness
- Power of Attraction
- Power of Happiness
- Power of Love
- Power of Marriage Success
- Power of Teacher
- Power of Visible Development
- Physical Desires
- Power of Broadcasting

Chart No. 5

The following is a list of a few of the POWERS attained when the MENTAL SOLAR PLEXUS IS opened:

Power of Super Mind
Power of Occult
Power of Mental Telepathy
Power of Psychic Development
Power of Psychic Clairvoyance
Power of Psychic Clairaudience
Power of Invisible Development
Power of Occult Science
Power of Appearing
Power of Disappearing
Power of Poetry
Power of Memory
Power of Mental Healing
Power of Mental Development
Power of Mental Concentration
Power of Mental Meditation
Power Over Five Passions
Power to Create Highly Developed Children
Power of Knowing Past, Present, Future
Power of Mental Levitation
Power of Imagination
Power of Broadcasting Mental Desires
Power of Business Success
Power of Brain Exercise
Power of Super Personality
Power of Cosmic Vibration
Power of Mental Magnetism
Power of Noble Deeds
Power of Mental Love
Power to Destroy Disturbing Actions
Power of Nectar-like Speech
Power of Changing Individual Form
Power to Create

Chart No. 6

The following is a list of a few of the POWERS attained when the SPIRITUAL SOLAR PLEXUS is opened:

Power of Super Spirituality

Power of Magnifying Holiness

Power to Meet the Kundalini

Power of Spiritual Clairvoyance

Power of Spiritual Clairaudience

Power of Broadcasting Spiritual Desires

Power of Spiritual Magnetism

Power to Go Where You Like Unseen

Power to Go Through Space

Power to Go Through Matter

Power Over Death

Power to Become All-knowing and All-seeing

Yogi Wassen Plans Hindu Yoga Yug

Yogi Wassan will shortly open a Yoga Center close to Denver to accommodate students. It will be named "Hindu Yoga Yug."

The word Yoga, which is derived from the Sanskrit root "Yug" to join, really means the merging of the lower self into the Higher Self—the Divine.

By the study of Yoga, darkness or ignorance is replaced by light, and undesirable tendencies are eliminated, and by degrees man becomes the master.

Opana Yama and the Soroda System of Yoga Philosophy will develop the individual to a Master within the shortest possible time. It is the daily automatic practice of these systems which enable an individual to develop even while busily engaged at his occupation.

Opana Yama and the Soroda System of Yoga Philosophy is the system used for Householders and is being revealed for the first time in America by Yogi Wassan.

Soroda System

CHART OF HOLY CHANT

Christian—Father in Heaven .... E
Hindu—O Ang Shantee .... E
Japanese—Devo Buddha Namo Amee .... E
Chinese—Shinto Ho .... E
Mohammedan—Allah Ho Akbar .... E
Sanskrit—A Hang Atma Brahm .... E
Hebrew—El-Oh-Im .... E

Chart

SORODA SYSTEM OF SUPER YOGA PHILOSOPHY
HINDU ANCIENT MYSTERY—OCCULT SCIENCE AND OPANA YAMA
TEMPLE OF HINDU YOGA YUG
YOGI WASSAN, *Founder and Teacher*

Ladder of Development

10	Cosmic	Consciousness
9	Self	State of Consciousness
8	Super	State of Consciousness
7	Astral	State of Consciousness
6	Spiritual	State of Consciousness
5	Mental	State of Consciousness
4	Occult	State of Consciousness
3	Dreaming	State of Consciousness
2	Physical	State of Consciousness
1	Ignorant	State of Consciousness

Ida, Pingala, Sushmuna

Climb the Ladder with the Secret Key of Opana Yama. Opana Yama is the System used by Householders to develop without excessive practice.

Yogi Wassan's teaching is different from any other and never before revealed in this country. This teaching opens up:

Physical Solar Plexus for Super Health.
Mental Solar Plexus for Super Mind.
Spiritual Solar Plexus for Cosmic Consciousness.

RESULT:

Super-Man   Super-Woman

100 Secret Keys of the Soroda System of Yoga Philosophy

BY

YOGI WASSAN, OF PUNJAB, INDIA

While chanting these keys the Yogis hold a small jug or glass of water in the palm of the left hand and use the palm of the right hand as a lid for the jug.

After chanting each key they breathe upon the hands and jug of water—thus magnetizing the water with the magnetic holy breath—and drink it for *every* need.

If there is no particular need, chant without magnetizing or drinking the water, for spiritual development.

Secret Keys of Ancient Wisdom

SECTION No. 1

How to Recharge and Vibrate Everything

Awakening of the Seven Spiritual Centers

Call   7 times ....Wake Up Myself, Sleep No More.
Knock 7 times......Wake Up Myself, Sleep No More.
Chant 7 times.....Wake Up Myself, Sleep No More.
Pray   7 times......Wake Up Myself, Sleep No More.

After *knocking* the 7 Spiritual Centers, which the Christians call the Hidden Lock, Moses called the 7 seals and Hindus call the 7 Chakras, with the tip of the five fingers, *will* and *vibrate* with the *action*.

Chant 7 times........................*O Ang Shantee*

Pray 7 times........................*Shantee Peace*

KEYS—SECTION No. 2

How to Chant Holy Word for Spirituality

Christian—Father in Heaven .... E
Hindu—O Ang Shantee .... E
Japanese—Devo Buddha Namo Amee .... E
Chinese—Shinto Ho .... E
Mohammedan—Allah Ho Akbar .... E
Sanskrit—A Hang Atma Brahm .... E
Hebrew—El-Oh-Im .... E
Ida, Pingala Sushmuna .... E
8 times—Ho-Ho-Ho-Ho .... Ho
8 times—Hu-Hu-Hu-Hu .... Hoon
8 times—Hoong-Yang-Yang-Yang .... Hoon

KEYS—SECTION No. 3

How to Chant Yoga Secret Mantram for Everything

So	Hoong	E
O	Hoong	E
Mo	Hoong	E
Ko	Hoong	E
Ro	Hoong	E
To	Hoong	E
Sho	Hoong	E

KEYS—SECTION No. 4

How to Chant for Mental and Spiritual Power

The Hindus call the Creative Power within "Chakra" and "Koola Kandlinee." Moses said the Creative Power within could be awakened through the 7 Spiritual Centers, 7 Seals and 7 Hidden Doors, 7 Colored Horses and 7 Lighted Lamps.

Mula............Dhara............E
Swadas............Astana............E
Mani............Pura............E
Ana............Hata............E
Washooda............E
Ka............La............E
Ajuna............E
Sahans............Ra Ra............E

KEYS—SECTION No. 5

Yoga Secret Mantram for Everything
How to Chant Mentally With Soundless Sound

Som............E
Om............E
Mom............E
Kom............E
Rom............E
Tom............E
Shom............E

KEYS—SECTION No. 6

SECRET KEYS FOR OPENING THE DOOR OF KNOWLEDGE, FOUNTAIN OF COSMIC VIBRATION AND COSMIC RAYS, ELEVATING YOU FROM THE IGNORANT STATE OF CONSCIOUSNESS TO THE COSMIC STATE OF CONSCIOUSNESS.

Wake Up Myself, Sleep No More

Sleep no more, sleep no more, sleep no more, sleep no more,
    My ignorant state of body,

Sleep no more, sleep no more, sleep no more, sleep no more,
Sleep no more, sleep no more, sleep no more, sleep no more,
   My ignorant state of brain,
Sleep no more, sleep no more, sleep no more, sleep no more,
Sleep no more, sleep no more, sleep no more, sleep no more,
   My ignorant state of mind,
Sleep no more, sleep no more, sleep no more, sleep no more,
Sleep no more, sleep no more, sleep no more, sleep no more,
   My ignorant state of soul,
Sleep no more, sleep no more, sleep no more, sleep no more,
Sleep no more, sleep no more, sleep no more, sleep no more,
   My ignorant state of consciousness,
Sleep no more, sleep no more, sleep no more, sleep no more,

Repeat the above, and substitute the words *physical, dreaming, occult, mental, spiritual, astral, super, self, cosmic,* for *"ignorant."*

Chant the above Health, Beauty, Wealth, Business, Love, Marriage, Music, Wisdom, Occult, Healing, Teaching, Mental Telepathy, Clairvoyance, Higher Spiritual Development, etc.

Wake Up Myself State of Consciousness Sleep No More, Sleep No More

BY

A MASTER OF ANCIENT MYSTERY

SUPER AKASHA YOGI WASSAN

SORODA SYSTEM OF YOGA PHILOSOPHY

AND

SUPER YOGA SCIENCE

Subject in This Book

How to get Occult Concentration, Power for recharging and magnetizing the optic nerve. Purifying the blood and blood circulation.

Grandma's secret for constipation. Will be of benefit to you for 100 years, and worth many thousands of dollars to you.

How I Get the Occult Power for Recharging the Optic Nerve

PRACTICE No. 1

Sit erect on chair.

Put left elbow on left knee, right elbow on right knee.

Place palms of hands over closed eyes.

Press head against the palms—but not enough to hurt.

PRACTICE No. 2

Hold palms over eyes for two minutes, quietly. With eyes closed, palms still over the eyes:

Look up into the forehead to the root of the nose. —Mentally see figure No. 1.

Look to the right forehead.—Mentally see figure No. 2.

Look to the right temple.—Mentally see figure No. 3.

Look to the right ear drum.—Mentally see figure No. 4.

Look to the lower right cheek.—Mentally see figure No. 5.

Look to the right chin.—Mentally see figure No. 6.

Look to the middle of chin.—Mentally see figure No. 7.

Look to the left chin.—Mentally see figure No. 8.

Look to the lower left cheek.—Mentally see figure No. 9.

Look to the left ear drum.—Mentally see figure No. 10.

Look to the left temple.—Mentally see figure No. 11.

Look to the left forehead.—Mentally see figure No. 12.

Look again to the root of the nose, in the middle of the forehead.—Mentally see figure No. 1.

Practice this exercise for 12 minutes, without looking anywhere.

Concentrate on each figure for one minute.

After completing the exercise from right to left, go over the same drill in the same manner, from left to right.

Roll eyeballs from left to right, from right to left, as fast as possible.

Close eyes for three minutes.

Open eyes for one-half minute.

Close eyes tightly for one-half minute. Contract fact as much as possible, for this pulls the optic nerve inward. Open eyes. Push them outward.

Open and close eyes for a half minute.

Gaze seriously ahead—tensing the muscles of the eyes.

Wink.

Gaze ahead.

While doing this exercise, keep the head in the same position—using the deep-thinking posture—that is:

Feet flat on floor.
Elbows on knees.
Chin in palms of hand—in the form of a "Y."

SECTION No. 2

Same position.

Hold eyelids open with tip of forefinger and thumb. Hold the eyes wide open. Keep the other three fingers of each hand closed tightly.

Place a golden, copper, or silver coin (gold is more magnetic than copper, copper than silver) about twelve inches in front of your feet, on the floor.

Look at that coin for a few minutes, while holding the eyes open.

Then revolve your eyes around the object in circles from left to right, mentally making a bigger picture of the circle each time, until it is about 14 inches in diameter.

Repeat exercise, from right to left.

Make each circle in about three minutes.

Again look at the coin. Look at it until the tears come to your eyes.

When tears come, close eyes. Rub eyes, using same motion as you would if they were itching. Rub gently, however, for you must not hurt the eyeball. Hands must be scrupulously clean.

Take hands away from eyes.

Look at coin with partially closed eyes.

(While doing this exercise, it is always necessary to keep your elbows on your knees—as this develops occult concentration power. Be very steady in your position.)

Now half close the eyes.
Concentrate again on the dollar.
Contract forehead and eyes.

Mentally try to pick that dollar up from the floor with your eyelids, just as if you were picking the coin up with your hand. Be sure to keep the same steady position.

Occult Concentration No. 3

Get a 200-watt blue electric lamp.
Place it three feet away from you.
Sit erect on chair.
Look into the light with eyes almost completely closed for one minute.
Close eyes for one minute.
Concentrate on the image of the light for one minute.
Mentally see figure No. 1 for one minute.
Open eyes.

The above exercise is to be carried out in 12 degrees—each time opening the eyes a little farther than before—each time concentrating on the image of the light, and mentally seeing a different figure —1 to 12.

Wear transparent green shade while performing this exercise.

Occult Concentration No. 4
Sun Practice

To be practiced between 8 A. M. and 10 A. M.
Hold both eyes open with tips of thumbs and forefingers.
Look straight into the sun for one minute.
Close eyes.
Concentrate on image of sun for one minute.
Mentally see figure 1 for one minute.

The above exercise is to be carried out in 12 degrees—each time opening the eyes a little farther than before—each time concentrating on the image of the light, and mentally seeing a different figure —1 to 12.

If eyes are very weak, wear a green shade for a week or two.

Do not practice in the sun after 10 o'clock A. M. or before 5 P. M.

Occult Concentration No. 5

Repeat Occult Concentration No. 4 after 5 o'clock P. M.

Occult Concentration No. 6

Repeat Occult Concentration No. 4 during Full Moon, but only during the night time. Do not wear eye shade for full moon exercise.

When there is neither sun nor moon, practice with the blue electric light. Electric light exercise should be practiced three times or more during every 24 hours.

Practice daily, until occult concentration is fully developed.

Then practice once a week to keep same degree of power forever.

Occult Concentration No. 7

Position:

Elbows on knees (feel pressure of elbows on knees.)

Neck crouched into the body.

Head bent toward the copy.

Push navel outward.

Eyes closed tightly—forehead contracted.

Wink eyes—fastly.

Take any first print you cannot read.

Cover everything on printed sheet except the word you want to read.

Hold sheet with forefinger and thumb finger of each hand.

While holding paper thusly, stretch it.

Gaze at uncovered *word* for one minute.

Sometimes you will see it—sometimes you will not.

Gaze at it until you can see it *clearly*.

Practice on this one word for two hours, and you will be able to read slowly all the print you want to —even the smallest.

While practicing, read the same copy *over* and *over again.* This will enable you to read *faster* in much less time than if you were to read different copy each time you practiced.

During the day, roll the eyes as much as possible —from right to left, from left to right. Always open eyes wide and hold them STEADY, every hour you are not sleeping. Try not to wink.

The more you practice this the sooner you will be able to develop complete occult concentration power.

How I Bathe My Eyes

Every night, before going to bed, I bathe my eyes with the following solution:

One teaspoonful of Table Salt in one cup of water.

After washing the eyes. I saturate a piece of cotton in the following solution, put on both eyes, under a bandage, and keep same on all night:

2 Tablespoons of Ground Nutmeg.

2 Tablespoons of Table Salt.

1 Pint of Water.

Boil together about five minutes. Let cool and strain, and keep in a bottle, ready for use.

How I Massage the Body

Massage every night before retiring with following solution:

1 Pint of Alcohol.

Rub on throat, chest, stomach, both arms, back of neck, shoulder blades, down to the kidneys, to the base of the spine, to the hips, legs, feet—top and bottom—medulla oblongata down to the ears, back of head to the upper forehead.

Do not rub on lower forehead, face, eyes, sexual organs, or open sores.

This massage is especially beneficial if troubled with Influenza, Bad Cold, Pneumonia, Rheumatism, Asthma, Bonchitis, Catarrh, Poor Eyesight, Black and Blue Marks, Baldness.

Do not use on children, for their skin is much too tender.

This massage limbers the body and the brain cells.

How I Make Home-Made Candy

Get two pounds of raisins (seeded or seedless) and eight ounces of senna leaves. Mix well and grind through meat grinder. Roll a piece of the mixture the size of a marble, lightly in flour, to make a smooth surface. Let dry for two or three days, and keep in fruit jar in cool place. Take one piece of this candy and a glass of hot water, every other night forever.

Use Star Chart No. 3

SHOWING PROPER METHOD FOR CONCENTRATION FOR OPENING THE THIRD EYE AND DEVELOPING THE SIXTH SENSE

Very Beneficial for Young People, School Children, Writers, Scientists, and Others

How I concentrate:—I take Yogi Wassan's Concentration Chart and paste in the middle of my dresser mirror, or attach by chewing gum, so it can be removed quickly. This mirror should be of a size 12 x 12 inches, or 18 x 18 inches, and be any mirror that is convenient. I then sit at a distance of six feet to ten feet away from the mirror, in a chair, erect, well forward in the chair, and not touching the back of the chair with my own back, feet flat on the floor, and hands placed at the back of my head, with fingers interlaced firmly, palmar surface of the hands pressing against the base of the head, or over the region of the medulla oblongata. When sitting in this position, I have the chart placed at a height or elevation level with my eyebrows, or on a level with my forehead, in a well-lighted room.

I lock my fingers first, and then press the palmar surface of my hands against the base of the occiput, and try to bring my elbows together in front of my face, making a scissor-pressure on the sides of the head with the forearms. I then look right into the middle of the black spot of the chart, and keep my eyes half closed, and wrinkle my forehead a little, just as a person would do when suddenly facing a strong light, or the glare of the sun and would wrinkle the forehead in contracting the eye for protection against the sudden exposure to the strong light. At the same time I am wrinkling my eyebrows in this manner, I am also pressing the temples with my forearms, and pressing the palmar surface of my hands against the base of the skull, just as if I was trying to crush something between the palms of my hands, so the back of my neck receives the effect of the pressing and pushing toward the forehead.

All this time I am gazing on the concentration spot of the chart, without winking my eyes, and if tears come into my eyes I let them come, but keep looking at the concentration spot of the chart. I continue this practice for five minutes, once a day, for one week, and after that, increase the time one minute each week, until I practice for a thirty-minute period on the Concentration chart.

In the beginning, when undertaking this practice, the tears will come somewhat freely, but I do not rub or wipe away these tears, but let them drop, and do not touch the eye at all. Then there will follow a feeling of drawing or pulling of the forehead right in the center, between and just above the root of the nose, and at this stage of the exercise, it may seem as if there are three or four charts, or five or six, or perhaps only two, and these other charts that come before the vision will not be black, like the original one upon which concentration is being made, but will appear all colors—yellow, white, golden, blue, or orange, etc., showing any or many of the seven colors, and these charts or colors can be seen even if the gaze is removed from the Concentration chart and placed upon the wall, or any other object in the room, by looking five minutes upon the Concentration chart, and then looking five minutes at some other surface in the room.

At this stage of the practice, when I look upon the original black spot of the Concentration chart, I find it seems to be changing color, getting lighter and lighter in shade, until it is almost a cream color, then a milky color, and at that stage the chart will seem to disappear entirely from the vision, just like everything is dark or invisible on a very foggy day. However, this should not be permitted to deceive the one practicing into thinking this effect is a condition outside, as of fog or darkness, for it is an effect within, invisible, inside, although the optical effect is as if looking through foggy or smoked glasses, but no glasses are there—only empty space.

At this stage of the practice, a copy of the chart may be made of paper, cut the same size as the chart. Upon this paper some words may be written by another person, the words entirely unknown to the person doing the concentration practice, and the piece of paper thus prepared and written upon, pasted upon the back of the chart and sealed. After this is done, the chart may now be placed against the wall of the room, and concentrated upon, just as was done with the chart against the mirror. Soon the chart will begin to appear cream colored, or milky in appearance; then foggy, and then will seem to disappear from the vision entirely, revealing the card or paper behind the chart, with the writing thereupon, in golden color, and the writing can be read. When that is accomplished through this method of Concentration, that means that one kind of Concentration has been accomplished, and the person so practicing is then ready for the "Higher Technique of Concentration" for opening the invisible, or "Spiritual Eye," which practice is outlined on Yogi Wassan Chart Number Three. These charts may be purchased by mail, by addressing

Chart No. 3

Yogi Wassan Sight-Renewing Chart
For Making the Eyes Strong for One Hundred Years Without Glasses

How I Make My Eyesight Strong:—I sit in a chair, facing the wall, erect, feet flat on the floor, hands on knees, and concentrate upon the Yogi Wassan Sight-Renewing Chart, which has been tacked carefully against the wall, at an elevation level with the top of my head. I sit four feet away from the wall, and look at the middle spot of the chart for fifteen or twenty seconds without winking my eyes, keeping eyes half closed. After fifteen or twenty seconds, I drop my head toward the Right Shoulder, but keep looking at the center of the chart as I commenced, never taking my vision off the center of the chart. Then drop the head forward, by touching my chin to my collar-bone; then roll head toward the left shoulder, always keeping the vision on the center of the chart, as I first began in the exercise. Then I let the head drop backward, lifting the chin high enough that my forehead will be facing the ceiling, but keeping my vision right on the center of the chart, all the time. I then let my head drop to the right shoulder again, and repeat two or three times, swinging the head to the left. Then reverse, and swing to the right in the same manner, always keeping my vision on the center of the chart.

I practice this exercise one or two minutes at a time, four or five times a day, drinking one glass of water before starting this exercise, and drinking one glass of water after I stop the exercise, but I do not get up from the chair until five minutes after stopping the exercise.

I then take the chart down, or use another chart, and put directly in front of me on a table, having the chart erect, as if supported by an easel. I then sit in chair in front of the chart, putting my elbows on the table, and hold my eyelids about half open with thumb and fingers, holding my vision right on the middle of the chart as I roll my head, first to the left, then down toward the chin, then to the right, then up, and thus around, twice, keeping vision always centered upon the central spot of the chart. Then I reverse the direction—I roll my head, and repeat the exercise. Then I look straight at the central spot of the chart for one or two minutes, until tears come into my eyes. Then I close my eyes slowly and cover with the palms of my hands, giving the magnetism of my hands to the eyes, and hold in this position for five minutes in concentration, inward. When I use this exercise at night, just before going to bed, I leave the tears in the eyes, and in the morning, upon arising, I bathe my eyes with a solution of salt and water.

Chart of Soroda System
RISHI AND DEVO SHAMADI
By Superakasha Yogi Wassan

Knock Seven Times each and call—Wake up myself 7 times each at

1. Heart—which Hindu calls Anhata Shabad.

2. Root of Nose — Hindu calls — Tricoatee and Shiva's Eye.

3. Top of head—Hindu calls—Daswa Dewara and Door of Brahm.

4. Back of Head at Medulla—Hindu calls—Sir of Mehar Dand.

5. Between the Shoulders—Hindu calls—Ghar of Atma.

6. Back of Kidney—Hindu calls—Ghar of Vishnu and Wisdom.

7. Base of Spine—Sacral Plexsus—Create and Creator — Hindu calls — Para-Brahma and Airavata, Coola Kundalini.

UPAR — KANCH — UPAN — KO — — — O
up / pull / exhale / it

PURAN — UPAN — MELAWAY — — — O
inhale / exhale / together

POORA — YOGI — JANIA — — — — A
highest / Yogi / demonstrates

TAKO — KAL — NA — KHAWAY — — — O
him / death / never / destroys

SHEA — CHAKAR — KO — FOR — KAR — O
  six   centres   it   hollow   making

SOON — SIKAR — KO — JAWAY — — O
  still   higher   it   get there

DHARNEE — BAND — LEGAY — KE — A
  ground   touch   making posture   to

DANE — BAWAY — KO — ROK — — — O
  right   left   it   stop

MUSTAK — PURAN — JHERAY — KE — A
above forehead life forces   raise   to

KARE - UMAR — BHAR — YOG — — O
  rest   clear   eternal and everlasting meditation

CHAND — CHELAWAY — DEVISKO — — O
  moon   driver   daytime

SOOR — CHELAWAY — NINE — — — O
  sun   driver   night

NET — SADHAN — AISE — KARE — — — A
  daily   practices   similar   dating

HOE — UMAR — BHAR — POOR — — — O
  will be   age   plentiful   full measure

AHE - PANCHO - MUNDRA - SAD - KE — A
  these   five   practices   control   to

PAWAY — GHUT — KO — BHED — — — O
  discover   chamber   it   secret

HOONG — YANG — YANG — YANG
great consciousness   eternal   eternal   eternal

As We Start on Our Journey

Modern archæological discovery reveals that at least ten thousand years ago there were *three* great centers of civilization and human development—Egypt, along the valley of the Nile; Babylon, on the banks of the Euphrates; and India, in the valley of the Indus.

What is not so generally known, however, is that, basically, the highest priesthood of each of these three great peoples hold almost identical conceptions of Deity, of the Universe, and of Man, in his relation to Deity. It has been found that the secret marks for conveying hidden meanings used by these ancient priests were common to twenty-six (26) of the languages of 2000 B. C.

Of that Higher Sacred Priesthood we read in the Christian Bible. The Book of Genesis tells of Abraham's visit to Melchizedek, Priest of Salem. "Melchizedek," however, was not the name of any one particular priest, but was the title held by the *head* of that sacred Priesthood, which is not to be confused with the "Aaronic" Priesthood of the Jews. Melchizedek means "Priest of the Most High God —King of the Upright One."

Moses, writer of the "Books of the Law" of the Hebrews, and learned in the mysteries of the Egyptian Priest-Craft, was a Melchizedek. The Apostle Paul states that Jesus was a Melchizedek. The Melchizedek Priesthood knew neither race nor nationality. The Melchizedek Priesthood is eternal.

The ancient Hindoos held the same conception of Deity, and in their sacred writings—the Vedas— they enunciated those same basic truths as given by Moses in the Book of Genesis.

Yoga Philosophy, built on this foundation, has sought to develop practical methods of application of laws whereby the earnest seeker after truth may attain the most perfect physical development, great length of life, increased mental power, unfailing happiness, and mental and spiritual unfoldment.

In the *Soroda* System of Yoga Philosophy, developed in India, and exemplified and taught in America by Yogi Wassan, the student is lead step by step away from weakness and inefficiency, unhappiness, inharmony, and want, to great physical and mental power, peace, poise, and harmony within, manifesting as joy, wealth, efficiency, spiritual unfoldment, and use of those higher occult forces, such as seeing, hearing, and knowing beyond the realm of the physical senses, and intuitive knowing of the past, present, and future.

To secure this attainment, the student must follow the *fourfold pathway* by earnest, conscientious meditation, systematic study, and by actually *doing* the exercises given in the following lessons.

In reality, science, religion, and philosophy are one. There can be no inharmony, no conflict. No more can one ray of God's sunshine, radiating out from its center—the Brahm—impinge or conflict with another ray of sunshine, than can one truth conflict or contradict another truth. Knowledge of truth—Law—shall make you free.

Basic Truths of Soroda System Yoga Philosophy

The Yogi recognizes that each and every individual in the Universe *must* have a conception of God which is *his own,* and that the breadth of conception of God and the Universe indicates the spiritual attainment and personal manifestation of power of the individual.

Recognizing God as *One,* the Supreme, Unified Consciousness, manifesting in and through everything in the *Universe,* knowing that the God which is in and which *is* everything in the Universe *is good;* looking through the seeming conflicts and seeming clashes, the *Yogi* sees *only* unfoldment, evolution, growth. He cannot conceive of this all-embracing God warring against Himself, breaking any of His laws, or being warred against or thwarted in the carrying out of any of His Divine plans by any other force, whether of the spirit world, or of the material world, or by man—His creation out of Himself. In fact, the Yogi cannot conceive of the existence or reality of any force other than that of the Infinite Creator of all.

Just as he sees God manifesting *as* all creation, evolving, unfolding age after age, expressing God-power more fully in each succeeding activity, so he recognizes that each individual God-created soul—*Atma*—created by God in the Beginning, with infinite possibilities of God-expression, must grow, must evolve, must unfold, and he *knows* that true happiness is found only in consciousness of *growth* and that happiness is the soul expression necessary for soul growth.

Conceiving God as Spirit, manifesting as Mind, Love, Life, Power, every form of energy, as material substance—conceiving the soul (*Atma*) of man as an integral *part* of God, and that *Adam* soul manifesting and using Mind, Love, Life, Power, and material, Yoga Philosophy sees the soul—Atma—as the *complete consciousness* of the individual, seen and unseen, *not* a minute spark of Divinity within the body, but as infinite divine power *within* and *without* the body, creating the body as the instrument for mind expression, love expression, and life expression, and he recognizes the *Absolute Power* of the soul—Atma—to change the body as needs require for greater expression, growth and unfoldment.

Yoga means "yoke" or "joining." Through concentration and meditation, the Yogi first recognizes God, spirit, essence, in every phase of universal manifestation.

Second, he becomes *conscious* of being *yoked-up* with that Universal Spirit, that Universal Power, Universal Intelligence, Universal Life, Universal Love. He becomes conscious that he is *one with it*, an integral part of it, and that thereby he becomes an open channel for its manifestation, resulting in increased understanding, increased love, life, power, and activity.

Third, by systematic exercise, he changes his body so that he manifests in the material world, bodily perfection, mental, and spiritual power, ever-continuing youth, and ultimately attains such growth that use of a physical body for further development is unnecessary.

Because of his consciousness of Unity of God and the Universe, of God and Man, of Soul and mind and body, in all truly Yogi practice and exercise for higher development, all phases of soul expression *must be unified by action.*

Unify bodily posture with thought; unify thought with feeling; unify feeling with action; and you will be amazed at the changes wrought within you.

Truly, there is nothing within the realm of human conception impossible to one who thus "Walks and communes *with* God," and "Becomes as God."

Padam—Asana—Uprightness of Power

Padam means Kingly. Asana means Posture.

Certain postures of the body give the impression of vitality, activity, capacity to endure and continue enduring. Summed up, all of these qualities mean *life*.

The *up* and *down* line, the vertical line, gives an impression of life. That is, it gives life to an idea or a proposition. Every indication of life in nature is indicated by movement up and down, or the upright line. You recognize the feeling of life conveyed to you by the posture of the man who stands upright and erect, with the shoulders back and down, the head *up*, because the line of the body is the symbol of the life line—the vertical line. Such a posture shows the longest up and down line of the body.

In contrast with this, you know the different effect produced upon your mind by the man who exhibits the bent back, stooped shoulders, and drooping head. The vertical line of his body is broken and bent, and, consciously or unconsciously, you immediately judge that there is less of life in him, less activity, less energy, and less endurance, than in the other man.

The strong, vibrant youth stands erect, shoulders back and down, head *up*, looking outward in an attitude of eager expectancy.

The old man—especially one who has failed and knows he has failed—slumps over, shoulders drooping, head toward the ground, showing an attitude of looking *backward* in dejected despondency.

The vital, living tree or plant stands erect, but, dying, its head droops toward the ground.

Law:—Mind attitude tends to express itself in bodily posture.

Law:—Bodily posture tends to create harmonious mental attitude.

Yoga Philosophy teaches that there are subtle forces in nature of infinite power which the soul, in its processes of unfoldment, must use—that within each body there are certain centers through which these forces manifest, and from which they radiate energy throughout the body.

One of these great power centers is located at the base of the spine. To permit the free radiation from this center, the spine *must* be held erect, the navel must be lifted up, and the head must be erect, and *there must be an eager, expectant mental attitude.*

Padam Asana or Posture

Stand *up*, bring arms behind the body, grasping left wrist with right hand, back of left hand touching the back, swinging elbows backward and bringing the hands upward as far as possible toward the shoulders.

Try to *push* the small of the back *away* from the hands.

Lift the head by pulling downward with the back muscles.

Push upper part of chest *outward* and *upward*.

Lift navel and draw in abdomen.

Straightening the Spine

Looking upward at the ceiling, gradually bend the head backward, so the eyes travel behind you along the ceiling, bending the neck first, then the space between the shoulders, then lower down, and finally at the waist, until your back is completely arched. Hold this position for a second. Then relax to Padam Asana. Then bend again slowly, and relax as before, repeating ten times. Each time you bend backwards inhale slowly until at the farthest point of your backward movement the lungs are completely filled with air, *especially* the upper part of the lungs. Exhale as the body returns to posture.

Stand before a mirror. First stand in your usual posture. Then assume Padam Asana. Note the *difference* in your appearance.

Try to *feel* power within you, power radiating upward and outward through your body from the base of the spine.

Walk about your room, expressing *power* in every step you take. Note how perfectly the body is *balanced*, and seemingly how much lighter your step.

Make your head say: *"I am a Superior Man."*

Every man of power easily balances his head upon his shoulders and holds his head well. The mere uplifting of the head gives an impression of superiority which no man in the world can misunderstand. You cannot succeed in leading others unless you can *cause them* to *feel* that you *are* superior.

If you undertake to say in words that you are superior, they will think you are a conceited fool.

Posture is the *only means* by which you can convey the feeling of your superiority.

Train yourself to *walk like a king*, like a *man* among men, strongly tensing the back thigh muscles so you seem to be pushing the earth away from you with each step.

Benefits of Rajana Asana

Why must the head be lifted upward in *expectant attitude?*

You assume the expectant attitude because *all life, all joy, youth* and *success* are *now* yours.

Not only must you *expect* them, but *you must begin to express them.* "To him that hath shall be given."

You have entered the path to *king power.* You must *now* begin to *express* that power.

By lifting the head you free the Thyroid Glands, so they can function freely, so the wonderful vital fluids which they secrete can flow freely throughout your entire body, bringing new life to every part of your body.

By keeping the spine, or vertebral column, erect, life energy flows upward and outward from the great nerve center (the life brain) at the base of the spine; tense muscles of your back, relax, and life energy flows more freely to every vital organ and tissue of the body.

You *lift the navel* so the vital organs (or viscera) of the abdominal cavity are relieved of pressure, the lower lobes of the lungs are brought into activity, and most important of all—pressure is removed from the great nerve center—the sacred *life center*—at the base of the spine.

Live *Padam Asana in thought*, and *feeling*, and *action, every waking hour of the day*.

Many men and women, especially those who have reached the half-century mark, find it very difficult to straighten the spine fully without assistance. Often some of the vertebræ have deflected somewhat from normal relationship, with a resultant squeezing and hardening of the cartilage pads between, and loss of volitional power of the muscles that extend along the vertebral column, so the individual experiences some difficulty in straightening the back sufficiently to permit assuming the correct posture. Under such circumstances, the assistance of someone skilled in the science and art of correction of the tissues and parts involved may be employed.

Certainly your soul *can*, in time and by sufficient effort on your part, gain control and bring your back and your body into correct posture without such help, *but* much time and labor and effort will be saved you (who may need such aid) by having any such distortions properly corrected by outside assistance, thereby permitting the free and unobstructed flow and radiation of all of the life elements throughout the body as it regains normal and correct posture.

Mantra Yoga

Everything in the universe is in vibration, and everything in the universe is inter-connected, one thing with another.

You seemingly live in a dark chamber—the skull. Apparently you are inside, with no means of getting out. Everything must *come* to you. Your soul-power of interpreting vibrations is the *one* means by which you form contact with that world of which you are a part.

When you hear a sound, it is because vibrations of the air are carried to your ears, thence to the hearing centers of your brain, and there interpreted as *sound*.

When you perceive anything through the eye, it is because light vibrations from the objects in your line of vision strike the retina of the eye, and are carried over the optic nerve to the sight centers of the brain, where they are interpreted as *pictures* or *visual images* of the objects from which the rays of light come.

When you touch anything, to determine roughness or smoothness, vibrations of the sensory nerve endings are carried over the sensory nerves to certain brain centers, and are there interpreted as roughness or smoothness.

All impressions which come to you are received as vibrations, and your brain interprets them more or less accurately, according to its sensitiveness and the training it has received.

All the universe is continuously in vibration, sending forth continuous impulses of power, radiating energy at varying rates and in varying forms of vibration. Your body is constantly in vibration, whether vibrating as a whole, in tune with the Universal symphonic harmony, or inharmoniously, dependent upon the conditions of body muscles, and upon mental and emotional conditions. Mental tenseness, emotional repression, and rigidity of body muscles, must be overcome before radiant health, increased mental development, or awakening of higher powers can be attained.

You cannot relax by willing, or ordering muscles to relax, or by any other kind of mental effort, because the vibratory effect of mind is to tense the muscles through which mind energy passes. This tensing effort of mind energy tends to *age* the cells of the body through which it flows. Whenever you *try* to relax the muscles which you can consciously move, you increase the tensity of the deep internal muscles of the body over which you have no conscious control.

But you can relax every muscle by appropriate *bodily action*—that is, by the use of *tones* which vibrate the body. As you bring the body into relaxation and rhythm through the use of *Mantra Yoga*, or Chants, you become "In Tune With the Infinite," and begin to feel yourself *one* with Infinite Mind, Infinite Love, Infinite Life, and Infinite Power—and you attain Radiant Youth, Health and Happiness.

The Seven Holy Words

The *Seven Holy Words,* taken from the *Seven Great Religions* of the world, represent God *within you,* manifesting in different phases of His Consciousness. As you chant these Mantrams, *feel* in every part of your body the particular phase of God Consciousness expressed by that chant.

Father in Heaven—(Christian—God of Harmony Within Me) .... E

O Ang Shantee—(Hindoo—God of Love Within Me) .... E

Devo Budha Namo Amee—(Japanese—God of Wisdom Within Me) .... E

Shintoo Ho—(Chinese—God of Peace Within Me) .... E

El-Oh-Im—(Hebrew—God of Creative Power Within Me) .... E

A-Hung-Atma—Buram—God Prideless Within Me) .... E

Ala-Ho-Akbar—(Mohammedan—God—Formless God Within Me) .... E

Using the Mantra Yoga

Assume the *Padam Asana,* but sitting in a chair, instead of standing. Have the feet flat on the floor, and body erect, *away* from the back of chair, hands behind back, navel lifted up, chest out and chin lifted slightly upward.

Confidently expect to *feel* the awakening of the body, the inflow of *power,* the relaxing of body and mind, and the growing realization of your *unity* with that Universal *Force* of which you are a part.

As you chant the first Mantram, "Father in Heaven," *feel* the God of Harmony manifesting in you; with the second Mantram, "O Ang Shantee," *feel* Love radiating through and from you, et cetera.

Close the eyes and mentally look into the middle of the forehead at the root of the nose. Take a long full breath through the nostrils before beginning each chant. After chanting the words, "Father in Heaven," sound the long "E"—prolonging it until you have expelled all the breath possible from the lungs. *Feel* the vibration:—(1) in the forehead; (2) in the roof of the mouth; (3) in the larynx, or "Adam's Apple;" (4) in the navel; (5) at the base of the spine.

1. Chant for Physical Power.
2. Chant for Dreaming Power.
3. Chant for Occult Power.
4. Chant for Mental Power.
5. Chant for Spiritual Power.
6. Chant for Astral Power.
7. Chant for Cosmic Power.

Yogi Method of Teaching

Development according to Yoga Philosophy is not by knowledge alone, but by faith and earnestness. In India, a student of Yoga (Yogishar Muni) may sit at the feet of his Master (or Guru) daily for months or years, absorbing knowledge telepathically, more by vibration and radiation from the Master than by spoken instruction. You know that if you want to warm yourself by a fire you do not need to jump into the fire, but you can sit near by, and you will receive the radiation of the heat from the fire. So it is with the higher philosophy. It is not altogether what you are receiving by word of mouth, or from the printed page, as it is what you are receiving telepathically from the Guru, or Teacher, by invisible thought and feeling through vibration—receiving the knowledge without words.

This philosophy is like a magnetic current in the atmosphere. Through certain chants, and the use of certain charts, upon which you concentrate, you receive the knowledge. This is one of the reasons why, in these classes, so much time is spent in the Chanting and Concentration exercises, much of the explanatory work being given in the lesson sheets in order to permit time for actual development through working together.

In all of our Chants and Exercises, both now, and as you continue your class work afterward, in groups or individually, I wish each student to develop as much Rhythm in practice as possible. Put rhythm in your chanting, rhythm in your walking, and in all of your daily work, whatever it is. Rhythm means *power*. It is a fact generally known that when soldiers are crossing a bridge that may not be safe, as they march, the order will go forward to "break the step"—the rhythm of the march, for fear of breaking down the bridge by the rhythmic vibration of the "step, step, step, step." Therefore, in walking or talking, in work or in play, if we develop rhythm we can hope to secure the greatest accomplishment of success or enjoyment in life.

The Robe

We use a Robe to represent the Flag of the Soroda System Yoga Philosophy, a robe of seven colors (yellow to represent the earth, white to represent water, red to represent fire, green to represent the air, blue to represent the ether, orange for the mental or intellectual color, and gold for the spiritual color)—with seven vibrations, seven powers. This is our visible robe for exercise and practice. As we practice, we develop an invisible robe within, or about ourselves, which you may have heard spoken of as the "Aura," showing many colors and blending of shades and tints, representing the vibrations of the individual radiating outside the body for a distance of from eighteen inches to three feet.

In the Christian Bible you will remember it is mentioned that Elijah cast his mantle (or robe) upon Elisha. In a like manner, it is a custom among the Yogis for each Yogi to conceal a piece of a robe of his Master in his own robe, for perpetuation of the vibration of his Master Teacher.

In our class work, we use the seven-colored robe for exercise and practice—for developing our inner selves, our inner vibrations, thereby developing the individual robe, invisible to the material eye, but which, nevertheless, radiates from us in Health,

Poise, Charm and Magnetic Power. After we develop those qualities, we can continue to wear the visible robe in our concentration and practice, or not wear it, as we choose.

Shrine for Concentration and Meditation

In India there are many Goofas (Gupha) or Shrines, used by the Yogis for mental and spiritual exercise, for concentration and meditation, just as a gymnasium is used by the western athlete for physical training. These Goofas are underground, or extend back into a cliff, or hillside, with a protected entrance. In the Goofa there is direct contact with the magnetism of the Earth, and all noises that might interfere with study, concentration and meditation are shut out.

In the western world, if individuals or members of a class could join together and build a Goofa somewhat removed from the noise of the city, to which a visit might be made on Saturday night, or Sunday, for Chanting or Meditation, with perhaps a Kitchen and Assembly room built above, the advantageous effects upon the health, mental development, spiritual development and business success of the individuals so practicing would be marvelous indeed.

Otherwise, each individual should have his or her own particular shrine in the home, in a closet that need not be disturbed by others, and which is large enough to permit sitting in posture—or by using an armchair in the corner of a room, with curtains of dark material (black or dark green) hung around. This shrine should be used by the individual, and by him or her only, for the practice of the Concentration, Meditation and Chanting exercises given in these lessons.

Padam Asana

Padam means concentration.

Hundreds of years ago, the ancient Yogis discovered, by long and continued experimentation, that certain postures of the body aided in Concentration and Meditation—that certain bodily positions obviated interruptions of consciousness during concentration upon any particular subject. Many of these postures are demonstrated by Yogi Wassan in his classes. To the people of the western world, some of those postures will, at first, seem very difficult to assume and master, but by gradual practice the body may be brought under such control that the postures can be assumed and held for considerable periods of time, during which the mind will not be interrupted by body sensations during its activity upon any particular question or problem.

Until these postures have been mastered, however, Yogi Wassan wishes his students to begin their Concentration and Meditation with the Modified Padam Asana.

Modified Padam Asana

Sit erect in your chair, with back, navel and head in the Padam Asana, but with arms folded so that fingers of right hand rest or enfold the left elbow, and the fingers of the left hand enfold the right elbow.

What Padam Concentration Really Is

What true concentration really is can best be illustrated by one of the methods of extracting gold from the quartz rock. When gold quartz is mined, tiny veins of the gold are mixed up with much larger quantities of the rock. First, the rock is crushed to powder, and, after being mixed with water, it flows over shallow pans containing quick-silver. The quick-silver catches the gold and rejects the rock. Through heating, this concentrated gold and quick-silver are separated, the gold being cast into bars and the quick-silver being put back into the pans to attract more gold.

Thus it is with the mind. Concentration is *not* mere *holding* of *one* thought, saying it over and over, parrot-like, or with machine-like affirmations, but *true concentration* is an *activity* of the mind, drawing to itself all kinds of thoughts *relating* to the subject, weighing them, retaining those of value, and rejecting the others—then, taking the retained ideas, relating them, re-forming them, and building them into pure gold of the complete *ideal*.

As you concentrate in this manner, day by day, your power of bringing to your mind *new* thoughts, of weighing them, analyzing them, relating them, and using them, will grow. New thinking is *creative* thinking. By this method, in a very short time you will discover that you are able to think more deeply and more completely about the problems of your business, of your every-day life; mistakes and mis-judgments due to partial thinking will be prevented; and you will move steadily forward toward financial success and material abundance.

Many Lessons In Soroda System Yoga Philosophy

BY

SUPER-AKASHA YOGI WASSAN

That Ye May Know Yourselves

In the preceding lessons we endeavored to understand the ideals of Vedic Philosophy in relation to God and the Universe—how God and the universe which He has created are *one*—just as the ocean, the bubble and the water are one, although until the realization is attained, there may seem to be a separation. We learned, too, that the Yogi recognizes that God, in every phase of His manifestation, *is good*, and *only good*.

The *real self—the complete consciousness* of each individual—the *ray* of God, radiated *out* from that God-Brahm-Center, possessing *all* the Powers and Attributes of God, the Yogi calls *Atma*.

God, *Ishara*, is Spirit. That Spirit manifests as energy which we cannot see, or know with our physical senses, as well as manifesting *as* matter, which we can touch, see, and know with our physical senses. So, also, *Atma*, the *you*, the *individualized ray* of God, *is spirit*, and the *you—Atma*—manifests as both *seen* and *unseen* energy, force, spirit, *as well as body*.

You, *Atma*, are a *soul-beam* of God, a radiation from God, and *you* have been from all eternity, are *now*, and Will Be to All Eternity *directly connected with God*. Neither you nor any other power—not even God Himself Can Sever that Connection. It is Eternal.

Atma is *not* a little spark of divinity hidden away somewhere within your body, any more than *all* there is of God is hidden within any one of His manifestations. Just as God is *limitless* in extent, as well as in power, love and activity, so also is *Atma* limitless, not only in Power, but in capacity to Love, and capacity for enjoyment of Life, and also *limitless in extent.*

You—Atma—always, at all times, *surround* your body and *you* extend miles and miles beyond it in *every direction.* *You—Atma—*are *not* confined within your body any more than *Atma* (spirit) is confined within your heart, or your liver, or your brain, or stomach, or any particular spot in your body.

*You—Atma—*are Limitless in *extension,* as well as in power, intelligence, and capacity for enjoyment. Your *body* is merely the *focal center,* through which *Atma* expresses in Physical activity. Only a small part of the activity of *Atma* ever manifests through your body at any one time.

Atma is *unity—*Unity *with* God, Unity *with* the Universe, and *unity within itself.*

Just as it is impossible to conceive of a *universe* divided against itself and still continuing to exist, so the thinking man or woman must recognize that it would be impossible for him or her to continue to exist were *Atma—*infinite power—divided against itself.

Now and for all time discard all thoughts of warfare between the God forces within yourself. And *know* that there are no forces in all the Universe which are *not* God forces.

Maya (illusion) has made you *think* of a divided universe, of certain forces as evil and of other forces as good. Maya has taught you to think of certain forces within yourself as good, and certain other phases of God expression as evil.

Awake! Oh Man, Oh Woman! Let the fogs of Maya be swept away and *know* Yourself as you *are* —a part of God—Universal Good—and begin to manifest that Good forever.

Laugh! Laugh! Laugh! Seven times laugh! Laugh your old pains, and fears, and worries out of existence.

This is not only the philosophy of the Soroda System Yoga, but it is also the philosophy of the Ancient Egyptians, of the Ancient Hebrews—of the Christ.

In Genesis we find that Moses, who was learned in all the mysteries of the Sacred Egyptian Priesthood, instead of using a Hebrew word for "man," used the Sacred Egyptian word, "Adam," which signified "That Part of God, given Particular God-Power, to Absorb God, to use God, to Radiate God."

In the Ancient Sanscrit, "*Adhim*—root word— means "first in origin; primeval force."

Jesus said. "The Father Within Me, He doeth the work." "Seek Ye First the Kingdom of Heaven."

Recognition of Adam's divinity is found in Luke 3:38, which gives the genealogy of Jesus, * * * * * "which was the son of Enos, which was the son of Seth, which was the son of Adam, which was the *son of God.*"

Atma, therefore, manifests in *you* as intelligence, as love, as life, as power, as action, *and* the *Atma* manifests in you and through you as *body*, which it has created as its means of physical manifestation and physical activity.

The *Atma—yourself*—is limitless in extent as well as in power—has created your body of itself. Your body, therefore, is just as spiritual as any other part of the Atma. "Know you not that your bodies are temples of the Living God?"—Paul.

The Atma—*yourself*—has always lived, always will live. Just as your *Atma* has created the body in which you *now* live, so it has created bodies in which you *have* lived, and it will create bodies in which you *will* live, and through which it will manifest itself.

The One Universal Law of All Life is *growth, change, evolution, unfoldment.*

Recognize that this law applies to *you*. Bring yourself into harmony with it. *Know* that you have power to change, to grow. Become filled with a burning *desire* to unfold. *Use* the God forces within you, consciously and discriminatively, and you will be *astounded* at the results in bodily health, mental superiority, success and happiness which will come to you.

The Three Great Vibratory Forces of the Atma

MIND

Mind energy is one form of God radiation.

The *brain* is the creation of the Atma as the organ, or center, for use of this particular energy.

You draw this mind-power from the Universe, and use it in thinking and you radiate it over the nerves of the body to bring about the intelligent activity of the cells of your body, to cause movement of the muscles, and you *radiate mind energy* directly to other minds, as well as manifesting it in speech, or other physical means.

EMOTIVE ENERGY (LOVE)

Love, or *emotive energy*, is the second form of God Radiation.

The Solar Plexus, or *love brain* (located behind the stomach), is the organ or center created by the *Atma* for use of this particular form of energy.

The *Atma* draws this Love Energy from the Universe and radiates it through the nerves to all parts of the body to bring about harmonious activity of the cells of the body; to bring about union of the cells, thereby continuing the life of the body; and from your body you radiate Love-Energy to other souls, thereby bringing you into harmonious relation with them. This Love-Energy radiates direct from Atma to Atma without physical contact, as well as being manifested through your words, tones and actions.

LIFE—OR CREATIVE ENERGY

Life, or *creative energy*, is a third form of God Radiation.

The Sacral Plexus, or Sacred Brain (Life Brain), situated within the pelvis and at the base of the spine, is the organ or center created by the *Atma* through which to radiate *life* to the cells of your body, bringing about the creation of *new* cells and continuing the life in your body. You also radiate *life* energy in every form of mental creative effort, in every form of physical creation—whether of literature, or invention, or art, or in the incarnation upon the earth of a new life.

You Are God of Your Body Universe

Your body, springing from a single cell—the union of two cells, male and female—is composed of cells—twenty billions or more of them.

Every cell of your body is an individual, possessing intelligence, possessing power to love and to respond to love, possessing life, with the life power of reproduction and increase. The cells of your body are male and female. These cells may reproduce themselves in either of two ways—by division or by union, with division again, after the union.

When cells reproduce by division, a male cell divides and produces two male cells, or a female cell divides and produces two female cells. Each of the cells so produced by division is *older,* and possess less life and power than the parent cell.

When cells reproduce by union, a male cell unites with a female cell and the *new* cell is a *youth* cell, younger and more powerful than the parent cells.

The *love* energy which radiates from the Love Brain causes these cells to be attracted to each other, and the *life* energy which radiates from the Life Brain causes these cells to *unite* and produce the Youth cells.

Think of your body as a whole world peopled by vast numbers of races of cells. There are only about two billion individuals in the whole world, but there are more than twenty billions of cell individuals in your body. Think of the cell empire of your Brain; the cell republic of your stomach; the cell kingdom of your liver; the vast number of cell states of each of the muscles of your body, et cetera.

As you attain harmony with God, harmony within yourself, and with all other individuals of God's universe, so will there be harmony manifested between the cells and organs of your body, between cell and cell, stomach and liver, brain and muscle, circulation and nerves.

The attainment of that inner harmony—that Kingdom of Heaven Within—is the first step in unfoldment as taught by Yoga Philosophy.

As you attain bodily harmony, you attain mental and emotional balance, and then you are ready for the higher unfoldment of mind and *Atma*.

Exercise for Awakening Consciousness of the Body Universe

As you perform this exercise, feel that you are supplying to each of these races of cells in the particular part of the body you are visiting, increased life, increased intelligence and love, and that you are awakening them to greater activity and power.

Feel *love* for the billions of individual cells composing these cell republics. As you actually feel (radiate) love to them, they will show their love for you and for each other by manifesting more nearly perfect health and bodily harmony.

Sit erect in chair, feet flat on floor, fingers clinched and little finger resting on lower thigh, just above the knees. Attention with the will, Low, Medium, High —Vibrate with the Action.

Think of your body as a great *temple*, with many special, separate rooms, each room having a number, one of the forty-nine numbers given in this particular exercise.

Close your eyes. Picture yourself at the entrance to this Great Temple. Relax, and look into the forehead at the root of the nose. Think that you are about to enter room Number 1—which is the Left Foot, and project yourself into the left foot for the moment, sitting very quietly, listening within and seeing within. *Feel* the Vibration within the foot, at first slowly, then more rapidly, and then still faster, like three speeds of an automobile.

Then go into Room Number 2, which is the Right Foot. With a feeling of love for the cells there, become conscious of the vibration of the foot, slow, medium and high speed.

Then visit the various parts of your Body Temple in the order given in this exercise:

Left Foot	1- 2	Right Foot
Left Calf	3- 4	Right Calf
Left Knee	5- 6	Right Knee
Left Thigh	7- 8	Right Thigh
Left Rump	9-10	Right Rump
Left Abdomen	11-12	Right Abdomen
Left Kidney	13-14	Right Kidney
Spleen	15-16	Liver
Left Ribs	17-18	Right Ribs
Left Lung	19-20	Right Lung
Left Collar Bone	21-22	Right Collar Bone
Left Shoulder	23-24	Right Shoulder
Left Upper Arm	25-26	Right Upper Arm
Left Forearm	27-28	Right Forearm
Left Hand	29-30	Right Hand
Left Thyroid	31-32	Right Thyroid
Left Ear Drum	33-34	Right Ear Drum
Left Eye	35-36	Right Eye
Left Temple	37-38	Right Temple

Left Cerebrum	39-40—	Right Cerebrum
Forehead, at Root of Nose	41-42—	Medulla Ob., Base of Head
Down through spinal cord to base of spine	43-44—	Around in front over Bladder and generative organs
To the Navel	45-46—	To the Stomach
To the Heart	47-48—	To "Adam's Apple" or Larynx
To the Top of the Head	49—	Straight through Door of Brahm

Feel that you are outside your body Temple and above the entrance through which you started when beginning this exercise.

Hold yourself in the attitude of meditation for a few minutes. Then, if you have time, reverse the exercise, beginning at the top of the head and going down to the foot. Always finish the exercise by mounting above your body, as it were, and sitting thus a few minutes in quiet meditation.

As you develop in this practice, school yourself to make quick changes, focusing your attention first in one part and then in another—as, for instance—projecting yourself from left knee (by number or name, or both) to right shoulder; then to stomach, then to left eye, etc.

This exercise will be very beneficial in stimulating the circulation throughout the body, in quickening the activity of all the cells of the body, giving power for Nerve-Control, Steadiness and Poise at all times. It will quicken the vibration of brain cells, thus quickening the thinking power, and stimulating memory cells for greater power of remembering.

The Tongue

People of the Western world have been accustomed to think of the tongue as the instrument of taste, or for use in moving food around in the mouth, or as an organ of speech. I give you here another use of the tongue which is almost magical in its results in making the body magnetic.

When not in use in speaking, or eating, the tongue should always be turned back in the mouth, and the tip of the tongue should be pressed against the roof of the mouth.

Why?—Placing the tip of the tongue against the roof of the mouth is like closing an electric switch, because then the nerve energy from the Love Brain (Solar Plexus) flows over the nerves, which extend from it to the tongue, and from the tongue these vibrations are carried to the brain over the nerves which come directly from the brain to the roof of the mouth. This love vibration relaxes the cells of the brain, awakens them to renewed activity and causes them to draw in more Mind-prana from the Universe, and to radiate it over the nerves to all parts of the body. Thus, the body is made more magnetic, and increased resistance to heat and cold is assured.

When the tip of the tongue is pressed against the roof of the mouth, the opening from the nose to the lungs is made larger, and the upper lobes of the lungs are more completely filled by air than when the tongue is permitted to lie flat in the mouth.

This practice is also of very great value to singers and speakers, because it brings the thyroid muscles into greater activity, and makes them stronger.

The Humming Breath

You can exercise your arms or your legs, or other muscles or parts of the body by making movements, as taught in gymnasiums; you can exercise your chest muscles by bending and deep breathing; but you cannot exercise the brain tissues in any such way because the brain is enclosed within a bony structure —the skull.

The chanting and humming, as taught in connection with these lessons, by vibrating the cells of the brain, frees them from congestion of blood by increasing the circulation, awakens the cells to greatly increased activity, and causes an increased radiation of Mind-Prana from the nerve centers to all parts of the body.

Think of your body Temple as a wonderful musical instrument, and that you are going to bring it into harmonious vibration through the use of the vocal cords in this humming exercise.

Hoong, Yang, Yang, Yang—"I am one with the great consciousness: always have been: am now: and always will be."

As you use this chant, realize the Power of the Thought. Realization of *oneness* with *all power* always causes increased inflow of Power through your body.

Feel that power flowing freely through you.

You can use this Humming Breath either while standing, sitting or walking, but *always*, when using it, keep the spine erect, shoulders back and down, head *up*, navel pulled *up* and *in* as though you were trying to *push out all the breath from the lungs.*

This exercise is the *first step* toward opening the Physical Solar Plexus, which will bring you radiant health, increased mental power, super-attraction, and great creative ability. It is also the first step towards clairvoyance and clairaudience, and all super-mental powers of Yogi.

1. Hold tongue firmly against the roof of the mouth while humming.
2. Pull navel in; at end of each breath pull navel in and up forcibly.
3. Hum slowly at first, then faster, and faster, like the three speeds of an automobile.
4. Continue the humming until you feel the vibration in the entire body—until every cell is in harmonious vibration.
5. Without making a sound, mentally hum, feeling the vibration in and throughout the entire body in every cell.

When you are making the sound, it is *visible* vibration; when mentally humming, without making sound, it is *invisible* vibration.

Practice the humming with the sound whenever you can, during the day, on the street cars, walking, wherever the sound will not annoy anyone. When unable to make the sound, practice the Invisible Humming. This is your first step to power.

Should you find your body tense, or feel lack of power, this humming, either visible or invisible, will aid you in regaining bodily and mental poise and harmony.

Stiff neck muscles, always present in cases of headache, eye-weakness, etc., can be quickly relaxed by placing the hand over the back of the neck, covering as great an area as possible, and vibrating the neck muscles under the hand with this humming breath.

Chant for Strengthening Eyes, Improving Hearing, and Relieving Catarrh

Sit erect in chair, eyes closed. Press small lobe in front portion of ear backward with thumbs, closing the auditory meatus. Place palms of hands over eyes to shut out light, with fingers over forehead. (If sitting at a table, elbows may be rested upon table, but keep erect posture.)

Hum the *Hoong, Yang, Yang, Yang,* strongly, and feel the vibration in nose, ears, eyes and throughout head.

Continue this practice in periods of five minutes at intervals during the day, during the first month, gradually increasing the time as you work for supermental development.

After humming, practice the Invisible Vibration, feeling the awakening of the cells in the ears, or the eyes, or at the root of the nose.

Hoong, Yang, Yang, Yang Chant for Power

Stand erect, arms dropped to sides and hands directly over the crotch, with fingers pointing inward, but not touching the body.

As you chant, gradually raise the hands upward toward the head, keeping the fingers pointing toward the body, but not touching it. Continue to elevate the hands until they are as high above the head as you can bring them. Rise on toes as you elevate the hands above the head.

Clinch the fists *tight*. Tense the arms *strongly,* and bring down *slowly,* swinging arms outward at the sides as though you were *pulling* power into your body. Drop on flat foot as arms are brought down.

Fill the lungs comfortably before beginning the humming, and gradually and slowly exhale as the arms are brought up. Hold the breath out as you bring the arms down.

Bring to relaxed posture over the groins and inhale quickly.

Repeat seven times.

Feel the *O-Ang-Shantee* Power (the impelling, out-going creative Power of the Atma) radiating upward from the base of the spine and spreading throughout the body.

This Chant for Power should be done in the privacy of your own room (it is truly your Prayer for Power), preferably in the morning when you arise. This will vitalize your body and make your work a joy throughout the entire day.

Physical Exercises—On Rising in Morning— For Relaxation

1. Sitting on edge of bed, grasp the mattress firmly with each hand, sitting erect and not moving the body, let your head drop to chest; then backward as far as possible. Then, without tensity, roll the head around in as large a circle as possible, rolling first to right, and then to the left.

Then rotate shoulders, making as large a circle as possible, rotating from left to right, and from right to left.

Then rotate entire chest from the waist, making as large a circle as possible, rotating in both directions.

2. Standing, with feet spread somewhat apart, clasp hands firmly behind head, forearms straight; rotate the body at the waist from left to right, and reverse. Keep navel pulled up *high* when performing this exercise.

CARE OF THE MOUTH

The first thing in the morning, upon arising, and after taking any preliminary exercises desired, clean the teeth and tonsils, brushing teeth thoroughly with your usual tooth-paste, or Hindoo Tooth Powder. Then dip the end of a clean towel in clear water, put over one finger, and rub the gums up, and away from the teeth with a brisk friction, and rub the teeth briskly in the direction away from the gums. Rub inside and outside until the gums (at first) bleed and the teeth feel hot from the rubbing.

Pull the tongue forward and rub top of tongue with a fresh portion of towel, as far back in the throat as it is possible to reach, cleaning all deposits off the tongue. Rub roof of mouth and tonsilar ring in the same thorough manner, cleaning out all mucus. This rubbing will strengthen the muscles of the throat and mouth, making them hold themselves firmly, thus warding off attacks from disease germs which might otherwise secure lodgment in the mouth.

Clean mucus from nasal passages with a Nasal Douche and warm water, to which has been added a pinch of salt or baking soda. This cleansing of the nasal passages is very necessary for anyone who has been troubled by catarrh. All mucus should be spit out; never swallowed.

Extend the tongue as far out of the mouth as possible; then draw it back into the larynx as far as possible. Make this movement rapidly and with force, at least twenty times. This brings the lower muscles of the mouth, and muscles of the tongue and larynx into action. Then grasp the tongue in the hand, which is covered by towel, and in a manner simulating "milking," draw the tongue as far out as possible without causing pain.

After this the throat may be gargled, if desired. Then drink a glass of lukewarm water, and make a slight effort to vomit, by tickling the throat with end of brush. To vomit a little of the water that has just been swallowed will bring up some of the poisonous residue that has accumulated in the stomach over night. Also, the effort to vomit will stimulate circulation to the head. After this drink two or three glasses of water. (Never drink iced water at any time.) This should be done at least a half-hour before any food is taken into the stomach, so the water, entering an approximately empty stomach, will pass on rapidly into the intestine, thus cleansing the stomach of any residue and mucus, and preparing for proper action of digestive juices upon the food that enters. This same method of cleansing the stomach may be used advantageously a half-hour before any meal that is to be taken during the day.

After the mouth and throat, nasal passages, etc., are thoroughly cleansed the first thing in the morning, and all mucus eliminated, then turn the tip of the tongue back against the roof of the mouth, and suck the tongue. This will stimulate the flow of Saliva, which is the "Nectar of Life." Swallow the saliva so digestion may be assisted.

Food

The subject of Food and Diet is ever with us, with a varied array of "Food Scientists," faddists and extreme theorists—each trotting out his own pet "hobby" or idea for our consideration and acceptance.

Diet Must Be Adapted to Individual Needs According to An Individual Analysis of Each Person

Visible Sineyas Yoga is the name applied to the Hindoo Science of Chemistry as applied to the vegetable, animal and mineral kingdoms—the science of botany, physiology and geology—and therefore embraces the subject of "Dietetics and Therapy"—or *chemicalization* of the body by the foods taken into the body.

While it is generally understood that Hindoo cookery embraces a non-meat diet, with a great variety of vegetable, grain and dairy combinations, and such a diet is recommended to all who may come to that idea, it is advised that such changes be made slowly and gradually. In this manner, any nervousness that might be caused by suddenly depriving the body of something to which it has been accustomed would be avoided, and at the same time a non-meat diet could be worked out to fit the needs of the individual, for securing in so far as possible the balance of proper equilibrium of the chemical elements of the blood— as to acidity, alkalinity, etc. In a Supplement to this lesson, this subject is handled in a little more detail, in connection with some fifty or more Combination Recipes which are given in such form that certain special uses of many of the recipes may be indicated in Individual Analysis.

In another Lesson of this Series, it has been mentioned that the word "Prana" was used by the Ancient Hindoo (Soroda Yoga) Philosophers to refer, not only to the energy or "Force" of the Air we breathe, rather than the Air itself, but also to the "life essence" of the food we eat and the water we drink. Modern Physiological scientists, in puzzling laboratory experiments, have verified this by having to accept the fact that there are certain subtle elements in food which are not simply *matter,* but which contain a "Life Spark" extending beyond the realm of matter, and therefore representing vital energy, which has led to the use of the term "Vitamins" with reference to these elements.

These Vitamins, designated as A, B, C, D, and E (with still others not yet differentiated) are found in various foods, including different kinds of raw foods, which fact has led to that modern slogan:— "Eat something raw every day." A few food faddists have gone to the extreme on this idea by recommending an exclusively raw diet, but in this, again, the individual case has to be studied as to whether or not the stomach can take care of raw food, either in small or larger quantities. However, by proper Chemicalization, the digestive system of most people can take care of at least small portions, either alone or in combinations, of some of the vegetables commonly eaten raw, such as lettuce, celery, watercress, onions, tomatoes, carrots, etc., as indicated in the Food Lesson.

For those who are endeavoring to re-build youthful bodies, the following general advice will be valuable:

1. It is not wise for adults to drink much cow's milk. This is because cow's milk contains a lime content greater than the needs of the adult body demand, and therefore have the effect of adding the element that will increase the hardness of bones, and of the arteries and walls of other vessels of the body as well. The cream, however, is very valuable, and should be used regularly, because it contains a vital essence (called in the Western world Vitamin A), which causes growth of cell tissue. Cod-liver oil also contains this vital essence.

2. Lettuce and cotton-seed oil (Wesson) both contain another vital essence, called Vitamin E, which greatly increases the mating activity of the cells of the body, causing them to unite to create new youth body cells. This element is also found in fresh egg-yolk.

In India there are many foods used for special purposes, but most of these are not easily obtainable in this country, so the best adaptation possible of American foods has been made.

Water

The composition of the human body is more than two-thirds fluid (usually given as 70% or over) so we can understand that Water is one of the principal ingredients of the body. The little individual cells of the body *must* live in fluid. With too small a proportion of fluid cell life is impaired, and elimination of waste materials from the body is interfered with.

Then the blood becomes too thick and too hot. Just how much water a person should drink in a day is often dependent upon certain individual conditions relative to the organs of elimination, and no universal rule can be applied for this reason.

Regulation of Eliminative Processes

Failure to eliminate the poisonous waste materials from the body is the chief cause of ageing of the body. Physical scientists of the western world have definitely proven (what the Hindoos have known for centuries—that with proper elimination of wastes from the body, there is no reason why the body should ever grow old.

The four great eliminative channels we find to be through—(1) the lungs or respiratory tract; (2) through the skin; (3) through the kidneys, or urinary tract; and (4) through the intestinal or digestive tract, in connection with which we find the liver, that wonderful chemical laboratory of the body.

The breathing exercises given in these lessons, if faithfully practiced, and the *habit* of deep and full breathing is attained, will insure fullest elimination possible through the respiratory tract.

The daily sponge bath, with friction of the skin by the hands (or a rough towel), and active physical exercises to produce perspiration, will provide proper elimination through the skin.

By drinking a sufficient quantity of water, the kidneys are provided with the fluid necessary for their share of elimination of body poisons.

Food is taken into the body in this western world usually *three* times a day, but in the matter of elimination there is frequently gross neglect, often with only one bowel action during the twenty-four hours, and sometimes not even that, with chronic impaction of the colon as a result. The too long retention of this fecal matter within the body results in reabsorption of poisons, which is one of the most direct causes of illness. There is *no* reason why this should be the case. On rising in the morning, as soon as the exercises here given have been performed (or before, which is better), the bowels should be completely emptied. Then again, before going to bed, there should be a complete evacuation of the bowels.

The habitual use of strong purgatives and mineral salts which are used by so many is very bad for the body and can be avoided by use of a food compound which acts also on the liver and insures frequent bowel activity. I herein give you a recipe for this laxative food, which you can use for the remainder of your life with the certainty of beneficial results. Eat one of the candies every other night as long as you live and you will avoid further troubles from constipation.

Before giving the recipe, however, I call your attention to another reason for emptying the colon at least twice daily. At the base of the spine, as you know, is the Sacral Plexus, or Sacred or Life Brain, which is the center of the Life energies of the Atma. When the colon is full, there is pressure upon this great nerve center, which thus *shuts* off the flow of life-giving energy throughout the body. When gas forms in the intestines, the pressure extends to the heart, lungs, solar brain, and sacral brain, which interferes with every physical activity of the body.

This stopping of the flow of energy from these

great energy centers interferes with development of the super-mental and spiritual functions of the Atma. Body and Mind and Atma are one. To secure greatest results the body *must be healthy.*

Home-Made Laxative Food Candy

Mix together two pounds of raisins (seeded or seedless) and eight ounces of dried senna leaves. Grind through food grinder, and make into small balls about the size of marbles, rolling in flour just enough to make the surface smooth. Let dry several days, after which keep in glass jars in a cool place. Eat one piece of this Laxative Food Candy every other night, chewing thoroughly, and drink a glass of hot water, before going to bed.

Many Lessons In Soroda System Yoga Philosophy

BY

SUPER-AKASHI YOGI WASSAN

The Seven Mantrams

TheseMantrams are to be used, first, for the opening of the inner self—for spiritualization of the body temple; and, second, for continued physical development.

So-Hoong—(Meaning *I Am* Unity with the Great Consciousness) .... E
O-Hoong—(Meaning *I Am* Unity with Physical Creation) .... E
Mo-Hoong—(Meaning *I Am Creator* of my own Universe. I create that which I desire) .... E
Ko-Hoong—(Meaning *I Am One* with Living Creation—animal and vegetable) .... E

Ro-Hoong—(Meaning *I Am* God of my Universe,
   I am Supreme in my Universe) ─────────── E
A-Hang—(Meaning Prideless God within me) ───── E
El-Oh-Tm—(Meaning Formless God within me) ─ E

Note:—Remember, that the *I Am* is the *Atma*, the complete consciousness, the *Soul*-Beam of the Universal, the *power* in and back of the Physical, which you are bringing into manifestation.

As you repeat the words and hum the "E" try to *feel* the thought expressed by the words.

Pranayama—Control of Prana

Prana is *not air*. *Prana* is the term used to refer to the finer forces of the Universe, these energies which your soul uses—mind energy, love energy, life force. It is the life essence of the air we breathe, the water we drink, and the food we eat.

As you inhale, *feel* that you are drawing into your body those finer forces, and as you exhale, *feel* that you are radiating those forces, not only through your body, but outward from your body—that you are a center of radiation force.

The Slow Breath—Storing Personal Magnetism

Inhale through the nose, filling first the lower part of the lungs, then middle lungs, then upper lungs, making special effort to fill the back of the lungs. As soon as the lungs are filled, begin to exhale, slowly contracting the chest, emptying the back of the lungs, and finally pulling up the diaphragm to force out all the air possible. Try to bring into action all the muscles of the chest, squeezing in and contracting the chest as much as possible.

As the air is inhaled, push out under the arms as

far as possible and lift the upper chest until the air seems to have filled up to the neck.

Keep head up, spine straight, and navel pulled in and up while taking the breathing exercise.

Note:—Very few people bring into action the back *half* of the lungs, thus cutting down the lung space and depleting the power supply which the body should receive.

Make a definite effort—even though it takes a considerable time—to use the back part of the lungs in breathing.

Practice drawing the air in *quickly* through the nose—then exhaling *slowly*, holding the breath *out* for a few moments before again inhaling. Do not hold the breath in.

Breathe rhythmically. A good time to practice rhythmic breathing is in walking. Breathing is a very *individual* matter, and no set count can be designated to fit all who may wish to practice a breathing exercise. Any breathing exercise designated should always be adapted very slowly and carefully to the individual rate of respiration of the individual, rather than by actual time or count.

Physical Benefits

First, there is a complete change of air by this thorough method of breathing, effecting removal of poisonous gases from the body. Every part of the lungs work, and therefore become strong and healthy. All the muscles of the back, between the vertebral column and the lungs, are used and relaxed, thus preventing congestion of the blood and tensity of muscles. Tensity of muscles prevents radiation of nerve energy throughout the body.

This rhythmic breathing also awakens all the solar plexus to greater activity, and the deep breathing also fills the lower lobes of the lungs, increasing the radiation of life energy from the Sacral Plexus.

The lifting up of the diaphragm and drawing in of the front walls of the abdomen at the end of the exhalation lifts the venous blood from the abdomen to the heart, strengthens the walls of the abdomen, thus giving greater support to the vital organs, lifts the navel, giving more room to the vital organs, and finally massages those organs by causing them to move one upon another.

The lifting up of the diaphragm and movement of the walls of the abdomen helps to correct Visceral Ptosis (dropping downward of vital organs). It increases digestive powers of both stomach and intestines and increases peristaltic movement, accelerating elimination.

By making the Humming Breath (Hoong Yang—3) as you exhale, you increase the physical benefit of the deep breathing, and at the same time you are freeing the Physical Solar Plexus for increase of mental power, by awakening and quickening the activity of the brain centers, thereby developing the power of magnetic attraction, and making yourself more sensitive to those higher vibrations which are called Telepathy, Clear-Vision, or Clair-audience.

Proportions of Various Parts of the Body

In the normal youth, the distance from navel to crotch should be one-fifth the total height of the body. As one grows older, there is a tendency to allow the upper part of the body to *press down*, to settle down on the pelvis and to shorten this distance.

This shortening of the distance crowds the vital organs and slows down their action, notably decreasing the power of these organs to eliminate waste elements from the body.

Physical scientists have stated there is *no* reason why the body should ever grow old except there is too much waste poison allowed to accumulate in the cell structure.

By continuously pulling the navel *up* and working to lengthen this distance from navel to crotch, this eliminative action is accelerated, and you can prevent largely this accumulation of poison.

The Exercise which follows, and many more given in this course of lessons, will be of great assistance in increasing this distance.

Rotating the Walls of the Abdomen

This exercise is particularly valuable for those who sit much of their time at work—office people particularly.

Sitting in a straight chair, with body erect, exercise, by pulling in the abdominal muscles, then rotate the walls of the abdomen from left to right, and then from right to left, for about three minutes. This exercise is particularly helpful in correcting constipation.

Early Morning Exercise

The first thing in the morning, put feet on the floor, sit on side of the bed, and take this exercise:

With elbows resting on thighs, hands up, fingers interlaced, try to reach the left shoulder to the right knee; and the right shoulder to the left knee, alternately, stretching all the muscles from the waist up. Then, with fingers interlaced in lap, rotate the head—first to the left shoulder, then back, then to right shoulder, then forward, slowly, pulling on the muscles of the neck as you rotate the head. Repeat this rotation four or five times for opening up the blood circulation to and from the head, for rejuvenating the scalp and preventing loss of hair; also for relaxing the tissues at the base of the skull, thereby freeing the medulla oblongata and nerves of the brain.

Then, with elbows on knees, hands up and fingers interlaced, tilt the head slowly backward, and gradually come forward again, dropping head forward a bit quickly on interlaced fingers—not too fast, or too forcibly. Then raise the head up straight again, and rotate again, slowly, to left, back, to right, and forward, pulling and stretching the neck muscles during the rotation.

Repeat the rotation of the head, this time letting the body follow the same path of rotation, from the waist up, stretching and pulling the muscles of both body and neck, to the left, backward, to the right, then forward, letting the head drop forward, stretching the muscles at back of head and body from the waist. Take this exercise a few minutes before going into the bath room in the morning, for waking up the muscles of the whole body.

Baths, Body Massage and Scalp Massage

Many people take too many tub baths. Bodily conditions should govern this matter, but ordinarily one or two cleansing baths each week are sufficient, with a quick shower and body massage morning or night, or both morning and night. For this, a shower spray is not absolutely necessary, but the hands should be dipped in water, which should be neither too hot nor too cold, and massaged over the body, the shoulders and arms, the chest, back, sides, and limbs, drying the body with the hands massage, and not by means of a towel. This gives a glow to the body that far surpasses the friction of a towel massage.

At night, the scalp should be massaged deeply with the finger tips before going to bed. For this, the fingers may be dipped in water, neither too hot nor too cold, and the scalp massaged deeply all over the head. Also the muscles at the back of the neck. This will free the circulation to the head and scalp, and will also make the finger tips strong. After completing the scalp and neck massage, then clasp the fingers, interlaced, at the back of the head, forearms tight against the temples, in a scissor-hold, and rock the head from side to side quickly but carefully; then backward; then letting it drop forward somewhat. This exercise relaxes the muscles of the neck, freeing the nerves to the head, permitting free circulation of blood to the scalp, and also to the brain and eyes.

Ida, Pingla, and Sukhmuna—for Personal Magnetism

AND

DEVELOPMENT OF TELEPATHY AND OTHER OCCULT POWERS

The Science of Magnetic Breath

Soroda System says: "The Yogi who has power over his breath can put it into any vibration he chooses, and the antagonistic effects of planetary positions, of adverse mental contacts, or thoughts of misfortune, will have no power whatsoever to affect that Yogi."

"This Science of the Rise of Breath is the highest of all sciences. It is a flame for illuminating the mansions of the soul."

"In the body are many Nadis (Nadi meaning river or vein in Sanskrit), having many forms and extensions. * * * The principal are the ten nadis in which act the ten forces, of which ten, three are the highest —Ida, Pingla, and Sukhmuna. Ida is the left part of the body, Pingla is in the right, and Sukhmuna in the middle. The left part of the body containing both the nerves and blood vessels may be called Ida— the right, Pingla. The Right and Left Bronchi form, as well, parts respectively of Pingla and Ida, as may other parts of the Right and Left divisions of the body." Sukhmuna may be said to be the place where the two—Ida and Pingla—join. It is really the place from which the Prana may move either way—right or left—or, under certain conditions—both ways.

Ida is the name given to the Negative Terrestrial magnetic force. Pingla is the name given to the Positive Terrestrial magnetic force. Sukhmuna is the name given to the Neutralization or balancing of these two forces.

For the purposes of practice and exercise, we may use the term Ida to refer to the left nostril; Pingla to the right nostril; and Sukhmuna to refer to the canal in the spinal cord. Likewise, we may use the terms Ida and Pingla to refer to the left and right divisions of the Sympathetic Nervous system, or to the currents as they pass, either on the left or right side of the body.

As the breath is taken into the body under scientific breathing, these Nadi (rivers of energy) open up through the Pranayama exercises just like a tube is opened up by being inflated with air.

The first work is the opening of the Nadi through the Physical Solar Plexus; after which the student will be prepared to learn the use of the positive and negative breathing, so that he may, at all times, be master of his condition—his inner conditions first, and then of outer or extraneous conditions.

Caution:—The positive and negative breathing here referred to does not mean that type of so-called "Positive and Negative, or Cross Breathing," which is being taught by so many teachers of "Psychology" or of certain phases of Yoga Philosophy in the Western World at this time; and which method of breathing is dangerous and detrimental to the health of the student in practically all cases. This subject is discussed fully in class.

Key for Opening These Nadi

Body erect, tip of tongue against roof of mouth, hands behind back, left wrist encircled by right hand. feet flat on floor, eyes closed, *navel pulled up and in.*

Hum "Hoong, Yang, Yang, Yang," feeling the vibration at these four points:—(1) the roof of the mouth; (2) root of the palate; (3) in the throat at the Adam's Apple; and (4) at the navel.

Start the humming in the throat, and as you continue to hum, you will feel the vibration go down the bronchial tubes, around the solar plexus, in the region of the navel, and then passing across in the region of the kidneys to the left side, then going up the left side (or Ida), into the head and around the pineal gland; then down the right side (or Pingla) to the tip of the base of the spine, and up the Sukhmuna, all the way through the medulla oblongata into the pineal gland.

At first your power of breath is too short to accomplish this entire circuit, but finally you will be able to open the door of Brahm, and meet the Kula Kundili, with this exercise, and you will fill the rivers, or Nadi, with this vibration. Start from the throat to make the physical body—every cell tissue, every gland and organ of the body—vibrate in harmony. Thus, you will be renewed physically and your body will be recharged with vital energy.

In about two months, or perhaps in ninety days, with sufficient practice, you may be able to make the entire circuit with the humming breath, and reach the pineal gland. (Then you should be able to see your own picture in the third eye.) Do not force this exercise, but take it gradually, and you will notice that your breath gradually becomes stronger, and you can prolong the vibration more and more, until finally you can get a breath five minutes long.

This opens up the Nadi, or Sympathetic Nerve Channels, and is for development of personal Magnetism, for unifying the whole body.

Set the chart up on the table in front of you, as you practice the humming breath for five or ten minutes before going to bed, and upon getting up in the morning. Trace with your finger the path of the vibration, as the currents flow around the line indicated on the chart. Then trace the path of the vibration mentally. After practicing a little while, you will begin to feel that you can detect the currents flowing in your body in the same directions.

Then your body will become the chart, and you will feel that you can detect the currents flowing in the directions you have been mentally tracing.

This is a continuous breath, and not "Cross-Breathing." Therefore, it is a safe method of breathing and exercise, and gives strength and power for overcoming disease, and for resisting adverse elements.

Should you feel mentally or emotionally depressed, there is not any exercise that will so quickly bring your inner nature into harmony and enable you to throw off the depression. These exercises will also give power for conquering the climate, so that rain, snow, wind, or storm will not bother. It will give power for resisting encroachment of any germs that may be breathed into the body, or taken into the body with food. It will vibrate the tissues of the brain as well as of the body. As you cannot exercise the brain as you would an arm or leg, this exercise was devised by the Yogis of India to strengthen and vitalize the tissues and cells of the brain. When tipping the tongue back in the roof of the mouth, you will be massaging the roof of the mouth, and also nerve filaments that return to the brain, which will have a very beneficial effect on the brain tissue within the skull cavity. Also, exercising the walls of the throat, especially at the back of the throat, will help keep them so strong and active that disease germs cannot find lodgment.

Massaging the roof of the mouth at the tip of the tongue will also increase the flow of saliva, which, being swallowed, will serve as an accelerator of stomach digestion.

Also, the thyroid glands will be vibrated from within. Congestions of blood or other fluids therein will begin to be dissolved, and the glands will be stimulated to create more of the vital life essence which they add to the chemistry of the body for rejuvenation.

By directing this vibration down around the navel, to the left, and up, around the pineal gland, and down the right side to the base of the spine, then up the Sukhmuna through the medulla into the pineal gland, you make the Ida and Pingla and Sukhmuna one, and thus prepare for the opening of the physical, or dreaming and occult Solar Plexus.

Invisible Vibration—For Concentration of All Forces to Resist Attack—or Make Grand Assault for Business Success

After you have practiced for some time this humming breath, make the sounds by voice, then breathing in the same manner but without making the audible sound and preferably at first with the eyes closed, try to *re-feel* the vibration and current passing around the course which you have traced on the chart and in your body. Soon, by merely doing this mental exercise, you will be able to vibrate the body and the vibration will become practically automatic, day and night, whether you are working or merely resting. Your body will then have attained inner harmony of function. Then, with your mind, body, and emotions in harmony, you will begin to enter the "Kingdom of Heaven (Harmony) Within."

The Magnetic Tones

Basic Law:—Like always creates Like, and Like is awakened by Like.

In many systems of philosophy, Thinking, Feeling (emotion), and Creative Life are confused.

As one thinks of certain people or certain events, he may also become conscious of the feelings which were associated with that person or event. The feeling, however, is not a product of the thought.

The focal point of thinking seems to be in the forehead just above the nose. The focal point of feeling seems to be close to the heart. The ancients, therefore, aptly considered the "Heart" as the center of feeling, of love, or emotion. In that they were far more correct than the modern idea that emotion, or love, is a product of the mind.

You have been given exercises which have made it possible for you to bring any part of your body into vibration by use of tone. Now, I give you an application of this exercise which you can make of wonderful value in your everyday Life—in dealing with people, in leading people, and in securing financial and social success.

First:—Let me again repeat the Basic Law:

Like creates Like, and Like is awakened by Like.

There are three basic tones of the human voice, dependent upon where the vibration of the body is centered.

When the vibration is centered in the head and upper chest (without vibration of the lower part of the chest)—the pure *mental* tone is produced. This tone is to be used to gain attention. It is a *fighting* tone—a tone which suggests *mental conflicts*.

This tone should be used *only* for these purposes. To attract attention; to present information; for explanations, and for awakening keener perception.

Remember this:—Mind is a separating force. Never use this tone when endeavoring to persuade someone to do the thing you wish to have done. If you do so, the person will always tend to react and reject your suggestion.

In presenting ideas, your words and your tones

should harmonize and you should use the *mental* tone.

The Feeling Tone. You should always convey your feelings to another primarily by your tones. The emotive, or feeling tone, should be used in conveying to the hearer's mind a true conception of your honor, of your kindness, of your courtesy, of your desire to serve. It should always be used when you are endeavoring to *persuade* someone to do as you desire.

Use the deep, emotive tone for elimination of all friction, and to aid you in working with others—that is, of rendering service in the position you occupy; as well as aiding you in any interviews relative to any position you may desire to secure.

The emotive tone cannot be produced—that is, it will not have the sincere emotive quality—unless the chest is set into vibration, so as to add many overtones.

Fill the upper portion of the chest with air, making the tone vibrant through the chest—desiring at the same time to express kindness and courtesy.

Place your hands at approximately the level of your heart. Then in speaking aloud, *lower* your voice so that you can *feel* the vibration of your tone underneath your *hands*. Talk as though you were talking quietly and lovingly to one who is very dear to you. Listen attentively to your tone.

No one can possibly quarrel with you when you are using this tone. No one can be annoyed with you. Moreover, *you* cannot be greatly annoyed with anyone else when you are using this *Love* tone.

The Power Tone

The Power tone should be used in commanding, and always to indicate your own solidarity, your capacity, your truthfulness, and to negate, with force, the objections of others.

Use the Power tone to secure justice. If you attempt to attain justice by profuse use of words, dwelling upon what you have done, and what you desire, you are wasting your breath, for the *means* you are using are not sufficient to convey your real soul quality to the soul listening to you.

Action is too effective to be used to secure justice, or the object you have in view. You would not think of beating up your employer to secure a raise in salary. The means to be used to secure justice is the Power tone, because it secures a more positive effect than words, and is less likely to cause difficulty than action.

The Power tone is always supported from the abdomen by the action of the big muscles at the waist line. The use of these muscles in supporting any phrase or sentence puts into such an expression a feeling and effect of power which no other support can give.

When you desire to make demands, or give commands, to others, image yourself as boxing, as actually engaged in a *friendly* bout, and with the intent of putting "punch" into your tone. With every phrase of your talk, image yourself landing a kindly, telling blow under the ear, or on the chest, or just under the jaw. Make these images clear so that ultimately you will grow into the habit of using a decisive, impelling power in your *tone*, and at the same time keep it *low-pitched*.

Practice for Developing the Three Tones

Mental Tone:—Take a very short breath, into top of chest, and keeping the tone in the head, chant the syllable "O-Ang," keeping the tone somewhat high-pitched. Note the vibration *in the head*, with no appreciable vibration in the chest.

Use the high-pitched mental tone *only* to gain attention. Then relax mind and body, and lower the tone somewhat in making presentation of your subject matter. *Vary the pitch of your voice.*

Emotive, or Love Tone:—Take a breath which fills the upper chest, placing your hands over the heart, and feel that you are making your tone express your kindness and love, chanting the syllable "O-Ang," keeping the tone medium low-pitched. Practice until you feel the vibration strongly in the heart region.

Power Tone:—Fill the chest full of air, placing hand over the navel, feeling that you are definitely and decisively stating your decision, chant the syllable "O-Ang." Keep the tone *low-pitched*.

Continue the practice until you can quite definitely feel the vibration of the lower part of your body, and contract the waist muscles firmly as you chant the "O-Ang."

Use this part of your lesson continuously, in all your conduct with people, until it becomes a part of your life.

In my contact with people, I find many who habitually speak in high-pitched, mental tone, and I have observed that these same people usually suffer on account of the tension of their neck muscles. They usually have difficulty in dealing with others, and a great many of them are under-weight; and many suffer frequently from headaches.

By changing the tone, lowering the pitch of the voice and vibration, relaxation of the throat muscles may be secured, with an accompanying relaxation of the neck muscles, so that fewer headaches (from this cause) will occur. Often this exercise alone is sufficiently effective to cause the body to take on the needed weight, and persons who practice this exercise will find that they are developing greater success in dealing with others.

How to Make the Ether Tube—for Occult and Mental Telepathy, Physical-Clairaudience, and Thought Transference

Of all exercises for attaining Occult Power, there is no other method which is nearly so valuable or effective as this one. Each student is cautioned not to impart the information given in this lesson to others who have not taken the steps for development outlined in the preceding lessons.

For best results, in fact for any results, the general tone of the body, and body harmony, must be obtained through the chanting and breathing exercises hereinbefore taught.

Before beginning the practice of this exercise, which is to be taken at night, the last thing before going to bed, Chant, Breathe, Exercise, and raise the vibration of the body through meditation, realizing that the purpose of this exercise is to awaken, and bring into vibration and functional activity, centers of the brain which have, heretofore, been asleep.

Definite Instructions for Forming the Ether Tube

1. Place a *blue* electric bulb, 100-Watt (Mazda) in the chandelier, or at least six or seven feet above the floor.

2. Place a straight-back chair (not a rocker) such a distance from the light that when sitting in the chair you will be directly facing the light, and eyes will be about eight feet away from the light.

3. Use a *transparent green eye shade over the eyes*.

4. Sitting in a low chair (or ordinary straight-chair with feet raised three or four inches from the floor by footstool or cushions) with knees about eighteen inches apart, rest the elbows on the knees, so the forearms will form an inverted "V."

5. Rest the chin firmly in the "cup" formed by the hands (heels of the hands together), thumbs touching the lower jaw bone, and palm surface of hands and fingers touching the cheeks.

6. Bend the head backward somewhat, not by merely tilting it at the first articulation with the neck, but more by contracting all the muscles of the back of the neck, which will thus give the effect of stretching the muscles in the front part of the neck or region of the throat.

7. Look *through the shade* at the light, so that the line of vision shall pass through the space between the eye-brows.

8. Sit *absolutely still*, breathing slow, quiet, long, steady breaths, *without winking the eyes* or moving a muscle of the body during the period of concentration.

9. As soon as you have completed the exercise, go to bed.

10. Spend *five* minutes each practice period the first week; no more. Spend six minutes each practice period the second week; no more. Spend eight minutes each practice period the third week; no more. Spend twelve minutes each practice period the fourth week; no more. Spend fifteen minutes each practice period the fifth week; no more.

After five weeks, the time of practice may be increased one minute each week, until the desired results are accomplished.

Some evening—it may be very soon, or it may not be until after weeks, or even months of practice—the light will *disappear,* and you will see your *face,* or your body in the posture in which you are sitting, just as though you were looking into a mirror.

This means that the *ether* has become a mirror, and is reflecting back the image of your body.

When the image of yourself replaces the light, you ARE telepathic.

Then, when you wish to send the message, first sit before the light until the image of your face or of your body replaces the vision of the light.

Then, substitute, in your mind, the vision or image of the person who is to receive the message.

Then, talk the message *entirely by thought,* neither speaking nor whispering the words. And the other person *will* receive the message. He will receive it as a "hunch," or as a very strong impression, as if coming from within himself.

Later, as you continue the practice and you use your new telepathic powers, which you can become able to do at will, you will find that you can project yourself—that is, your ethereal body—wherever you wish to be, and you may be seen there as a shape or a shadow. You will see what is going on there, hear, and know.

Wherever ether is—and that is everywhere—there you can project yourself (on this planet). Seeing and Hearing become one. In the physical body, seeing and hearing are two functions, but in the psychic, or spiritual, there is only *"knowing."* By this practice you develop "all-knowing" power for use both with the visible and the invisible.

Then you have the power of knowing what other people are thinking; power of diagnosing disease; power of understanding motives and feelings, and intentions of people with whom you deal; and eventually you will become aware of events which are about to happen, as well as be aware of events which have happened, both in your own life, or the life of others.

This power must be used only for *good*, for giving messages of love, for giving spiritual healing, or for some other good purpose, as for help, for unity, or for brotherly love.

You *must* always hold inviolate information which comes to you through the invisible. Misuse of such information is *un*spiritual, and will cause the loss of power, as well as bring unpleasant conditions upon yourself.

This exercise causes very rapid vibration of the optic nerve, and the brain centers connected therewith, thus awakening them to higher and greater activity.

The sitting in posture overcomes nervousness, and causes freedom from leakage of personal magnetism from the body.

The sense of "Knowing" developed by this practice is a wonderful help to the parent, teacher, lawyers, judge, or business man, giving a quality of "Judgment" in affairs of life and activity that makes for great success.

Many Lessons in Soroda System Yoga Philosophy

BY

SUPER-AKASHA YOGI WASSAN

Charging the Body with Atmic Energy

O-Ang-Shantee—the Sacred Word of the Yogis—signifies consciousness of *unity* with all the Universe.

Attain now, and for all time, a consciousness of Unity—unity as pertaining to the Universe, as to the manifestations of the One God—unity of the Atma with the Spiritual Buram Center which is forever *pushing* His power outward into expression through *you*—Unity of Atma, Mind, Love, Body, Life, Action.

As you bring your body into harmonious vibration through the chanting of this sacred word, think and feel yourself as united, or joined with Universal Power, and with all other individuals of the Universe through the radiation of the Love Energy of God, radiating out through you.

In India, when a baby is born, the *O-Ang-Shantee* chant is repeated many times by those around, signifying creative activity, the incarnation of God in man.

Beginning this chant in a high, mental tone, feel the resonance in the larynx, roof of the mouth, the nasal cavity, and head.

Then, pitching the tone slightly lower, feel the vibration in the upper chest; again dropping the tone slightly lower, feel the love vibration in the mid-chest, and finally, with a very low, deep tone, feel the vibration in the lowest part of the chest—the power tone.

Chant seven times, each time dropping the tone slightly, and feeling the vibration in the lower part of the body.

Chant seven times, beginning with the lowest tone —the Power tone—then elevating the tone a little higher to the Love tone, and finally to the high Mental tone in the head.

As you strike the *Ang,* pull up the navel and give a definite strong impulse to the breath.

Repeat and repeat until the entire body is in harmonious vibration.

INTENSIFYING DYNAMIC ACTIVITY OF MIND EMOTIVE FORCE
OR
CREATIVE CENTERS—AT WILL
DYNAMIC MENTAL POWER—STORING MIND-PRANA
(Preparation for Telepathic Thought Transference)

Mind Prana has a mode of vibration which is peculiar to itself. The force is impulsive, moving in straight lines, each particle of Ether seemingly striking the particle next to it in such a way that motion, or vibration, is continued in a straight line.

With *eyes closed,* mentally picture your brain as the focal center into which an infinite number of mind energy-rays from the great spiritual Buram-Center are converging; mentally seeing this Mind-Prana being conveyed to your brain by straight line blows.

With elbows extended on level with the shoulders, thumbs pressing in the small lobes in front of the ears, with fingers spread fan-wise over upper part of face and forehead:

Sound *"O-Ang-Shantee," using Mental Tone*, feeling the vibration in throat, medulla oblongata, nasal passages, ears, and forehead.

With eyebrows slightly tensed, and mentally looking intently into forehead at the root of the nose—

Sitting erect in chair, with navel pulled up and in—

Fill *upper* part of chest by breathing in *short*, quick breaths, and exhale strongly and forcibly as you make the sound.

Begin with seven breaths.

Invisible Vibration

There are times when it is necessary to give a message to another, and the conditions make it impossible to chant the mystic *"O-Ang-Shantee."* By practice of Invisible Vibration—immediately after using the visible vibration with the sound, the student will become able, within a few seconds, to vibrate the brain, and thus store Mind-Prana without either the vocal vibration, the closing of the eyes, or the use of the hands over the eyes.

At first, however, the eyes should be closed and the hands placed as in the preceding exercise.

Always, however, the mental picture of the inflow of *rays* of Mind-Prana from the Great Burma-

Center to the brain should be created, and the *feeling* of inflowing power should be attained.

Mentally *feel* the vibration in the throat, roof of the mouth, medulla oblongata, nasal passages, and forehead.

Breathe the short, quick breaths into the upper part of the lungs, and exhale with strength and force.

Begin with seven breaths.

DYNAMIC EMOTIVE (ATTRACTIVE) POWER
(Preparation for Awakening *Feeling* in Another)

Love, or Attractive energy, is the one attractive power of the Universe. When this Emotive, or Love-Prana acts between planets, it is called gravitation; when between atoms, it is called atomic attraction; when between souls, it is called Love, or Emotive Force.

Love-Prana has a mode of vibration peculiar to itself. This force always acts in *waves* of energy. To form the picture in your mind, image the rays of Love-energy coming to your entire body in ripples (as the surface of water would move if a stone were thrown into the middle of a quiet pond).

Feel this Love-Prana flowing into the body, vibrating every cell of the body, and focusing in the solar plexus, or solar brain.

With *eyes closed,* form the mental picture of the Love-Prana inflowing in waves to your body, and centering in the solar brain.

Spread fingers fan-wise, and place against the chest over the heart.

Sit erect in chair, with navel pulled in and back.

Fill *middle chest,* trying to extend the chest at this point in every direction—back, sides, and front.

Then sound "*O-Ang-Shantee,*" feeling the vibration strongly under the hands and throughout the mid-chest .

When the vibration is strongly felt, then add to the mental picture as follows:

Picture yourself a focal center, a dynamo of emotive energy, with power being drawn in as before. Then picture the rays of emotive energy are going, in waves, outward from the solar brain through your body in all directions, and particularly to someone whom you do love. *Feel* those rays charged with the *love* which you feel. See that one vibrating in harmony with your vibration, and, in turn, sending out rays like your own, to you.

INVISIBLE VIBRATION

(Charging the Love-Brain for Telepathic Love Transference)

With eyes closed, hands and body in position given above—Create the mental picture of the Love-rays rippling from the Great Burma-Center to your body and converging in the Solar Brain.

Fill the middle-chest with air as indicated in previous exercise, centering consciousness where the hands touch the chest—over the heart region.

Then *mentally* chant the "*O-Ang-Shantee,*" and mentally feel the vibration of the body under the hands. In a few moments you *will feel* the vibration. That is, the body will actually vibrate, and you will actually store the Love-Prana in the Love-Brain, ready for use in sending the telepathic message.

Feel the ripples of Love-Prana radiating out through your entire body, bathing every cell individual in love, and radiating out from your body in all directions.

Mentally *vision* the person to whom you wish to send the message as being actually with you, either as holding the hand, or with arm thrown lovingly around the shoulders.

Feel love radiating from you to that one, and *feel* love radiating from that one to you.

Whisper or speak the message which you desire that one to receive. Then, when you have done so, *know* that your loving message has been received, or will be received, as soon as that one is sufficiently relaxed to be open to reception.

Remember that Love is the one *attractive force* in the Universe, and that because *You*—Atma—do actually extend far beyond your body, you actually *do* contact the one you love, and thereby, your message is actually received by that one.

Remember, also, that *you* have *no* right, or power, or dominion over any other person; that you should not take such a privilege, and that you must not try to force any other person to do anything which that person does not truly desire to do, whether you think it might be of real benefit to that person, or not. (This does not mean that a parent should not guide and direct the conduct of a child, or children.)

Remember:—*That you have no right to endeavor to force another person to love you.*

Remember, also, that each individual in the world has just as truly a right to be different from you in thought, and feeling, and beliefs, and actions, as you have a right to your own thoughts, desires, beliefs, and actions.

Advanced Practice

After you have practiced sending the telepathic love message, as above directed for some time, you will find that you can create the vibration, and store the Love-Prana, and radiate it without the closing of the eyes, or the placing of the hand.

Then you will be able to *give* (not send) the *love* message by merely mentally *seeing* and *feeling* the contact with the Loved One, and *mentally* repeating the words which you wish to be received.

Methods for giving other messages, and for clairvoyance and clairaudience, will be given in later lessons of this course, but this method should be practiced as a means for developing your powers, and for constantly feeling the spiritual contact with those you love.

Dynamic Creative Power—Storing Life-Prana

Life, or Creative Energy, has a mode of vibration peculiar to itself. This force moves in spiral form —which explains the reason it is symbolized in Hindoo Philosophy as the "Serpent-Power"—the Kundalini.

There is but one Life or Creative force in the Universe. This manifests in every form of creation —invention, or art, or literature, or birth of new cell structure in the body, or the incarnation of a soul for a new life upon earth.

With eyes closed, sit erect in chair, with hands spread out over abdomen, just under the navel, or below the navel.

Breathe *deeply*, filling the lower lobes of the lungs, pressing outward strongly against the hands.

Chant the "*O-Ang-Shantee*," using the Power Tone, feeling the vibration strongly under the hands.

Each time you repeat the syllable "*O-Ang-Shantee,*" press in strongly with the hands, tense the muscles of the abdomen, the muscles of the buttocks, and of the thighs—thus putting *power* into your tones, and awakening the Sacral Brain to greatly increased activity.

As you complete the exhalation of the breath, try to draw the navel *up* and *in,* as though pressing it against the back-bone, and tense all the muscles as strongly as you can, endeavoring to empty the lungs as completely as possible.

Form the mental picture in your mind of an infinite number of Spiral-moving Life-rays, radiating out from the Buram-Center, converging to your body-focal-center, radiating into your body, and being focused in your Life-Brain at the base of the Spinal Column—thence diverging (radiating) outward throughout your body, to every part of the body, bathing every individual cell of the body in its life-giving rays; causing the union of cells in your body—causing the birth of new-youth cells in your body for its rejuvenation.

If you have formed an ideal of some work of Art, or Invention, or Writing, or whatever it may be that you may desire to bring into manifestation, picture these life-rays pouring into this ideal, bringing it to life and activity.

Invisible Vibration
(Charging the Body for Creative Effort)

Carry out the mental picturing, the posture, and the breathing as directed in the previous exercise, chanting the "*O-Ang-Shantee*" mentally, feeling the vibration under the hands, and feeling the out-flowing rays going to every part of the body, and to the particular ideal which you desire to create.

Then, *with earnest consciousness of power, actually begin to do definite work to bring your ideal into manifestation*—that is, begin to write, or paint, or work with your hands whatever you wish to do by hand, or whatever you wish to create.

This exercise is *not* to be used except for your own personal invigoration, or personal development—with the single exception of a Healer, who may be endeavoring to awaken *Life* activity within a patient.

Opening the Solar Plexus

Many people make the mistake of trying to open the solar plexus through the forehead first (by thinking and concentrating). This is a common mistake of Occidental teachers and philosophers who call themselves "Applied Psychologists." Many such teachers also undertake to develop students by teaching them "Cross Breathing," which is not only injurious physically, in most cases, but may also cause the individual to become insane.

When you open the solar plexus through the navel, you secure greatly increased physical power. Then the plexus at the base of the spine should be freed, and finally the plexus at the base of the skull (the medulla oblongata) will open of itself.

The navel is in the middle of the body. Near it is the Solar Plexus (emotional brain). At the end of the spine is the Sacral or Sacred Plexus (the life or sex brain). At the top of the spine is the Mental Brain. In addition to these three great centers of activity through which *Atma* expresses, every cell and every pore of the body is also a center for receiving and radiating *Atmic* energy.

Turn the tip of the tongue back into the roof of the mouth, and sound the humming breath (Hoong, Yang, Yang, Yang), bringing the sound up into the nose, in Padam Asana (Posture) keeping navel up and in.

Then place the tips of the fingers of one hand over the navel, and with the other hand over that one, pressing in on the navel with both hands as you exhale, drinking in the nectar of life(sucking the tip of the tongue and drinking the saliva as you hum). Chant "Hoong, Yang, Yang, Yang" as you push the navel in and try to feel the vibration under the hands.

Remove the hands, pull the navel in by mental effort, as you exhale, and practice the humming breath.

Keep pulling the navel in and up each time you exhale. Practice until the vibration is felt strongly at the navel and throughout the entire abdominal region.

Grunting Breath

As you chant the Humming Breath, *grunt* hard, as you pronounce the "Hoong," and pull the navel back with a shock.

Grunt like a pig grunts, and imagine that the force of that grunt is *hitting* at some particular spot along the spinal column—at one of the seven centers beginning at the base of the spine, and going upward step by step.

Repeat seven times, centering in each of the seven steps.

First chant slowly, in a low key; then in a higher key; then in a still higher key—remembering the three keys—mental, love, and power tones. Then chant faster and faster, and still faster, like the three speeds of an automobile.

The use the grunting breath, one, two, three, four, five, six and seven, making the seventh a hard grunt as you finally expel all the air from the lungs.

Invisible Chanting

After you have completed one round of the chanting as above directed, close the eyes, and *without making a sound*, try to *feel* the vibration of the body in the navel, at the "Adam's Apple," and in the roof of the mouth. Try to re-feel the grunting breath. Do this again and again, mentally, until you can instantly re-image the feeling of both the vibration and the grunting.

Etheric Vibration

The vibration of the air and ether during the twenty-four hours which we call a day varies quite considerably. The vibration of the human body—when not changed by these exercises—varies in accord with the earth vibration.

The lowest vibration of the day is from 4:00 P. M. until midnight.

The highest vibration of the day is from midnight until 8 A. M.

The intermediate vibration is from 8:00 A. M. until 4:00 P. M.

The best time for spiritual and mental development by practice is from 2:00 A. M. until 6:00 or 7:00 A. M.

Far more quickly will you secure results through your practice if you arrange your day so that you can rise at 5:00 or 6:00 o'clock in the morning, and spend an hour in practice. One hour then is better than several hours just before going to bed, although there are certain exercises which I wish you to practice just before going to bed, such as exercises for the eyes, and others as aids for development while you are sleeping as well as for the purpose of insuring quiet and restful sleep.

Balance—or Poise—of the Body

Soroda System Yoga Philosophy is a system of training which gives the student physical, mental, emotional, and spiritual control over himself.

The only way in which you can grow mentally is through bodily activity of the muscles which are connected with the centers of the brain. You might *read* these lessons over and over until you had committed them to memory, and still *not* attain physical or mental power in accordance with their teachings —*but*, when you actually *begin* to do the exercises, to use your body, then you *change*, and *change mightily*.

This is true of all study. Study in itself may give you information, but stuffing the mind does not develop brain structure. *Only action* can do that.

You desire to become *master* of your body. You desire to secure *poise* of body. You desire to secure *mental poise*. You desire to attain greater power to weigh problems and make correct decisions.

This attainment comes only as you develop your sense of *balance* in the body, through *bodily exercise*.

It is a proven fact that jugglers, acrobats, tight-rope walkers, and others who have gained the power of balancing the body, are better judges of value even than bankers and business men who are *not* masters of balance of their bodies.

Every lack of balance in your physical body tells the other person that your mentality is unbalanced to just that degree—that your plans and judgments are unsafe to just that degree.

Practice the following exercises regularly each day, and practice walking and standing in a well-balanced posture, until that well-balanced posture becomes a habit.

Exercises for Developing Poise or Balance

1. Stand *erect,* head up, feet close together, arms clasped behind head. Sway the body forward and backward, then to the left, then to the right, as far as you can without falling. Rotate your body from left to right, and from right to left, in as large a circle from the hips as you can make.

2. Stand on one foot, head and back erect, hands on waist. Swing the other foot in front of the body, then behind the body, then to the sides—at first slowly, and then as you gain control—swing with greater speed. Alternate, standing first on right foot, and then on left.

3. Standing on one foot, swing the other foot behind you and bend forward until your body from head to foot is a straight line. Then swing the body, rotating on the upright leg. Change to other foot and repeat the exercise.

Advanced Exercise—Vibrating Mind Brain

Stand erect, feet close together, head up, navel pulled *high.*

Bring hands to level of collar bone in front of

throat, arms horizontal. Inhale a short, quick breath into upper chest.

Swing arms upward and outward (to form letter "Y"), rising on toes as you reach upward, and at the same time take long, high step.

Swing the arms and hands back to starting point, and at the same time drop the body till heels touch the floor, and inhale a quick, short breath into the upper chest.

Pull navel up and in sharply as you elevate the arms.

Repeat seven times, feeling the vibration in throat and head. Feel that you are drawing in Prana with each inhalation. Feel that you are radiating it through the body as you exhale.

Shoes—A Factor in Bodily Poise

The very high-heeled shoes which are being worn by so many American women today have a very detrimental effect upon their health, because the extremely high heels not only throw the spine and body generally into wrong posture, but they also cause a jarring of the whole vertebral column in walking, and there is a continuous pressure on the nerves of the heels, and those in the ball of the foot just behind the toes. In addition to producing a nervousness through constant fear of falling, or of turning the ankles, this pressure on the nerves of the foot causes a great deal of bodily discomfort by reflex-irritation to the brain and other parts of the body.

I recommend flat-heeled shoes for every-day wear —a good sensible heel. Reserve the spool-heeled shoes for "special occasions" where ultra-fastidious custom demands, and even then, in buying a "spool-heel" shoe a little caution may be used in getting the heel not "too high."

I further most earnestly recommend that everyone should go barefoot part of each day when around home, or in their own rooms.

When you come in from the street, take off the shoes you have worn during the day, and either go barefoot for a while, or at least put on soft flat-bottomed house slippers, and give your feet a chance to be natural.

Spiritual Breath—For Telepathic Development

Either sitting or lying down (not standing), and not until all the preceding exercises have been practiced, and your lungs have become strengthened, practice the following breathing for opening the *mental solar plexus*.

Inhale a quick, smooth breath, not trying to fill the lungs completely, pulling in the navel as you inhale. Then quickly exhale, again pulling the navel in, as though you were trying to force it against the backbone, and trying to pull yourself up over the top of the head, as though levitating yourself.

Repeat three or four times, somewhat forcibly. Then as you exhale, make the grunting sound—grunt, and grunt, and grunt—pulling in the navel sharply each time the grunting sound is made. This tends to elevate the navel and to awaken the sacred or life brain, stimulating the flow of Life-Prana throughout the body.

Advanced Exercise—Humming Breath for Clairaudience

First, practice the Humming Breath, with thumbs pressing in or against the little lobes at the front of the ear, and palms of hands over eyes, as previously directed in earlier lessons, all the while listening and becoming conscious of the vibration in nose, eyes, ears, roof of mouth, and "Adam's Apple" or larynx.

Then listen to the invisible humming for a few moments without moving the thumbs.

Now change position of the thumbs, so the small lobe is freed, and the ends of the thumbs close up the passage into the ears. Listen intently, and as your development comes (sometimes after a few weeks—often longer) you will hear the *cosmic sounds* of your own body. There may be many variations of the sounds heard, but generally they may be described something like this:

1. Sound like listening into a sea-shell, or a scratching sound (which is the "Earth" sound).

2. A sound like church bells.

3. A triple sound—like a drum, like a horse walking on a sidewalk, and another sound like a newspaper being crumpled up.

4. A sound like music of Hawaiian guitar.

5. A sound like Scotch bagpipes, or the Krishna flute (this same sound can be made by humming).

6. A sound like whip-poor-will birds singing.

7. The seventh sound is like thunder and lightning.

Many Lessons in Soroda System Yoga Philosophy

BY

SUPER-AKASHA YOGI WASSAN

EXERCISES FOR IMPROVING EYESIGHT AND HEARING
EXERCISES FOR DEVELOPING OCCULT POWERS

O-Ang-Shantee—The Chant for Power

There is nothing the soul desires so much as the consciousness of power—because when it is lacking one feels so deficient—so unequal to others. Consciousness of power makes life glorious!

You *know* that *you* (the *Atma*) are unlimited in power because you are a *ray* of power forever shining out from the infinite *Buram Center* of Power.

What you desire is to *feel* constantly that Power *within you*—always on tap (as it were)—ready for instantaneous expression.

To attain that *feeling* of power within, you *must* unify the *thought* of power, the *feeling* of power, and the *action* of power, expressing all three phases at the same time in *one* activity.

First, I give you the meaning of the Power Chant, and the use to which it is put by the Hindoos, with its application to you. Then I give you the posture and actions of power; and finally, I teach you to unify this *thought* with *feeling* in *action*. Thus you actually *change* your body and register the feeling of Power within the body temple so that always you will *feel* power, and with that feeling will come *poise, calmness, soul serenity*.

O-Ang-Shantee means: "I have power over wild beasts." In other words: "I am *master*." In India this chant is used by travelers through the forests to make the singer *feel* his own power and thus overcome fear within himself—also to drive away the wild animals by making them fear him.

The position of the fingers—second and third finger pressed against the thumb, and first and fourth finger extended—is in imitation of the head and ears of a wild beast—and may be called the "Cat Head."

In the action, the effort is to feel the body being lifted up above the hands—not the hands lowered (during the chanting as will be described)—thus symbolizing Man as being lifted up over the beasts of the field.

In modern life, far removed from the forests, we feel no need of protecting ourselves against wild animals, but we have *other fears* that may be just as destructive. There are many times when we are worried, when we do not feel strong enough to overcome conditions in which we find ourselves, relative to the people we contact, or thoughts which come to us, and it is at such times that we desire greatly to feel consciousness of power within. By chanting this Mantram, we can raise the vibration of our bodies from the low vibration of weakness to the high vibration of power.

The Hero Posture

Stand erect, heels together, hands loosely at sides, head *up*, *spine straight* (or not stooped), navel lifted *up*.

Inhale a full quick breath, lifting the arms with hands outstretched so that the body forms the letter "Y." As you raise the arms, rise on tip-toes, pulling the navel up as far as possible, and stretching *up* as far as you can.

Press second and third fingers of each hand against their respective thumbs, straightening first and fourth fingers (pushing them back as far as possible).

Chant "*O-Ang-Shantee* . . . E" prolonging the "E," making the sound vibrate through the entire chest (using the Power tone of the lower chest).

As you begin the chant, gradually *pull* the arms downward, feeling that you are *pulling* the body up, as though lifting it through an opening by the lifting power of your arms. Arms should be tensed, but the rest of the body should be relaxed as much as possible. Continue until the arms are extended full length at the sides. Gradually lower the body as the arms descend, and keep pulling the navel *up* and *in*, pushing the tone outward forcibly by the power of the diaphragm and abdominal muscles.

Note:—Because this Chant for Power is so wonderfully effective when correctly performed, I have given you these minute directions. Take time enough to master the movement before actually beginning the chant. Then you will be able to give your attention to the mental and emotional part of the devotional exercise.

Thinking of *yourself* as a *power-ray* of God, *feeling* God-Power (the Atma) within, standing erect as a god, chanting with full voice of power, and making the movements with force, you *change* the vibrations of your body; you become conscious of your *union* with the source of all power, and make that feeling of *in-dwelling power* an ever-present reality.

Use this chant every morning as a part of your devotion, repeating the movement and the chant *seven times.*

Before beginning this chant, it is well to chant either the "Five Holy Words," or the "*O-Ang-Shan-tee*" for a few moments to awaken the body.

After chanting, close the eyes, and mentally *live* the chant in thought and feeling and action, without moving or chanting.

When you shall have gained the power to do this, you will have ever at hand the means of overcoming fear or worry wherever you may be, for even though you cannot actually make the movements and chant audibly, you *can* chant mentally and emotionally, and by so doing, the whole vibration of your body will be changed. You will become conscious again of the power to overcome all obstacles. You will *feel* the Power of the Master.

Strengthening the Eyes

Any person who can see at all with the aid of glasses, and who is earnestly following the training given in these lessons, can so completely strengthen the eyes that glasses may be thrown away.

Whether you are a young man or woman who has been told by the "Specialist" that your eyes are so permanently impaired that you must always wear spectacles, or even though you *were* one of those who lived in the reminiscences of past joy, never expecting again to *feel* vibrant life within you—whoever you are—you *can* so strengthen your eyes and make them permanently strong, that you will never need the aid of glasses (crutches), either for close reading or for seeing at a distance, provided you actually practice the following exercises steadily until actual results are secured—which will usually be within a month or six weeks at the most.

Modern city life has a detrimental effect upon the eyes, in several different ways:—The city dweller no longer recognizes the necessity for continually *moving* the eyes in all directions to preserve life, as was the custom of his forest-dwelling ancestors. Instead of *moving* the eyes about, the city dweller, as he walks down the street in crowded traffic, moves his head about quickly and in jerks, thereby permitting the muscles of the neck to perform the movements that could otherwise be performed by the muscles of the eye-balls, and with benefit to the eyes. Likewise, too frequent attendance at moving picture shows and prolonged watching of flickering scenes has had a very injurious effect upon the eyes of the American people, especially upon the eyes of children, who are permitted to attend such places when very young, and before the eyes are sufficiently strong to withstand the strain of the high-powered and flickering lights.

Seeing is a much more complex operation of the mind than most people think. It is commonly supposed that the images of the objects looked upon photograph themselves upon the retina of the eye, and are carried directly to the brain center of sight, and there re-imaged in that one brain center.

However, the fact of the matter is that there are three different centers of the brain activity employed in the function of seeing. One of these centers is connected with the retina of the eye. The other two sets of brain cells are connected with the *muscles* which *move* the eyes. The consciousness of *shape* and *form* of objects is recognized by the brain centers connected with the muscles of the eyes, rather than with the optic nerve.

Six small muscles are attached to the eye-ball. These are in pairs and are arranged in such a way that they can move the eye-ball not only from side to side, or up and down, but can also lengthen or shorten the distance from the cornea of the eye to the retina. Thus they can change the focus of the eye-ball, so that images *will* be correctly focused on the retina.

When mankind lived in the forest the preservation of his life depended upon the activity of these muscles. He was compelled continuously to move his eyes from side to side, up and down, or sweeping the entire field of vision to ward off attacks of wild beasts, serpents or other forms of life which might injure him. Also, he had to exercise this same muscular activity in searching for food. Thus, those muscles were continually active, and the eye-sight continued unimpaired as long as the rest of the body organism of the individual continued in a state of normal activity and function.

In your own life, how much exercise do these eye-muscles get? You look almost constantly in only one direction—straight before you. Your eye-muscles do not wear out. They *rust out*. Then, because they are weak from *lack* of exercise, the power of changing the shape of the eye-ball is lost to a degree, and as a result you say your vision is impaired.

Then what do you do? You go to an oculist, or an optometrist. And what does he do? He puts a pair of glasses on you and tells you to look *only* through the center of the glasses. He actually causes you to discontinue all exercise of these eye-muscles, and shortly you are compelled to use stronger (?) glasses.

Another cause of impaired eye-sight is *tensity* and *rigidity* of the muscles of the *neck*. The blood supply of the head comes through arteries, which are deep within the neck, but the blood returns from the head through veins, which pass through the tissues of the neck nearer to the surface than do the arteries, and are also of not such a rigid structure as to their walls as are the arteries. Therefore, when the outer muscles of the neck become tensed, they press against the veins, causing a back-pressure on the veins and capillaries of the head, lessening the rapidity of the return flow of blood from the head. As a result the brain suffers, the eyes suffer, and the mucous membrane of the nose and larynx, so that the entire body is affected by the congestion in this area, with "headache" as a very common symptom, as well as extreme nervousness, which also usually manifests itself.

I have given you an exercise for "rotation of the head" to help overcome this tensity. I have called your attention to the necessity for change of tone of voice from "tense mental tone" to "low-pitched emotional tone"; and I have given you mantrams and chants for use in vibrating the body. Now I *add* other definite exercises for the particular purpose of relaxing the neck muscles.

Massage for Relaxing Neck Muscles

Reaching up to the back of the neck, first with one hand and then with the other, grasp the muscles of the back of the neck firmly between the heel of the hand and the fingers, pulling the fleshy part of the muscles up into the hand, holding firmly, and then relax. Then grasp as much of the fleshy part of the neck as you can and try to pull it *away* from the bones, out from the back of the neck. Grasp the flesh of the neck, and while holding it firmly in the hand, rotate the head first to one side and then to the other.

(If the *tensity* of the neck is too great to be freed in this manner, it may be well to secure the services of one who is skilled in spinal manipulation to render some assistance, as there may be a deep condition which should be adjusted.)

Massage around the eyes, the cheeks, the forehead, the temples and around behind the ears to the base of the skull.

When you have completed the active movement of the eye-muscles, as directed by "Yogi Wassan," for making the eyes strong without glasses, and have closed the eyes, and have covered the eyes with the palms of the hands, then *feel* that you are now sending the life blood of the body to these eye-muscles; that this life blood is removing the worn out tissues of the eyes, and that the thousands of cells which compose the eye-muscles are now receiving new life elements—that the nerve energy of your body is flowing freely to them, and that they are actually being reborn and renewed to the fullest extent.

Use the Humming Breath (Hoong, Yang, Yang, Yang) and feel the vibration in the eyes, in the neck, and back part of the head.

Eye Exercise to Be Taken Without Chart
(For Opening the "Inner Eye")

Close the eyes. Then look toward the left (that is, turn the eye-balls to the left), then into the head, making as strong a "cross-eye" motion as possible. Then look or turn the eye-balls to the right; then backward; then inward; then to the root of the nose. Roll the eyes around, first in one direction, and then reverse.

Practice this exercise for two minutes, and then

cover the eyes with the palms of the hands, holding for a few moments for magnetizing the eyes.

This exercise is particularly helpful when the eyes have become fatigued from close application.

Eye Exercise to Be Taken Out of Doors

This is *more than* a mere eye-exercise. This is mental development, and increased joy and appreciation of life to be secured by those who are willing to *look* for the beautiful.

General Exercise for Quickening the Activity of the Brain Centers of Motion, Color, Sound, and Direction

1. Arrange your daily schedule so that you can walk at least a couple of blocks every day, and during that walk:—

(A) Assume an attitude of intense alertness. Lay aside, for the time, all thoughts of everything except the *expression* of the most intense mental activity through *increasing* the perception of everything which goes on around you during the time spent in this drill.

(B) Cast the eyes quickly, first in one direction and then in another; first on one object and then on another. *See fully each thing your eyes rest upon.* Look at something close to you and then look as quickly as possible at something away off in the distance. See something in a window on one side of the street—and then give a lightning glance at something on the opposite side of the street.

In each case, observe every detail of each thing you look at—color, form, symmetry—etc., but do so quickly. See something on the top of a building near you, then something at the ground at your side. Keep the eyes (not the head) moving from one spot to another.

Use the full mind. Turn on the full current of your mind. Try to see everything you can possibly see as quickly as possible, and as completely as possible. Try not to miss a single thing.

At night, as a memory training, try to *reimage* as much of what you saw as possible.

As a general attitude: Feel *alive*. Pretend that you are interested in everything that is going on. *Observe everything*. If you continue this assumption by muscle action, using your muscles in the *intent* and *desire* to become more alive, the brain centers respond, and soon the aessumption becomes a reality.

Not only keep the eyes active, every moment of the day, and keep the body awake, but keep the *face* expressive, responding to everything you see and everything you hear. Keep the lips and eyes in action, expressing the interest you feel in the things presented to your mind.

The muscle action of the tissues of the face produces an effect upon the brain centers, and aids them in more rapidly changing, so that you rapidly attain increased joy and happiness in living.

Color

Many people have eye trouble because they live in a world of their own making—which is devoid of color. They do not observe color, they do not love color, they do not revel in the beauties of color. Their world is a white and black world—mostly black.

Think what a dreary, drab-looking world it would be if God had not expressed himself through color.

Think of the trees with white leaves, of white grass, white flowers, and white earth—everything in the home, at the table, on the street, the physical body, and the whole universe just ghastly white.

In order *really to live* and *enjoy life* to the *fullest* extent, you must *love color*, and you must *love activity*. Love of color and love of activity are the soul's expressions which are absolutely necessary if you are to remain youthful and healthy and happy.

Remember, that the optic nerve is the channel through which the color vibrations of objects reach the brain. If you persist in refusing to see color, can you really complain if this nerve ceases to function?

Exercise for Improving the Hearing

1. Each day, for about ten minutes, walk along the street or out in the fields in the country, and try to *hear* all the sounds you can possibly hear. Pretend that you are a *scout*, and that your life depends upon the acuteness of your hearing. If the streets are not too crowded, as you walk along, lean forward slightly, walking on the forepart of the foot, so as to bring the muscles of the ankles and lower legs into activity.

2. Listen, not only for sounds, but try to locate the direction of the sound, and try to determine, from the sound, what is producing the sound. For instance, in walking down a city street, hear the sounds of the street cars—the grind of the brakes; the rattle of a milk wagon; the distant grind-organ; the paper boy—and this and that. Break up the city's roar into its component parts, and become conscious of each sound.

3. In beginning this practice it is best to begin on a street that is comparatively quiet, until the brain

centers have begun to function discriminatively. Each evening try to recall some sounds you have heard during the day.

Strengthening the Eyes
THE BLUE LIGHT
(For use at night before retiring)

Procure an eight-watt *blue* electric light bulb, connect by extension cord, and set on dresser or table on a level of the eyes, when sitting comfortably erect in a chair. Sit about three feet away from the light and hold the eyelids open by thumb and forefinger, so as not to wink the lids while looking at the light. Gaze steadily at the light for about two minutes, or until tears come into the eyes.

Do not wipe away the tears, but go to bed immediately.

Take this exercise every other night, gradually increasing the length of time that you look upon the light, until you can gaze at the light steadily for five minutes.

In the morning the eyes can be bathed by use of eye-cups with a salt solution (one-half teaspoonful of salt to one cup of warm water).

First Concentration Exercise—For Clairvoyance

FIRST CONCENTRATION EXERCISE—FOR CLAIRVOYANCE AND CLAIRAUDIENCE

CHART NUMBER TWO—FOR OPENING THIRD EYE AND DEVELOPING SIXTH SENSE

The exercise outlined on this Chart should be practiced for several weeks before beginning the practice of the exercises given below:

Second Concentration Exercise for Developing Clairaudience, Etc.

This exercise is to be taken at night before going to bed, or in the morning upon arising.

Paste a piece of orange paper the size of a dime upon the forehead, at the root of the nose.

With the blue electric light placed behind the head so that it shines upon the mirror, sit about eight to ten or twelve inches away from the mirror. Gaze, without winking, upon the orange spot, which is reflected from the forehead.

This exercise should be continued not longer than five minutes each practice period the first week; and after that two minutes may be added to the practice period each week until a fifteen-minute practice period is reached.

Chant, look into the mirror for the length of time desired (as directed) and then turn off the light and close the eyes. After practicing this exercise for awhile in this manner, you may seem to see a hollow tube when the eyes are closed, with your own face at the far end of the tube. This tube is called the "Ether Tube." When you see your own face in this tube, with the eyes closed, as you sit in the dark, you can then substitute the image of the face of a friend, to whom you may wish to send a telepathic message, and by thinking the message, send that message by telepathy, or thought transference.

This exercise helps to open up the mental solar plexus, and to help develop the powers of clairvoyance and clairaudience.

Exercise with Blue Light for Vibrating Retina of Eye and for Strengthening Eye Muscles

Drop the head far down upon the chest (as you sit in chair) and look at the blue light. Turn the head and look at the light from different angles, keeping the light always in the range of vision, but turning the head in different directions. When you drop the head down that necessitates your rolling the eyes upward to see the light. Then, when you turn the head to one side, you have to roll the eyes sidewise. Then, when you drop the head backward, the eyeballs have to be directed more downward to keep the range of vision upon the light. And when the head is turned toward the other side, the eyeballs have to be rolled sidewise again.

This practice gives a wonderful exercise for the accommodative muscle fibres of the iris of the eye, as well as to the muscles that control the movements of the eyeballs. This exercise can be taken once or twice daily (or nightly) with great benefit.

VITALIZING EYE-MUSCLES AND BRAIN CENTERS BY ROTARY EXERCISE AND SPIRITUAL BREATH
Without Light

With lights out, sit erect in chair, feet flat upon floor, fingers interlaced in lap—with chin down upon breast-bone. Inhale by nostrils, and exhale by nostrils, somewhat forcibly, pulling the navel in during the prolonged exhalation. Then sit very erect away from the back of the chair, raising the head well up. Continue breathing by nostrils, slowly but forcibly.

Try to turn the eyeballs up into the forehead for a few seconds; then turn the eyeballs to the right; then up; then to the left ;then down toward the chin.

Then roll the eyeballs around, somewhat more rapidly, looking upward first, then inside to the top of the head, then toward left ear, then to left side of the cheek, then down to chin, then to right of cheek, then to right ear, then between eye and nose; then to root of nose, converging the vision as much as possible between the eyebrows.

Then look right up to the ceiling and hold the eyes open as long as possible, without winking, and breathe deeply.

Now repeat the exercise of rolling the eyeballs around, this time reversing the direction, looking upward first; then inside to the top of the head, and then toward the right ear first; then to right cheek; then down to chin; then to left cheek; then to left ear; then between eye and nose; and then to root of nose.

This exercise is very valuable for developing the "Magnetic Eye," which is such a valuable asset both to business and social success.

Exercise for the Muscles of the Eyes
With "Black Star" Chart

Place a "Black Star" Concentration Chart upon the wall at the height of the head, so the nose will touch the black spot in the center of the chart. Stand for this exercise, with hands behind the back, fingers of right hand around left wrist. With the tip of the nose touching the middle of the chart against the wall, roll the eyes upward; then to the left; then down; then to the right; then up again—all the time with a feeling as if the eyes are being pushed (by the mind) in the direction they are being rolled.

Then focus the vision on the point at the right side of the chart, holding the concentration upon that point for about one second; then roll the eyes and fix the gaze upon the upper point of the chart, tensing the muscle of the eyeballs as the gaze is so fixed upon the point of the chart. Then roll the eyes to the left point of the chart, and fix the gaze there for the same length of time, tensing the muscles of the eyeball in the same manner. Then roll the eyes downward, and fix the gaze upon the lower point of the chart, and hold in concentration in the same manner and for the same length of time.

Then roll the eyes to the point at the right side of the chart again, and hold in concentration in the same manner, but this time reverse the order, and look down at the lower point next; then to the left; then to the upper point; and back to the right again —holding the concentration upon each spot for about one second during the first week of this practice. Increase the time of concentration upon each point of the chart about one second each week as you practice, until you can hold the eye in concentration for one minute on each spot.

This exercise will not only strengthen the muscles of the eyeballs, but will also strengthen the vision, or eyesight. This exercise should be taken daily, and may be taken more frequently if desired, espcially as a relaxing exercise after periods of close application of the eyes in close work. At such times it will be very beneficial.

"Levitation Exercise" for Developing Occult Power

For those who may wish to develop *occult* powers to a greater extent this exercise may be practiced as an aid to Mental Telepathy and Thought Transference. For this the practice should be continued for a period of six months, the first month sitting in a chair, and after that, standing in five-minute periods, twice a day. After practicing for six months a sensation of floating up may sometimes be experienced during sleep, and if, through practice, you develop to the point where you feel as if you were projecting yourself ten, fifteen or twenty-five feet, that is enough. You do not need to undertake to develop yourself into an "astral traveler" and undertake an "astral trip" to India, or to some other country, because—by developing yourself in accordance with the exercises given in these lessons, you will be able to bring everything to you—within you, within yourself. You can then be able to bring everything outside inside, and into the realm of consciousness.

Do not let yourself be deceived by teachers who claim that they can make you an "astral traveler" in a short time, or who claim to be doing "astral traveling" themselves, in demonstrations upon the stage. If you want to put such teachers to the test, inflict some kind of bodily pain upon such a person, and see if he is "there." Such conditions *can* be attained, and the body brought to a state similar to that which exists when under an anesthetic for an operation, but in order to develop the proper power for real "astral traveling," the right "Key" has to be learned, and in order to come to the state where that "Key" will be operative there has to be renunciation of the material world, as well as a great deal of practice with certain definite exercises designed for the particular purposes of developing this particular power.

However, this exercise for "Levitation" can be practiced in one's room at two o'clock in the morning, without bothering anyone in the next room, letting the humming be not too loud. It can be practiced at night upon going to bed and upon getting up in the morning. For best results, take the exercise in the room with the body entirely nude, letting the body touch the wall without any cloth intervening, in order to let the body get the magnetism from the wall, which connects with the earth, like the ground-wire of a radio system.

Then, every time you get an opportunity to go out into the woods, practice this exercise for developing physical power—for attaining real *physical prowess*, letting your tones come good and strong in chanting, and contact the earth with the bare feet if at all possible.

This exercise, with others given in these lessons, if properly practiced, will enable the Western student to make as extended a developmnt along occult lines as may be desired for practically any purpose. All exercises given are not only absolutely safe, but they are also beneficial, both for physical and mental development.

This Lesson is to be used by student of Yogi Wassan, for his or her personal use—*only*.

Advanced Course—Soroda-Yoga Philosophy

BY

SUPER-AKASHA YOGI WASSAN

There are many different kinds of Yoga Philosophy, six main branches or divisions being the number usually given by writers on the subject—but there are many, many different variations, just as there are many different churches in the western world—all representing the Christian religion.

By the Soroda System, the highest and most complete physical control and development, mental development, and spiritual development are attained. In the Soroda System full symbolic charts are used, combined with a study of breathing, concentration and meditation, and a consideration of the different states of consciousness, together with chants, exercises, and postures that are most adaptable for securing the results desired. This adaption has made this System safe for use by the householder people—men, women (even if pregnant), and children. For that reason, it is the System that is adaptable, and can be used with benefit by the practical Western student.

There are some eighty-four distinctive postures included in the Pranayama System of Yoga Philosophy, but in the Soroda System only a few of these are used, and in this course for opening up the Chakras, I give you a few of these, partly in a modified form that will make them usable by the Western student. The purpose of posture is to prevent thoughts, or feelings, or consciousness of the existence of the body from interfering with concentration and meditation.

In taking up the study, and practice, for opening each chakra, draw the picture of the chakra (from the chart) on a piece of paper, placing this on your forehead, and repeat the Bija Mantranm for that Chakra over and over, as you will be taught in class, with one full breath. Then swallow the saliva that comes in the mouth during the humming of that mantranm, and with another full breath repeat again and again, for one hour in the twenty-four.

"Bija" means "root of" the mantranm, and there will be seven Bija mantranms given with seven chakras. The practice can be with each Bija mantranm separately, and then combining all in a chant, as will be given in class.

Chanting the name of the chakra calls to the chakra to wake up, and chanting the Bija mantranm (the sound of the chakra) vibrates the chakra. This practice can be performed as you walk, or sit, or work, day or night, as you wish, quietly, without disturbing anyone else. For best development, of course, with this as with other concentration and meditation exercises, practice may be performed between the hours of 12:30 midnight, and 8 o'clock in the morning, in the goofa, or shrine, quietly, alone, putting a pail or glass of water (covered by a cloth) nearby. Then look right in the middle of the picture of the chakra, on the chart, or the picture you have drawn and placed on your forehead, and from which you make the reflection in the mirror, sitting straight in chair, or in posture on floor of shrine.

Every petal of the lotus of each chakra has its own sound, and when you open up the chakra, and see the chakra yourself, you will hear the sound of each petal, which is a *cosmic sound*.

The chakras are not considered as being in the physical plane, but are behind or beyond the physical plane. However, for the purpose of study and practice, we have to locate them in certain regions of the physical body. In taking up each Chakra separately, the name, shape, color, element, sense stimulated, Bija mantranm for opening, and qualities developed by opening, will be given.

POSTURES

(1) Inner tuberosity (or knob) of left ankle under outer tuberosity of right ankle—or, outer tub-

erosity of right ankle on top of and touching inner tuberosity of left ankle; arms against the sides of the body, elbows resting on thighs, wrists dropping slightly outward, thumb and forefinger touching; other fingers in repose. During the chanting of the Bija mantranm ("Lang, Lang, Lang, Lang," etc.) the elbows may be elevated from the thighs, and the hands held, palms upward, and fingers outward from the body. Then, upon the repetition, the elbows may be rested upon the thighs; and, another time, the wholeforearm may be extended along the thigh, and the fingers allowed to drop over the knees, for resting. In this posture let the head drop forward, with chin on breast-bone part of the time during chanting.

(2) Sit on floor of shrine, heels and soles of feet flat together, fingers grasping the toes or ankles—the right hand grasping toes or ankle of right foot, and left hand grasping left toes or ankle—grasping the ankle from above, or by running the fingers underneath the ankle, and grasping from below, as the ankle lies on the floor. At first the feet will necessarily be quite well extended in front of the body, but each day the feet may be brought a little nearer to center of the body, with practice, as the body becomes more supple. Head as in Posture No. 1.

(3) Press the palm of the hand flat against the floor under the full length of the foot, on each side (right hand for right foot, etc.)—as the foot lies on the floor, as in Posture No. 2. Or the palm of hand may be against the foot, instead of resting flat upon the floor, and this is a very good posture, as it holds the body steady. Head as No. 1.

(4) Sit on floor, locking the hands in front of the knees, with knees either somewhat close together, or

apart, soles of feet on the floor. Head as in No. 1.

These four postures can be used for practice with each or all of the Chakras. Of course, there are many other postures, but these are easier ones for beginning study and practice.

(5) Padam Asana is used for most practice exercises, but this posture can hardly be assumed by Western men, although some Western women can assume this posture quite easily after a little practice. The complete and correct Padam Asana is holding the left toe with the left hand, with arm back of the body, and the right toes with the right hand, which is brought around back of the body, with right foot up, and crossed over to left side of the body in front; and left foot brought across to right side of body in same manner. In this exercise the head is held slightly backward, for drinking the nectar of life.

A modified Padam Asana may be used, by sitting on floor, with ankles crossed, and hands behind back, fingers of right hand encircling the left wrist. This position of the hands may also be held when walking, or when sitting in chair or on edge of bed.

In chanting "Upar Kanch Upan Ko—O; Puran Upan Melaway, O—" to make "Puran Upan Melaway" or inhaling and exhaling together, sit in posture on floor, or bed, with ankles crossed, humming the chant, and finally the two will come together, and the body will become supple. Practice ten or fifteen minutes, exhaling with a grunt and pulling the navel in. You can sit in this posture and even sleep in this posture for hours, which will bring you not to the dreaming state, but to the Mental state or plane, and you will see and know many things and will be very happy. This practice is not to be used until after you have practiced for some time all the exercises given you in the Beginning Series, and is to be used sometime when you are not too tired from working, or when you can go out into the woods.

Another posture for use when out in the woods is to make "Puran Upan" one, exhaling with a grunt, pulling the navel in, and then sit, in posture, with thumbs in ears, and palms over the eyes. Soon everything will become light, and you will be able to feel the vibrations through the spinal column.

In this life we find our physical bodies, our mental activities and our spiritual vibrations are affected by:—the world we live in—the earth planet (of which the physical body is a part), called Agni Khanda—by the sun, called Sooriya Khanda, and by the moon, called Chanda Khanda. The Chakras are, likewise, in three groups, two in the Agni Khanda, two in the Sooriya Khanda, two in the Chandra Khanda, and one outside.

In this world the Agni Khanda, the fires are burning, and people, having this element strong within, experience this burning in forms of physical expression, or mental clashing oftentimes in contact with other individuals. Therefore, if this fire, which is augmented in strength by the vibration of the sun during the daytime, can be cooled down, then there will be less fire within to stir up anger between people, and we can have a more harmonious world.

To accomplish this the Yogis, in their practice, developed a secret method of reversing the vibrations of the physical body (which is in accord with the vibrations of the earth) so as to get the vibration of the moon by day, and of the sun by night, thus developing an *individual* vibration for each individual, in which state fires do not bother, and sorrow and pain do not affect deleteriously, so everything will be a success, and the individual can elevate himself from the subconscious mind to the conscious mind, and into superconsciousness. The key for this practice will be given in the class work.

In all chanting and humming exercises practice to prolong the breath, or length of respiration, stressing the prolonged exhalation, in accordance with what you have been taught in earlier lessons. As you increase the length of respiration in this manner, just so you increase the span of healthy normal life and activity.

    Lang   Vang   Shang   Shang   Sang

Chakra—Muladhara.
Situation—Spinal Center, region below genitals.
Number of Petals—Four.
Regnant Tattva and its qualities—Prithivi (Earth) Cohesion; stimulating sense of Smell.
Color of Tattva—Yellow—flowing forward.
Taste of Tattva—Sweet.
Number of Rays of Tattva—Thirty-four.
Name of Group—Agni Khanda.
Name of Meeting Point—Rudra Granthi (opened by).
Shape of Mandala—Square.
Bija and its Vahana—*Lang*, on the Airavata (elephant), representing strength, firmness and solidarity.
Devata and its Vahana—Brahma (creative force), presides on Hangsa (or the Bird—Swan), transporting across the river of knowledge.

Shakti of the Dhatu—Dakini (creative) (power of).
Linga and Yoni—Svayambhu and Traipura Trikona.
Other Tattvas—Gandha (smell), in organ of sensation.
Centered here—Pau—Feet (organ of action).

QUALITIES DEVELOPED

Kavishar-ho-jana—Become a poet.
Vidwan-hona—Become learned.
Bismari-dur-hona—All diseases dispelled.
Maut-jitna—Gives power over death.
Dise-bina-har-jaga-jana—Power to go where you like unseen.
Prithivi-van-hona—Power over all the earth; no earth element can injure. Gives steadiness.

The qualities developed by opening this Chakra will be:—Power for becoming a poet, or become learned, or know all knowledge, and become creator of knowledge; power of health and healing; power over death; power of disappearing and appearing, or going unseen; power over all the earth, and earthly beings, animals or man—no earthly element can destroy—gives great power of steadiness.

Vang: Bang Bhang Mang Yang Rang Lang
Chakra—Svadisthana.
Situation—Spinal center, region above the genitals.
Number of Petals—Six.
Regnant Tattva and its qualities—Pani (Water)—
Contraction—stimulating the sense of Taste.
Color of Tattva—White—moving downward.
Taste of Tattva—Salty.
Number of Rays—Forty-four.

Name of Group—Angi Khanda.
Name of Meeting Point—Rudra Granthi.
Shape of Mandala—Same as Petals.
Bija and its Vahana—*Vang* on Makara (fish).
Devata and its Vahana—Vishnu, of furious aspect, presides on Garuda (Eagle).
Shakti of the Dhatu—Rakini (Fury).
Other Tattvas here dissolved—Rasa Tattva (Taste) —taste being situated in an organ of sensation.
Hath—Hand (organ of action).

Qualities Developed

Panch-bhut-bas men hona—Become Master of the five passions: Anger (karod), Greed (lobh), Love (moha), Pride (hankar), and material (or sex) desires (kam).

Sab-se-bari-Mudra—This is the highest Mudra or exercise.

Sab-Dukh-dard-dur—Practice of this Mudra gives freedom from all sensual desires, sorrows and fears.

Gyan-hona—Opens the inner self to all knowledge, giving knowledge of great things.

Amrit-barash—Gives nectar-like speech. (Literally, "like perfume rain."—Therefore giving power of beautiful speech.)

Rang: Dang Dhang Anang Tang Thang Dong
       Dhang Nang Pang Phang

Chakra—Manipura.

Situation—Spinal Center, region above the navel.

Number of Petals—Ten.

Regnant Tattva and its qualities—Tejas, or Agni (Fire)—Expansion, producing heat, and stimulating sense of sight—sense of color and form (also suspending animation).

Color of Tattva—Red, like fire, or cochineal bug—lightning red.

Taste of Tattva—Bitter—flowing upward.

Number of Rays of Tattva—Fifty-four.

Name of Group—Surya Khanda.

Name of Meeting Point—Vishnu Granthi.

Shape of Mandala—Same as petals, all together.

Bija and its Vahana—*Rang* on a Ram (Bhody), representing strength.

Devata and its Vahana—Rudra presides on a Bull (powerful as fire in creating and destroying).

Shakti of the Dhatu—Lakini (dispels fear and grants boons of favors).

Other Tattvas here dissolved—Rupra Tattra (form, color and sight)—Rupa meaning beauty, or—Roop—sight (organ of sensation).

Guda (bowel or anus—organ of action).

Qualities Developed

Viryawan-Hona—Acquire power to create and destroy; power of creation, as if by magic. Also gives power in the face of danger—the hero power, or power of rescue.

Saraswati-rup-hona—Blessed by the Goddess of Knowledge. Also, the power of changing form in different places or surroundings, as practiced by Yogis—a young man today in one place, and an old man tomorrow in a different place, by power of control over physical body.

Maut-ka-dar-dur-hona—Frees from fear of death.

Ag-ka-dar-dur-hona—Gives power over fire, which

cannot injure in any way; and death cannot destroy. Gives power of spiritual magnetism and power to become Healer and Teacher.

Yang: Kang Khang Gang Ghang Nang Chang Chhang Jang Jhang Jnang Tang Thang

Chakra—Anahata.
Situation—Spinal Center, region of the heart.
Number of Petals—Twelve.
Regnant Tattva and its qualities—Vayu (Air)—movement is its quality; stimulating sense of Touch.
Color of Tattva—Bright green.
Taste of Tattva—Sour—direction, flows side to side, or across.
Number of Rays—Sixty-four.
Name of Group—Surya Khanda.
Name of Meeting Point—Vishnu Granthi.
Shape of Mandala—Same as petals, all together.
Bija and its Vahana—*Yang* on an antelope, representing fleetness, or swiftness.
Devata and its Vahana—Ishara presides (protector and destroyer of the world).
Shakti of the Dhatu—Kakini (kind-hearted).
Linga and Yoni—Bana and Trikona.
Other Tattvas here dissolved—Sparsha Tattva (Touch and Feel).
   Touch—organ of sensation.
   Linga (penis)—organ of action.

Qualities Developed

Buddhman-hona—Becomes wise and full of noble deeds.

Indri-jit-hona—To have the five Knowing senses (Giyan Indriya), Seeing, Hearing, Smelling, Tasting and Feeling—completely under control.

Lakshmi-sarup-hona—Become prosperous. Turn yourself into mayeya (money).

Hava-men-chalna—With this power one can travel in the air; wind cannot harm.

Hang: Ang Ang Ing Ing Ung Ung Ring Ring Lring Lring Aing Aing Aung Aoung Anang Anghah

Chakra—Vishuddha (Washooda).

Situation—Spinal Center, region of Throat.

Number of Petals—Sixteen.

Regnant Tattva and its qualities—Akasha (Ether) —space-giving; stimulating the sense of Hearing.

Color of Tattva—Like that of deep-blue sky, or ocean water.

Taste of Tattva—Perfume-like. Direction of movement, inward, within.

Number of Rays—Seventy-four.

Name of Group—Chandra Khanda.

Name of Meeting Point—Brahma Granthi.

Shape of Mandala—Same as petals, all together.

Bija and its Vahana—*Hang*, on a white elephant, representing purity and firmness.

Devata and its Vahana—Sadashiva presides (all beneficence)—giving favors.

Shakti of the Dhatu—Shankini—(Light itself).

Other Tattvas here dissolved—Shabda Tattva (Sound), Hearing (Organ of Sensation).

Muhk (Mouth), Organ of Action.

Qualities Developed

Kavi-Hona—Become eloquent and wise.

Bari-umar-hona—Become long-lived.

Tin-kal-Dekhna—Be able to see the three periods (Past, Present and Future).

Sab-se-bara-Yog—Highest powers of Yoga; can conjure Ether Tattva; can go through matter; and all open space becomes as an open door—nothing can be locked or barred. Power of disappearing. Death cannot destroy, even though the world is destroyed.

Brahm-pana—One comes to Brahm.

Oang

Hang   Kshang

Chakra—Ajna (Ajuna) or Tricotte (Shiva-Eye) (Past, Present and Future).

Situation—Center of region between the eyebrows or root of nose.

Number of Petals—Two.

Regnant Tattva and its qualities—Manas, or Mun (Mind)—Mental faculties.

Number of Rays—Eighty-four.

Name of Group—Chandra Khanda.

Name of Meeting Place—Brahma Granthi.

Bija and its Vahana—*Oang*.

Devata and its Vahana—Shambhu (all powerful).

Shakti of the Dhatu—Hakini (pure-hearted).

Linga and Yoni—Itara and Trikona.

Other Tattvas here dissolved—Mahat (great or large), the Sukhmuna Prakriti, called Hiranya (negative).

Garbha (born of womb)—therefore, birthless and deathless.

Tircotteo (Three-eyes)—become one—Brahm, Vishnu and Mehesha.

QUALITIES DEVELOPED

Shuddh-chit-hona—Become pure of mind.

Muni-ban-jana—Become all-knowing and all-seeing —the highest state of mind.

Brahm-giyana-hona—Acquire unity with Brahma, or Par-brahm.

Chakras—*Kala* and *Sahansrara*

The Sahansrara Chakra may be said to be situated above the head, with the base three inches inside the skull cavity, like one big lotus, with countless rays or petals, very shiny and shimmery in appearance, like gold, or more like the luster of diamonds, or star-shine. This chakra cannot be opened until all the other chakras are opened, and no special exercise or practice is neccesary when the other chakras are opened.

The Ka-La chakra opens first, and then the Sahansrara opens. The exercise for opening the Ka-La chakra can be given only by word of mouth, the Ka-La chakra being situated in the door of Nirbana, and that is not given in writing. Kala is the key for opening Nirbana, and the practice is not given in writing—only by word of mouth, after the very highest state of development is reached by the Chela. When all other chakras have been opened, and the Chela can make certain demonstrations to the Guru, then the secret for opening the Kala will be given.

As long as you wish to develop one power better, or

to a higher degree than another, and try to make one thing better than another thing, then that is only Brahm or Par Brahm, but Nirbana is Cosmic Consciousness.

It is very dangerous to undertake to open the Sahansrara chakra until all other chakras are opened, including Ajuna. Then the key for opening Kala can be given, by word, and that is the key for opening Sahansrara, called Nirbana.

The Sahansrara chakra is situated half in the brain and half above the head, is of countless petals and countless rays. When you open the Sahansrara chakra through Kala, then you are in pad Nirbana. (Pad, meaning state of.)

Many Western students undertake to open Sahansrara chakra first, or more often the Ajuna chakra first, but this is a very dangerous practice. It is very necessary and important that the lower chakras be opened first, and on up in their order, beginning with Muladhara. Get the physical body strong first; then open the chakras in their order, beginning with the lower ones and proceeding upward. In this manner you will be able to maintain the greatest possible degree of steadiness and poise and equilibrium of body, mind and superconsciousness.

There is no Bija Mantranm for the Kala chakra.

The Bija Mantranm for Sahansrara is a sacred word and is never spoken aloud by the Hindoo; but only spoken by the mind.

No.
74. Bhujamgini Mudra—this destroys old age and death, all sicknesses (especially indigestion) and does it quickly.
73. Matangini Mudra—Drink water through nostril and reverse the action. This gives strength like an elephant and this Yogi achieves unending happiness.
72. Kaki Mudra—Drink air like a crow. One will never get sick.
71 and 70. (See No. 38.)
Chakra.
69. Akasi Dharana Mudra—Color like the wonderful pure water in the ocean, or the deep sky. Symbol "H." With this Dharana one opens the portals to Heaven and Deliverance. Death does not come to him even with the destruction of the world.
Chakra.
68. Vayavi Dharana Mudra—Color black like eye-cream, or smoky black. Symbol "Y"—Deity Isvara—Has Sattva quality. Gives the adept power to walk in the air. He can destroy age and death; the wind cannot harm in any manner. He can walk in the air.
Chakra.
67. Agneyi Dharana Mudra—Color Red—Symbol "R" Figure "△" triangle—Deity—Rudra. Gives perfection in the Agni Tattva, takes away the fear of death. An adept in this Dharana if he falls in burning, flaming fire, remains alive and will not die.
Chakra.
66. Ambhasi Dharana Mudra—White (like the moon, a sea-shell, or the Jasmine flower). Letter "V"—Deity Vishnu. This Dharnana takes away unbearable pain and sins. One cannot be injured or drowned in the deepest water.
Chakra.
65. Prithivi Dharana Mudra—Color Yellow—Letter "La" —Symbol is four-sided. Deity—Brahma. The residence of Prithivi Tattva. By this one conquers death. One conquers the earth and brings himself to absolute

No.

steadiness, all success and happiness. One can visit with the physical body the Heavens, he can go where he will with the quickness of a thought. He can walk in the air.

64. Sambhavi Mudra—This brings a high state of happiness. He is a Brahman who knows this Mudra.
63. Manduki Mudra—Gives eternal youth—freedom from wrinkles and gray hair.
62. (Same as No. 61.)
61. Tadagi Mudra—Take pascimottana position and pull stomach in like a water-hole.
60. Sakticalini Mudra—Use Sidda posture. Gives success in Yoni Mudra—removes fear of death and gives the magical powers.
59. Vajroli Mudra—A wonderful exercise. Gives perfection and happiness while still indulging the sensual world.
58. Yoni Mudra—Take Siddhasana posture. Its secrets only through a teacher.
57. Viparitakarani—By this practice one becomes a perfect human. An adept in this exercise is not destroyed when the world is destroyed. The digestive fire is greatly increased. Can only get the secret of this practice through a teacher.

56—54—53—52. (See 36.)

51. Kapalabhati—This destroys phlegm, prevents old age and fever. Cures all diseases of the mucus.

50—49. (See 36.)

48. (See 34.)

47—46. (See 36.)

45. Tratakan—This cures eye diseases, gives a Godly look, and magic powers.

44. Vahnisara or Agnisara—This gives success to the Yogi, increases the digestive fire, cures all diseases. A very difficult Mudra.

43—42—41. (See 34.)

No.
40. Varisara—This cleanses the body. This is the highest process of purifying the blood.
39. Vatasara—Increases the digestive fire. All sickness disappears. Cleanses the dirt from the body.
38. Basti—Increases the digestive fire, prevents constipation, flatulency, and kidney diseases. The body becomes beautiful, gives strength to the senses, and multiplies all the bodily humors.
37. Bahiskrtam—Washing the bowels.
36. Dauta-Dhauti—This is the cleaning of the teeth, tongue, ears, forehead. This corrects the lymph, prevents old age and death.
35. Neti—This gives magic powers and clairvoyance. Cures all diseases above the neck.
34. Hrddhuti—This destroys phlegm and gall, skin diseases and worms.
33. Yogasana—Gives health and poise.
32. Bhujamg-asana—Bodily fire consantly grows, cures all sicknesses, Kundalini wakes up.
31. Ustrasana (Camel posture).
30. Makarasana (Fish posture). This stills the bodily fire.
29. Salabh-asana (Lizard posture).
28. Vrsasana (Stern posture).
27. Garudasana (Eagle posture).
26. Urksana (Tree posture).
25. Uttanaman-duk-asana (Stretched frog).
24. Manduk-asana (Frog posture).
23. Uttanakurmasana (Stretched turtle).
22. Kurmasana (Turtle posture).
21. Kukkutasana (Rooster posture).
20. Mayurasana (Peacock posture).
19. Samkat-asana (Klatra posture).
18. Utkal-asana (High posture).
17. Matsyendrasana—This stills the digestive power and gives the power to fight off all the disease.
16. Goraksasana (Nath posture).

No.
15. Pascimottanasana.
14. Guptasana (Hidden posture)
13. Savasana (Maot posture).
12. Dhanurasana (Arrow posture).
11. Virasana (Hero posture).
10. Gomukhasana (Cow face posture).
9. Simhasana (Lion posture). This destroys all sicknesses.
8. Svastikasana (Happiness-promoting posture).
7. Secret.
6. Vajrasana (Cement posture). This gives magic powers to Yogis.
5. Muktasana (Free posture). Gives magic powers.
4. Bhadrasana (Noble posture). Destroys all sickness.
3.
2. Siddhasana (The perfect posture). Twelve years of this practice gives the person perfection. It opens the portals to deliverance.
1. Laukiki. This multiplies the digestive fire and cures all sicknesses. Drives out the three humors.

The practices for these postures and mudras cannot be given in this book. Under the Soroda System of Yoga Philosophy, these postures and mudras must be practiced with Opana Yama Breathing, the key to which can only be given in the classes, under the instruction of a teacher.

Yogis Automatic Divine Healing and Self Healing Which Is Called Mantram Yoga in Sanscrit

Opening Affirmation:

O Spirit—eternal—energy—awaken within me—
Conscious will, conscious will, conscious will.
Conscious vitality, conscious health.
Good will to all, Vitality to all, Good health to all.

O Spirit—eternal energy—by thy power I command my Will—

O Spirit—my mind is awake—

> Awake to sleep no more —
> Awake to sleep no more —
> Awake to sleep no more —

Forever, forever, forever.

> Peace—peace—peace.

Closing Affirmation:

> I am strong—I am strength—
> I am healthy—I am health—
> I am joyful—I am joy—
> I am peaceful—I am peace—
> I am successful—I am success—
> I am blessed—I am bliss—
> I am immortal—I am immortality—
> Peace, bliss, peace, bliss, peace, bliss.

Exercise for Awakening Consciousness of the Body Universe

As you perform this exercise, feel that you are supplying to each of these races of cells in the particular part of the body you are visiting, increased life, increased intelligence and love, and that you are awakening them to greater activity and power.

Feel love for the billions of individual cells composing these cell republics. As you actually feel (radiate) love to them, they will show their love for you and for each other by manifesting more nearly perfect health and bodily harmony.

Sit erect in chair, feet flat on floor, fingers clinched and little finger resting on lower thigh, just above the knees. Attention with the will, Low, Medium, High—Vibrate with the Action.

Think of your body as a great temple, with many special, separate rooms, each room having a number, one of the forty-nine numbers given in this particular exercise.

Close your eyes. Picture yourself at the entrance to this Great Temple. Relax, and look into the forehead at the root of the nose. Think that you are about to enter room Number 1—which is the Left Foot, and project yourself into the left foot for the moment, sitting very quietly, listening within and seeing within. Feel the Vibration within the foot, at first slowly, then more rapidly, and still faster, like three speeds of an automobile.

Then go into Room Number 2, which is the Right Foot. With a feeling of love for the cells there, become conscious of the vibration of the foot, slow, medium and high speed.

Then visit the various parts of your Body Temple in the order given in this exercise:

Left Foot	1- 2—	Right Foot
Left Calf	3- 4—	Right Calf
Left Knee	5- 6—	Right Knee
Left Thigh	7- 8—	Right Thigh
Left Rump	9-10—	Right Rump
Left Abdomen	11-12—	Right Abdomen
Left Kidney	13-14—	Right Kidney
Spleen	15-16—	Liver
Left Ribs	17-18—	Right Ribs
Left Lung	19-20—	Right Lung
Left Collar Bone	21-22—	Right Collar Bone
Left Shoulder	23-24—	Right Shoulder
Left Upper Arm	25-26—	Right Upper Arm
Left Forearm	27-28—	Right Forearm
Left Hand	29-30—	Right Hand
Left Thyroid	31-32—	Right Thyroid
Left Ear Drum	33-34—	Right Ear Drum
Left Eye	35-36—	Right Eye
Left Temple	37-38—	Right Temple
Left Cerebrum	39-40—	Right Cerebrum
Forehead, at Root of Nose	41-42—	Medulla Ob., Base of Head
Down through spinal cord to base of spine	43-44—	Around in front over Bladder and generative organs
To the Navel	45-46—	To the Stomach
To the Heart	47-48—	To "Adam's Apple" or Larynx
To the Top of the Head	49—	Straight through Door of Brahm

Yogis Auto Suggestion	Mantram
Liver	O M
Left Lung	M U M
Right Eyebrow	S U M
Root of the nose	S A W
Left Eyebrow	O M
Right Lung	M U M
Spleen	S U M
Navel	S A W

Mantra Yoga

How To Chant Holy Word for Cosmic Vibration

Christian—Father in Heaven	E
Hindu—O Ang Shantee	E
Japanese—Devo Buddha Namo Amee	E
Chinese—Shinto Ho	E
Mohammedan—Allah Ho Akbar	E
Sanscrit—A Hang Atma Brahm	E
Hebrew—El-Oh-Im	E
Hoong Yang-Yang-Yang	HOON
O Ang Shantee	HE

You have ten states of consciousness. How to climb them by Mantra Yoga.

Sleep No More   Sleep No More

My Ignorant State of Consciousness
My Physical State of Consciousness
My Dreaming State of Consciousness
My Occult State of Consciousness
My Mental State of Consciousness
My Spiritual State of Consciousness
My Astral State of Consciousness
My Super State of Consciousness
My Self State of Consciousness
My Cosmic State of Consciousness

Now you have the Power to use on everything, health, wealth, beauty, charmingness, etc.

Maha Atma Brahmvidya
Brahm Giyan, Vigiyan, Jeven Mukti

(Means cosmic consciousness, cosmic vibration and cosmic ray.)

RAJAH YOGA SYSTEM OF MUNEE AND RISHEE PHILOSOPHY FOR HOUSE HOLDER

TATTWA PIRKIRTEE?, PIRKIRTEE PURUSHA?, MANISH AVATARA

By MAHA ATMA MASTER WASSAN

First seal—Body of Bead, Temple of God, Holy City.

An exposition of the "Finer Forces of Nature." The ordinary expanse of life should be one hundred and twenty years but through our ignorance of these forces we shorten that period by short respiration.

920,000,000 respirations equal 120 years of life.
   21,600   "   "   24 hours of life.
       15   "   "   1 minute of life.

From Brahma came forth Ether.
From Ether came forth Air.
From Air came forth Fire.
From Fire came forth Water.
From Water the Earth was produced.

From these elements Nature produces the body in nine months.

—THREE GUN—

The three abstract qualities in Nature: Causative, primary, the root of all substances.

"RAJO"	SATO	TAMO
"BRAHMA"	"VISHNU"	"MAHESHA"

(Three deities symbolizing the above qualities)

Rajo Gun: Power of Activity. Sato Gun: Perfecting, preserving, bringing to maturity. Tamo Gun: Cessation, checking activity.

Five Organs

Roop	Fire	Eye
Gandha	Earth	Nose
Ras	Water	Tongue
Sparsha	Air	Skin
Shabda	Ether	Ear

ETHER	BLUE	PERFUME	BACKWARD
AIR	GREEN	SOUR	LEFT OR RIGHT CIRCLES
FIRE	RED	BITTER	UPWARD
WATER	WHITE	SALTY	DOWNWARD
EARTH	YELLOW	SWEET	FORWARD

Five actions of Fire — AGNEE DEVTA:
    angry
    hungry
    sleepy
    yawning
    thirsty

Five actions of Water — JAL DEVTA:
    blood
    perspiring
    coughing
    mucus
    semen

Five actions of Air — PAWAN DEVTA:
    running   growing
    jumping   quietness
    gripping

Five actions of Earth—DHARTEE DEVTA:
- bone
- hair
- skin
- veins
- flesh

Five actions of Ether—AKASHA DEVTA:
- greed
- jealousy
- material love
- agony
- pride

NUN————MIND
BHUDEE————UNDERSTANDING
ATMA————SOUL
ISHRA————UNIVERSAL MIND AND CONSCIOUSNESS
NIRVANA————COSMIC CONSCIOUSNESS AND COSMIC RAY

These 25 functions and vibrations are called the body. The body being composed of bones, flesh, veins and glands. Hindus call "Tattwa Pirkirtee," which means combinations in the body.

The human body has no name or nationality—no male or female, sickness, anger and jealousy. It being composed of the same cells, tissues and organs governed by the same emotions. Because we are all children of God.

Truth belongs to everyone, dedicated to everyone by God. Hindu YOGA Philosophy is the truth and technique for human education. Recommended all over the entire world, by its foremost learned men

5	0	0	0	0	0

By Yogi Wassan, from Punjab, India

#			
1	Hindoo	O Ang Shantee	E / O
2	Japanese	Devo Budha Namo Amee	E / O
3	Chinese	Shintoo HO	E / O
4	Mohammedan	Alla HO Ackbar	E / O
5	Christian	Father in Heaven	E / O
6	Gurroo	Kar Guroo	O / E
6	Gurroo	HO Guroo	O / E
4	Plan of Consciousness	Jagrat Soopan Sakopat Tooria	O / E
3	Plane of Mind	Ida Pingla Sookmuna	E / O

Mahan Wakia of the 4-Vedas of the Sanscrit

Rigvedas	Pragiya Nama Nad Buranm	E / O
Jujar Vedas	A Hang Buramn us mee	E / O
Shanman Vedas	Tat Twang Masee	E / O
Atharban Vedas	A ing Attma Buranm	E / O

KABIT

Sir. Hai. Akas-Suwas Naska Pawan Was	E / O
Soor sus Nain Mukh Analko Karl Hain	E / O
Har-Har-Bhaj Daoo-Hea Chatranan Hai	E / O
Udar Sakal Ved Banee Mukh Rare Hai	E / O
Parbat ust Ronm Sokal Benas Pat	E / O
Meng Mal Beeraj Petal Paw Dhare Hai	E / O
Alakh Aroop Jakee Malma Anoop Dekho	E / O
Voho Sive Bhoot Wisaw Roop Ap Dhare Hai	E / O

1 Hoon.   3 Yung.

and women. Such as Prof. Max Mueller, Annie Besant, Professor Leadbeater, Baird T. Spaulding, Manly Hall, Swami Yogananda, Swami Parmananda and countless others.

Practical Breathing for Health

How I Breathe:

1. I inhale breath through nostrils, keeping mouth closed until lungs are half filled, then swallow, which locks breath, and then exhale through nostrils, and hum like a bee.

2. How to drink the Nectar of Life and gain strength of physical voice and the power of word: I inhale breath through nostrils, keeping mouth closed until the lungs are half filled, then swallow breath and exhale by making sound like hoon, young, young.

3. Inhale breath through nostrils, keeping mouth closed until lungs are half filled, then swallow, which locks breath, then exhale through pursed lips and distended cheeks with a whistling sound. Do this all night while in bed.

And the Lord God formed man of the dust of the ground, and breathed into his nostrils the breath of life, and man became a living soul.—Gen. 2:7.

Then said Jesus to them again, Peace be unto you: as my Father has sent me, even so send I you.

And when he had said this, he BREATHED on them, and saith unto them, Receive ye the Holy Breath.—St. John 20:21-22.

Secret Key of the Yoga Philosophy
IDA, PINGLA, SUKHMUNA

The word Yoga, which is derived from the Sanscrit root "Yug" (to join), really means the merging of the lower self into the higher self, the Divine. By the study of Yoga, darkness or ignorance is replaced with light, all undesirable tendencies are eliminated, and by degrees man becomes the Master. Any philosophy which teaches man to do this is worthy of study.

Three qualifications are absolutely necessary for the student of the Yoga Philosophy, namely, Patience, Perseverance and Earnestness. With these three well in mind, there is no reason why any Westerner cannot only develop the higher phases of Yoga, but that he can do so while in his usual life, and while following any occupation. The Hindoo adept, of course, devotes all his time to practice, but the average Westerner cannot do that, and it is not necessary.

Again, the student must learn contentment, and be free from complaining when experiences come, analyze and weigh them well—the bruises of the so-called hard knocks will soon be erased by turning the mind to what you are trying to attain. This will soon prove that even in the *attempt* to realize the Divine Spirit, the "hard knocks" will lessen in significance and gradually disappear.

The student must remember his duty to dumb beasts as well as to man, and that he must not hurt any of these, by thought or deed. He must not think evil. The mind must be free from *malice, hatred* and all uncharitableness. It should be kept as placid and calm as possible.

For this the science of Breathing, which the Yoga teaches, will be found very beneficial, as its mission is to steady the action of the brain, to overcome the crowded and uncontrolled thought forms that congregate there, and to regulate the action of the heart so as to insure a steady and constant flow of blood to the brain.

As the Bible teaches us that all things apparently real are only temporary, so Yoga maintains that the only things that are real are spiritual. From Spirit (Brahma) came forth Ether, from Ether came forth Air, from Air came Fire, from Fire came Water, and from Water the Earth was produced. The student of Yoga will find certain parts of the human anatomy very interesting and to which he should pay attention. While the spinal column is the center around which all else revolves, the various other nerve centers have their specific value. It is not only the object of the exercises, etc., to develop these centers, but to free them, more especially to free the passage within the spinal cord.

The vertebral, or spinal column, forms the center, at the top of which and at the base of the brain is one important nerve center. At the base of the spinal column in the region of the Sacral plexus is another.

The principal nerves taken under consideration are twenty-three, but of these only three are of real importance—the Ida, Pingla, and Sukhmuna. Of these the Sukhmuna or passage through the spinal cord is the principal. The importance of this passage will be noticed when practice begins. All the nerves are like threads branching from the spine by which they are supported. The principal nerve centers represent the Sun, Moon and Fire. The center at the top of the spine represents the Moon, IDA. The one at the base of the spine, the Sun, PINGLA, and the SUKHMUNA is called Chittra.

At the base of the spinal column, the region of the sacral plexus, is the Kundalini, which represents creative force. The awakening of this force, under proper guidance, gives one all the knowledge and power. Through proper guidance one attains this knowledge consciously and retains it. One does not merely stumble upon it and then forget it.

While intelligent questions are advisable and to be encouraged in a student of the Yoga Philosophy, when he comes to a Guro or Teacher he should come with all due humility, not only to learn what he can from the teaching, but to serve and look after the Guro in every way possible, with devotion and reverence.

When the student arrives at the stage of development when he can hold his breath for five minutes, nothing is impossible to him. By drinking air daily the student can destroy all feeling of fatigue and old age, and when he can drink the fluid (air) day and night, the powers of clairvoyance and clairaudience are fully acquired. Anybody who practices this regularly for a few months can destroy diseases and free himself from sin. Then it will not be long before he can conquer the elements and make them obey his commands.

By continual meditation upon things divine the student forgets the worldly things. This once done he can obtain wonderful powers by which he becomes the Master and is no longer the slave of the nine senses. The previously unseen realm becomes visible and bows down before him, his vision clears, and all knowledge, all power are his. He acquires all psychic powers, walks on air and on water, heals the sick, rids himself of sorrow, sin and disease—in fact, he proves that to him who has Faith and Energy and Love nothing is impossible.

Mahan Wack of the Four Vedas of the Sanscrit Reg Veda, Pragiya, Nama, Nad Barum

Pragiya means God is too far away, until we see it. God is not distant and is in no one direction.

Nama means that there is no use praying to God in words. Realize and feel that we are one with Him and in that realization one's prayers are answered.

Nad means to be peaceful and satisfied. To see God.

Barum means when you see what God is. That He is all in all and everywhere. To be one with God—the Absolute—the Universal.

Vojar Veda
Ahang Burum Usmee

Ahang means that God is not proud, and has no enemies or friends. God is Universal Love.

Burum means that God is in everyone, just like the thread in the pearls.

Usmee means who is that God? The real self, the one in all.

Shaman Veda
Tat Twang Masee

Tat means the earth.

Twang means the 84,000 individual life on the earth and how they came to life.

21,000 came to life through eggs, and these are the different species of birds, fish, etc.

21,000 came to life through wombs or were born of mammals. Human beings belong to this species.

21,000 came to life through pores, through sweat,

such as worms and larvas. There is no male or female in this species.

21,000 came from seeds, all plants and vegetation growing on the earth belong to this species.

This 84,000 individual life is one flesh, one life, one breath. There is one God in everyone, just like the thread in the pearls, the fire in the wood or the butter in the milk.

Tat means ocean. Twang means bubble on the ocean. Masee means water in both. One water in both. The ocean, water and bubble are one, but we call them three until we know.

Earth and the 84,000 individual life on the earth and God are One, but we call them three until we know the true God.

The Eastern mother teaches her children from ten years of age this Mahan Wack of the four Vedas of the Sanscrit, to bring Universal Brotherhood to the world and Universal Love to all Mankind.

Atharban Veda
Aing Atma Buram

Aing means that God is birthless and deathless, eternal and changeless.

Atma means that I am that God, the real Self, just as the ocean and the bubble are of one water.

Buram means the absolute. The Great all in all, which we call God. God is in all like the thread in the pearls.

The four bodies of man, which the Yoga calls Jagrat-Supan-Saikhopat Tooriya.

Jagrat is the physical body, and is the vehicle of action. It eats, walks, works and plays. When the body gets tired we think of rest and sleep.

Supan is the sleeping body or dreaming body, a counterpart of the physical body. When we dream we often travel in the air or dream that we swim. We often have wealth and happiness and waken to find it gone.

The physical and dreaming body respond to the sub-conscious mind. When we use the physical body and dreaming body we can live to be fifty or sixty years of age, and have to leave this earth life. We use only the sub-conscious mind and low vibrations. We do not know about the higher mind. Man is not the Master in this state, he is the slave of the nine senses. Sakhopat is the third or mental body. The Yoga calls this the conscious mind, and teaches in the Secret Key how this body can be used and developed.

Tooriya is the fourth body and the Yoga calls this the spiritual body, and the super-conscious mind. After the third body is properly developed, the fourth body unfolds itself, and then we know the real self and the union with the Divine Spirit takes place.

The physical and dreaming body is the dark consciousness, and when we use them we can see only the physical and earthly objects and forms. We can not see the higher forms until we develop the third body and the conscious mind. When man develops the Tooriya, or fourth body, he knows and sees the real self and is One with all there is in the Universe.

IDA, PINGLA, SUKHMUNA

These are the three vibrations, and the map for the knowledge. This knowledge is the ocean. The teacher is the captain. The teacher's mind is the boat. The pupils are the passengers. When the teacher has a good map he takes the pupil to the end of the knowledge, but a teacher without a map takes a pupil to the ocean only and leaves him to drift with the tide.

When you study with a teacher be sure you have one who has a real map for the knowledge. The Yoga uses the map called Ida, Pingla, Sukhmuna for the knowledge. These are the three breaths in the body.

The breath called Ida runs in the left nostril for eight hours, from four p. m. until midnight. This is the sub-conscious mind and low vibrations. When the breath goes through the left nostril we are using the physical and dreaming body, and feel the inharmony and worry of the material world.

The breath called Pingla runs in the right nostril for eight hours, from midnight until eight a. m. This is the breath of the third body, or conscious mind. This brings high vibrations and raises the consciousness from the physical and dreaming state of the sub-conscious mind. These vibrations cause the body to feel lighter and freer and full of health and harmony.

The breath called Sukhmuna runs through both nostrils eight hours, from eight a. m. to four p. m. This is the breath for the fourth or Spiritual Body, and the super-conscious mind. When this stage of development is reached the pupil is free from the physical body, also the conscious and sub-conscious mind.

The Ida and Pingla is no longer used, only the Sukhmuna breathing is necessary in this super-conscious mind and spiritual body—then you are the real self. Ida, Pingla and Sukhmuna is the real map for the knowledge—which knowledge is given in the Secret Key of the Yoga Philosophy.

Only a Super Kasha Yogi knows how to use the Secret Key of Ida, Pingla, Sukhmuna, and this secret cannot be written. It must be given by word.

The student is warned that Yoga can only be practiced, after direct study with a teacher. If a pupil has a strong desire for this knowledge he will find his teacher.

A great many Western teachers claim that Yoga breathing is dangerous. When studied and practiced the correct way, it is a great benefit to the health, and it will also develop the latent powers. It will develop the sixth sense by opening the Pineal Gland. Super Kasha Yogi claims it has taken 1,768,000 years of practice to perfect this method of development through breathing.

The Yogi proves that this breathing is a great benefit to the health, by the way animals breathe.

Snake Breathing

The cobra snake inhales 24 hours and exhales 90 days. At the end of 90 days of exhaling nature has provided a new skin. By this method of breathing he has drawn enough magnetism from the air to renew his body. This snake lives to be 5,000 years old, and looks just like he did when he was one year old, and is clairaudient and clairvoyant. This breathing keeps the pineal gland open. If this snake inhaled and exhaled every five minutes he would live to be only 100 years old. He knows how to control his breath, so he can live as long as he desires. The cobra does not eat or drink. He takes his nourishment from the liquid that is contained in the air.

Cat Breathing

The cat breathes by purring. This sends the magnetism to the solar plexus and makes the stomach strong. For this reason the cat can eat four rats without being poisoned.

Dog Breathing

The dog does not live to be very old because his breath is short. He also draws magnetism from the air, and has a strong solar plexus, so that he can run a great distance without fatigue. The dog is clairaudient and clairvoyant. He is not proud, and a good friend to man even when he is abused.

Frog Breathing

The frog sits in the water and looks at the stars, without winking his eye. The croaking he does is deep breathing. He is drawing magnetism from the moon and stars, water and air. The frog dies in the summer when the water dries up, but in the fall, when the rain comes, there is a new frog for every piece of the dried body. Frogs are neither male nor female.

Leach Breathing

The leach walks with his breathing. He is so strong he can lift with his body more than one hundred times his own weight. The leach never exhales —he only inhales. This breathing draws much magnetism and makes the body very strong. It will keep alive in the different parts twenty-four hours after it has been cut to pieces.

So each animal has a lesson for us, by which we can derive a benefit. If the Yoga breathing is studied and practiced by the human race the results will be a strong, pure body, and the pupil will also be brought into greater knowledge and power.

There are different ways of developing the higher self practiced by the different Yogis.

The Super Kasha Yogi develops the higher self by reading the Ida, Pingla, Sukhmuna. By doing this he can live 500 years in the same body.

The Prana Yama Yogi controls his breath until he can hold it for twenty-four hours. By this practice he develops great powers and can live 500 years in the same body without eating or drinking.

The Nevely Karma Yogi preserves his body in an air-tight stone vault. He permits himself to be buried alive, while in a high state of consciousness, and sets a date when he wishes to come out of this state. Sometimes the Nevely Karma Yogi remains buried for 500,000 years, and is found still alive when people are digging wells or excavating in India.

The Nevely Karma Yogi does this so the records of the Sanscrit can be proven.

The Balnath Yogi develops his higher self by sitting in the fire in the summer and in a lake in the winter. He draws the magnetism from the fire and water; this gives him great healing power. He can cut his body into five different pieces and put them together again in five minutes. He can walk in the air and walk on the water and control wild beasts. This Yogi can be seen in Kajley Ban in India.

The Ramata Yogi develops his higher self by walking day and night, without sleeping or sitting down for 36 years. This gives him the power of sleeping on nails without feeling any pain. This Yogi can control pain in others and heal diseases.

The Raj Yogi develops his higher powers by controlling the sex forces and renouncing the world. He develops all knowledge and all power.

The Western people can do the Super Kasha and Prana Yama Yoga without harm. Only the Hindoos are prepared to do the other kinds of Yoga, because they live a pure life and do not harm anything.

All those different kinds of Yoga are called Yoga Abiasa. Ida, Pingla, Sukhmuna is the Key for all the Yoga Abiasa.

The Sanscrit is the oldest language on the earth for reading or writing. The Sanscrit alphabet contains 37 letters, each letter having 14 sounds. There are 518 sounds in this language. It is a very rich language and hard to translate into any other language. The English language has 26 letters, the letter a having five sounds, and the whole alphabet 85 sounds. So anything from Sanscrit we have to teach by word.

The earth remains in the light 5,000,000,000 years, and in the dark 5,000,000,000 years. The reason for this is that the mountains get too high, and the rivers too deep, and the inside of the earth too hot. So nature repairs and tightens up the damage by floods. This has been done many times and is proven by the Sanscrit.

The Sanscrit also teaches that the earth breathes. The ebb and flow of the tides is the earth's breathing. The earth has open pores and long breath. She can be trusted with our treasures.

The human body is made of five elements, fire, air, earth, water and ether. There is not disease in any of these elements, so the body must necessarily be free from disease. The Yogi claims that if no decayed flesh is eaten to build disease into the body, man can live as long as he desires without bodily suffering.

The human body comes and goes through birth and death, just as long as man uses only the physical and dreaming body and sub-conscious mind. These are the low vibrations.

When man uses the mental body, conscious mind and the spiritual body or super-conscious mind, there is no more birth or death. There is no more day and night, light or darkness. There is only the One, the Real Self.

FROM 8 A. M. TO 4 P. M.	SUKHMUNA	TOORIYA	4	14 / 13 / 12 / 11 / 10 / 9 / 8	SUPER-CONSCIOUS	REAL SELF
FROM 12 M. TO 8 A. M.	PINGLA	SAKHOPAT	3	7 / 6 / 5 / 4 / 3 / 2 / 1	CONSCIOUS MIND	MENTAL BODY
10TH DOOR		TRICOTEE				PINEAL GLAND
FROM 4 P. M. TO 12 M.	IDA	SOCPAN	2	9 / 8 / 7 / 6 / 5	SUB-CONSCIOUS MIND	DREAMING BODY
FROM 4 P. M. TO 12 M.	IDA	JAGRAT	1	4 / 3 / 2 / 1		PHYSICAL BODY

1. PRAGIYA NAMA NAD BURAM
2. AHANG BURAM USMEE
3. TAT TWANG MASEE
4. AING ATMA BURAM

JAGRAT SOOPAN SAKHOPAT TOORIYA
IDA PINGLA SUKHMUNA

The Optic Nerve

O ANG SHANTEE

O ANG SHANTEE

MY 10 STATES OF CONSCIOUSNESS

SLEEP NO MORE

SLEEP NO MORE

How to get Occult concentration power for recharging and magnetizing the optic nerve and restoring the eyesight for a hundred years.

ENGINEER NO. 1

Sit erect on chair.

Put left elbow on left knee, right elbow on right knee.

Place palms of hands over closed eyes.

Press head against the palms—but not enough to hurt.

ENGINEER NO. 2

Hold palms over eyes for two minutes, quietly.

With eyes closed, palms still over the eyes:

> Look up into the forehead to the root of the nose.—Mentally see figure No. 1.
>
> Look to the right forehead.—Mentally see figure No. 2.
>
> Look to the right temple.—Mentally see figure No. 3.
>
> Look to the right ear drum.—Mentally see figure No. 4.
>
> Look to the lower right cheek.—Mentally see figure No. 5.
>
> Look to the right chin.—Mentally see figure No. 6.
>
> Look to the middle of chin.—Mentally see figure No. 7.

Look to the left chin.—Mentally see figure No. 8.

Look to the lower left cheek.—Mentally see figure No. 9.

Look to the left ear drum.—Mentally see figure No. 10.

Look to the left temple.—Mentally see figure No. 11.

Look to the left forehead.—Mentally see figure No. 12.

Look again to the root of the nose, in the middle of the forehead.—Mentally see figure No. 1.

Practice this exercise for 12 minutes, without looking anywhere.

Concentrate on each figure for one minute.

After completing the exercise from right to left, go over the same drill in the same manner, from left to right.

Roll eyeballs from left to right, from right to left, as fast as possible.

Close eyes for three minutes.

Open eyes for one-half minute.

Close eyes tightly for one-half minute. Contract face as much as possible for this pulls the optic nerve inward. Open eyes. Push them outward.
Open and close eyes for a half minute.

Gaze seriously ahead—tensing the muscles of the eyes.

Wink.

Gaze ahead.

While doing this exercise, keep the head in the same position—using the deep-thinking posture—that is:

Feet flat on floor.

Elbows on knees.

Chin in palms of hand—in the form of a "Y."

SECTION 2

Same position.

Hold eyelids open with tip of forefinger and thumb. Hold the eyes wide open. Keep the other three fingers of each hand closed tightly.

Place a golden, copper, or silver coin (gold is more magnetic than copper, copper than silver) about twelve inches in front of your feet, on the floor.

Look at that coin for a few minutes, while holding the eyes open.

Then revolve your eyes around the object in circles from left to right, mentally making a bigger picture of the circle each time, until it is about 14 inches in diameter.

Repeat exercise, from right to left.

The Ear

O ANG SHANTEE

O ANG SHANTEE

MY 10 STATES OF CONSCIOUSNESS

SLEEP NO MORE

SLEEP NO MORE

WHAT I DO FOR DEAFNESS AND BUZZING IN EAR— I lie on my side and put in three (3) drops of homemade oil (No. 11) in outer ear. Then I put finger in entrance to the ear and shake for one minute. Then I apply hot wet towel to ear and use hot water bag on ear to give heat. I continue this treatment while I remain lying upon my side for twenty or twenty-five minutes. The same night I treat the other, or opposite ear, whether affected or not. I continue this method until well. Use once a month, but not for children.

How to make homemade oil:

½ oz. olive oil

½ oz. oil of nutmeg

Stir together, mixing thoroughly, bottle and keep. Put this mixture into your ears at least once a month.

Lay flat on your back, placing hands and arms on a pillow and put a forefinger in each ear. Let the arms rest at side of body. Now hum:—Hoon, Yang, Yang, etc., for about five minutes. Do this about two or three times daily.

This will vibrate the ear drum and both cerebrums. Making your hearing very sensitive so that it will catch all sounds.

O ANG SHANTEE

O ANG SHANTEE

MY 10 STATES OF CONSCIOUSNESS

SLEEP NO MORE

SLEEP NO MORE

Copyrighted by Yogi Wassen 1916.

The Adenoids

ENGINEER NO. 1

By Yogi Wassan

CHANG SHANTEE

CHANG SHANTEE

SLEEP NO MORE

SLEEP NO MORE

I feel sorry for the people because they don't know enough about adenoids. They are one of the gates to the body. If they are not kept open, the life of Prana can not get into the body. Life of Prana purifies the blood and throws the mucus into and out the nostrils, through the throat, Adenoids and palate cavity.

If the Adenoids are clogging the nostrils, the mucus drops down into the stomach. That creates Cancer, Consumption and open sores in and out of body. It is the cause of many sicknesses being created.

It is very essential to know more about the Adenoids, more fuller details will be given in the classes.

HOW TO APPLY ENGINEER NO. 1 FOR THE ADENOIDS

Procure the largest handkerchief you can buy. Then taking this handkerchief, blow your nose into it as hard as you can. Now roll the handkerchief on your fore-finger, and stick into your outside nostril entrance and clean the walls of the nose. Now blow your nose again, bringing all the mucus from the Adenoid cavity.

Take a small piece of cotton and roll it into a ball the size of a pea. Stick it into one nostril as far as you can, leave it there for 2 or 3 hours at a time and breathe through one nostril.

This will give Automatic deep-breathing exercise, making the suction force deeper and stronger, also drying the mucus. It purifies the blood in the lungs, making the lungs and heart very, very strong.

This is a method of breathing, giving Automatic physical exercise, while you engage in business. You are using $\frac{1}{2}$ of the body while the other $\frac{1}{2}$ is resting. Blow the cotton ball out of your nose every 2 or 3 hours and change it for a clean one. Do it one day in one nostril from 6:00 in the morning to 6:00 at night. The next day do it with the other nostril.

1. This is called, "Rava Yoga cross breathing."
2. This is called, "Sun and Moon Breathing."
3. This is called, "Positive and Negative Magnetism Breathing."

4. This is called, "Mental, Spiritual, Physical, Clairvoyant, and Clairaudient Breathing."

This breathing is a very high, safe and harmless breathing, used through out India by the Householder. It fits to any age or vitality, can be used by the weak or strong person alike. This breathing gives a new life, recharging the Sympathetic system nerve center, waking the Eight (8) Glands and Plexuses, putting them all into action.

Helping you to all the success you need, because it rejuvenates the body for everything; very wonderful for any kind of fever, I have met people who have had adenoid trouble for 10 years and by doing this were freed from that trouble in one month.

The Adenoids

O ANG SHANTEE	SLEEP NO MORE
O ANG SHANTEE	SLEEP NO MORE

ENGINEER NO. 2

By Master Wassan of India

TAKE   1 qt. of water
¼ cup of table salt

Put the salt into the water and boil for about five minutes. Let it cool, then put in a jar and keep airtight. Fill a "Nasal Douche" with a quantity of this water and pour it into your nostrils. Pour this thru the nostrils and down into the throat. Avoid swallowing if possible.

Do this twice a day:—

1st. In the morning upon arising.

2nd. At night, just before going to bed.

Sleep on the left side or on the stomach all you can. Always use these 2, "Adenoid Engineers." Forever.

O ANG SHANTEE*!*
O ANG SHANTEE*!*
SLEEP NO MORE*!*
SLEEP NO MORE*!*

Coyprighted 1920 by Yogi Wassan.

The Mouth, Throat, Tonsils and Teeth

O ANG SHANTEE
O ANG SHANTEE
MY 10 STATES OF CONSCIOUSNESS
SLEEP NO MORE
SLEEP NO MORE

Hindoo Tooth Powder—For relief and prevention of pyorrhea, toothache, decay, and germ encroachment, removal of tartar, for sore and bleeding gums, for preserving the enamel, and for making the teeth white and beautiful. Also for promoting even growth of teeth in children.

4 ounces Areca nut, powdered

¼ oz. powdered borax thoroughly mixed

Use three times daily, on tooth brush, with a little water to moisten, rubbing vigorously, morning, noon and night. If not possible to use three times daily, use at least twice daily. This powder should preserve the teeth, beautiful and white, for one hundred years. Good teeth are powerful agents for the prevention of all diseases in the human body.

After the teeth are thoroughly cleaned by using this powder on the tooth-brush, a pinch of this powder may be used, with a little water, for a throat gargle, for cleansing around the tonsils. Do not swallow the liquid thus used. After using this gargle, the mouth may be rinsed with clear water.

O ANG SHANTEE

O ANG SHANTEE

My 10 States of Consciousness
SLEEP NO MORE
SLEEP NO MORE
Copyright 1916 by Yogi Wassan.

The Thyroid Gland
Engineer No. 1
O ANG SHANTEE
O ANG SHANTEE
My 10 States of Consciousness
SLEEP NO MORE
SLEEP NO MORE

You strengthen and magnetize the thyroid gland and put power into the voice by—

Humming Hoong, Yang, Yang, Yang, chanting O Ang Shantee, My 10 States of Consciousness:—

(1) My Ignorant .... State of Consciousness
(2) My Physical .... State of Consciousness
(3) My Dreaming .... State of Consciousness
(4) My Occult .... State of Consciousness
(5) My Mental .... State of Consciousness
(6) My Spiritual .... State of Consciousness
(7) My Astral .... State of Consciousness
(8) My Super .... State of Consciousness
(9) My Self .... State of Consciousness
(10) My Cosmic .... Consciousness

SLEEP NO MORE
SLEEP NO MORE

Also chant the seven (7) holy words from the seven (7) holy bibles:—

Christian—Father in Heaven .... E
Hindu—O Ang Shantee .... E
Japanese—Devo Buddha Namo Amee .... E
Chinese—Shinto Ho .... E

Mohammedan—Allah Ho Akbar .... E
Sanscrit—A Hang Atma Brahm .... E
Acblew—El-Oh-Im .... E

Ida, Pingala, Sushmuna

Use the "Blood Irrigation Button," and cotton cross breathing exercise in Engine No. Engineer No. 1. This will vibrate, magnetize and recharge the thyroid gland, with the magnetic current. It will keep the Thyroid Gland stronger, younger and perfect in action. Also helps to vibrate all the cells in the body and open the fountain of cosmic vibration. Which is a protection against disturbing actions in you and your daily life.

Copyrighted 1916 by Yogi Wassan.

The Liver
Engineer

O ANG SHANTEE

O ANG SHANTEE

MY 10 STATES OF CONSCIOUSNESS

SLEEP NO MORE

SLEEP NO MORE

Liver is the biggest engine in the human body and is the most sensitive. It runs without an engineer. When anything goes wrong with this engine all the other twelve engines stop at once and body starts to die. Which means it gets sick. Master Wassan Human Engineer knows the technique of all the human factory. Thousands and millions of engines running in this human factory. He will give the complete key, how you can be engineer yourself for your own factory.

This is one of the many engineer's given you

Engineer No. 4

Take 4 oz. of shredded cocoanut

4 oz. of almonds
4 oz. of Pistachio
4 oz. of senna leaves
4 oz. dried seedless raisins

Take all of these and mix well before grinding. Then take a food grinding machine and grind this slowly, pinch by pinch. Use the coarsest grinder you have. After finishing grinding, kneed the mixture together and roll with rolling pin, making it ½ inch thick. Cut into one inch squares like candy. Let it get dry for a half day. Then put in a fruit jar and keep air tight. This will keep it for a year without spoiling. Chew one every night at bedtime forever as long as you live and more if necessary. This is one engineer of the other 12 which will be given in the classes. Also has been given in "The Secrets of the Himalaya Mountain Masters and Ladder to Cosmic Consciousness."

O ANG SHANTEE

O ANG SHANTEE

MY 10 STATES OF CONSCIOUSNESS

SLEEP NO MORE

SLEEP NO MORE

Copyrighted 1916 by Yogi Wassan.

The Stomach

O ANG SHANTEE

O ANG SHANTEE

MY 10 STATES OF CONSCIOUSNESS

SLEEP NO MORE

SLEEP NO MORE

The stomach is the food dish of the human body. People have an ignorant idea, they wash the dishes they eat in, but they do not try to wash the walls of the stomach. The stomach lining is very brushy, and the food gets stuck to the cells and pores of the lining. This is the cause of many sickness. When people get sick they run to a mineral springs, or change of climate.

They do not know that there is plenty of Natural Sulphur and 16 mineral salts in the food they eat. This is all unknown to them because they do not study chemical diet and food remedies with some one who knows all about it. Yogi Wassan has learned from Raja Yoga Science of Super Health Study that it is not necessary to go to Sulphur Mineral Springs or to change the climate.

Following is the stomach engineer and sulphur drink. This receipt will wash the stomach and keep its pores open. Giving healing power any place that it may be needed inside or outside of the body. It penetrates and purifies the whole body, circulating and purifying the blood throughout it.

1 glass Grapefruit juice
1 glass Orange juice
Underweight put in 2 glasses of cream
Overweight put in 2 glasses of water
3 yolks of eggs
½ cup honey

Mix all these things together in a milk shaker and drink one (1) glass before eating, drink the balance any time during the day. This will make you reduce or gain which ever you need most. This is called 16 salt or sulphur drink in the Raja Yoga Super health study. It is wonderful for lungs, consumption, consumption fever, dropsy, sugar diabetes and strengthens the heart, kidneys, liver, bladder and bowels. Purifies the blood and rejuvenates the 8 glands in the human factory.

If you don't like to drink it every day, drink it every other day, or every third day. You can drink this throughout one week and quit during the next week. By drinking it in this manner you have it do wonders by giving you an automatic house cleaning.

Do this:—1 week a month, 1 month every 6 months, 6 weeks every year.

I am telling you this because I know it is very, very wonderful and is the truth. This will give you the power of automatic self-healing. If you give this attention as long as you live, you will always enjoy super-health.

Also use the Liver Engineer with this.

O ANG SHANTEE
O ANG SHANTEE
MY 10 STATES OF CONSCIOUSNESS
SLEEP NO MORE
SLEEP NO MORE

Copyrighted 1916 by Yogi Wassan.

The Heart and Blood Purifier

O ANG SHANTEE
O ANG SHANTEE
MY 10 STATES OF CONSCIOUSNESS
SLEEP NO MORE
SLEEP NO MORE

When all the other engines and engineers are working perfectly that means pure blood and a powerful heart and body. Also a good physique and super mind. When you have mental and physical power you can create super-consciousness, everlasting youth, super-man, or super-woman, power of knowing visible and invisible, see all, hear all, know all called, "LIFE IMMORTAL."

This is given in the Booklet of Engines and Engineers, for super health, super mind, and super consciousness. It is given in the advance course mouth to ear, written copy and gold bound book, "Secrets of the HIMALAYA MOUNTAIN MASTER AND LADDER TO COSMIC CONSCIOUSNESS." "BLOOD IRRIGATION" and "ATTENTION CONCENTRATION," button sold here or sent by mail fro mheadquarters. Yogi Wassan, P. O. Box 373, Chicago, Ill.

There are two causes for heart trouble, too much blood and being too fat. The second is not enough blood, making heart trouble and underweight.

If you have heart trouble analyse yourself and see if you are underweight and lack blood:—

FOR UNDERWEIGHT PERSONS

1 gallon milk. Let it stand for two or three days until it gets sour. Now take ½ gallon of that sour milk and put in ½ gallon sweet milk and let it stand 1 day. Take the two quarts that you have taken from the gallon and put one cup of honey into it and mix well with a milk shaker. Drink this before every meal every day for about six months.

FOR OVERWEIGHT HEART TROUBLE

Use all the other engineers, drink ginger tea according engineer No. 7.

O ANG SHANTEE
O ANG SHANTEE
MY 10 STATES OF CONSCIOUSNESS
SLEEP NO MORE
SLEEP NO MORE
Copyrighted 1916 by Yogi Wassan

Kidney, Spleen, Bladder, Bowels and Blood Circulation

O ANG SHANTEE
O ANG SHANTEE

My 10 States of Consciousness
Sleep No More
Sleep No More

When the kidneys catch cold, the spleen does not work properly, the bladder freezes and locks up the urinating action. Making you urinate very often and only a few drops each time. I know why I am talking about this matter, and so do you—because it is highly important. Most ruptured testicles, and lame-sicknesses are caused by it. All sicknesses of this origin belong to a changeable climate, such as exists in America.

This is the Engineer for that:—

    1 teaspoonful dri-powdered ginger
    1 quart water
    ½ cup honey
    ½ cup milk

Pour all this into a teakettle and boil for a few minutes like coffee. Don't drink it hot, let it cool till it is lukewarm, then drink. Drink it like water, do not sip.

This engineer keeps spleen, kidneys, bladder and bowels warm. It guards you from being paralyzed and keeps the blood in good circulation. Wonderful remedy for aenemic blood, sugar diabetis, dropsy, Adenoids, Thyroid gland, lungs, bronchial tubes, sore-throat, bad cold, and sleep sickness. Drink this once a day, about ½ of the solution.

I am sure you will appreciate what I have given to you. Drink every day or every other day, when any of the above ills affect you. Drink every day until you get better. Always don't forget to take this if you care for super-health.

                      O ANG SHANTEE

O ANG SHANTEE
MY 10 STATES OF CONSCIOUSNESS
SLEEP NO MORE
SLEEP NO MORE
Copyrighted 1916 by Yogi Wassan.

All Over the Body

O ANG SHANTEE
O ANG SHANTEE
MY 10 STATES OF CONSCIOUSNESS
SLEEP NO MORE
SLEEP NO MORE

ENGINEER No. 1

This engineer consists of the button exercise.

ENGINEER No. 2

Take a sponge bath, two times a day, morning and night. Take a tub bath once a week, because too many tub baths weaken the body. Swim outdoors as much as you can, because it is more magnetic. Don't go swimming too much at the sea shore, for the salt water contains fever. The ocean becomes purer about two or three hundred miles from land.

Use this following massage. Massage every night before retiring with following solution:

1 Pint of Alcohol.

Rub on throat, chest, stomach, both arms, back of neck, shoulder blades, down to the kidneys, to the base of the spine, to the hips, legs, feet—top and bottom—medulla oblongata down to the ears, back of head to the upper forehead.

Do not rub on lower forehead, face, eyes, sexual organs, or open sores.

This massage is especially beneficial if troubled with Influenza, Bad Cold, Pneumonia, Rheumatism,

Asthma, Bronchitis, Catarrh, Poor Eyesight, Black and Blue Marks, Baldness.

Do not use on children, for their skin is much too tender.

This massage limbers the body and the brain cells.

In taking your weekly tub bath use the following salts, alternating each week:

   1 lb. table salt
   1 lb. Epsom salts
   1 lb. saltpeter
   1 lb. powdered alum

  O ANG SHANTEE
  O ANG SHANTEE
MY 10 STATES OF CONSCIOUSNESS
  SLEEP NO MORE
  SLEEP NO MORE

Copyrighted 1916 by Yogi Wassan.

Eight Glands and Plexuses

  O ANG SHANTEE
  O ANG SHANTEE
MY 10 STATES OF CONSCIOUSNESS
  SLEEP NO MORE
  SLEEP NO MORE

1. Pituitary Gland and Plexus
2. Pineal Gland and Plexus
3. and 4. Thyroid Gland and Pharyngeai Plexus
5. Cardiac Plexus and Gland
6. Solar Plexus and Gland
7. Hypo Gastric Plexus and Gland.
8. Pelvic Plexus and Gland

These are known as: 7 holy temples, 7 holy cities, 7 lighted candles. Moses calls these the 7 seals and hidden locks and keys. Hindus call them the chakras.

O ANG SHANTEE
O ANG SHANTEE
MY 10 STATES OF CONSCIOUSNESS
SLEEP NO MORE
SLEEP NO MORE

This will be given in the Classes by Human Engineer Master Wassan. Truth belongs to everyone, dedicated to everyone by God. Yogi Wassan's Cosmic Concentration and Blood Irrigation Button of Opana.

YOGI WASSAN and RAJA YOGA

Concentration of serpent wisdom. Rejuvenation food remedy will cancel healing sensation, and exercise auto suggestion, raw food, climate change and mineral water for super-health.

Why cancel the will power? Because by using the will power, not help.

For purifying blood, because will power is not a laxative for purifying blood and equalizing the bowel action.

Why cancel the mental treatment? Because mental treatment is not salve or rubbing alcohol.

Why cancel the faith healing Because it is too slow, the sickness grows like water sinks in the sand.

Why cancel the physical culture exercise? Because sickness makes more pain by doing so. Body is too weak for exercise, that will do it more injury.

Why cancel horseback riding? Through cause it will make bladder trouble if you never had it before. Make heart trouble, if you never had it before. Takes extra time to do it and very expensive. Does not belong to a sick person or old age. Only young person can do it.

Why cancel golf, tennis, football and all other athletic exercise for health? Because it takes a healthy and strong body to do it. Another reason, because it belongs to rich people, takes extra time and money to afford to do it.

Why cancel raw food? Eating raw food produces twice more gas in your stomach. Because your stomach is not strong enough to digest raw food. It will create more gas.

Why cancel fasting? Because you need more nourishment and vitality from food to build the body. So fasting is not a remedy for a sick person. Only an overweight person can use it. By fasting you become underweight, very thin and nervous, and never regain your health again, because oxygen burns the stomach lining out.

Why cancel auto-suggestion with spoken word? Spoken word means some kind of power in the word, so there cannot be power in the word if there is no power in the body. Because if you are very sick and you cannot repeat a word and have sore throat and hoarseness, how can you repeat the word. Auto-suggestion treatment is worse than none.

Why cancel the climate change? First cause, expensive; second cause, sick person cannot make money to go; third cause, may be no body vitality to go; fourth cause, may be you are too young or too old or business reasons; fifth cause, you depend on climate and drop everything else. When you build up in good climate, you have to come back in same climate and have same trouble as before.

Why cancel going to mineral springs? Because you never had mineral water before. By greed or craving, you drink too much. Before going you needed it and now you have too much. You are drinking too much because you have the opportunity. Also you have to come back and by not drinking you run out of reserve what you had in your body.

Why not cancel prayer, chanting, breathing and magnetism, meditation and concentration and diet? Diet spices salt for super-health. Will be given in the classes called super-health class.

Copyright, 1928, applied for by Yogi Wassan.

Raja Yoga is the highest teaching of all source of Yoga.

First, from all religious teaching; second, from all Christian Meta-physical teaching and all Astrology and Numerology, Phrenology and Psycho-Analysis and Mystic Psychology; third, from Hindo Theosphist teaching; fourth, Karma Yoga; fifth, Bhagdee-Yoga; sixth, Kukarma Yoga; seventh, Giyana Yoga; eighth, Dharana Yoga; ninth, Mantra Yoga science study; tenth, Purana Yama 84 posture study; eleventh, Soroda Yoga-Panta-jalee system; twelfth, Raja Yoga-Panta-jalee system; thirteenth, Maha Atma Braahm-Vidya study; fourteenth, Brahm Gyan study; fifteenth, Vigiyan study; sixteenth, Jeven Muktum study; seventeenth, Jeven Shuma-dee study.

These all bring life immortal—means freedom from—

This teaching is spiritual education and is non-sectarian.

Hindu Raja and Hindu mystic lectures by Human Engineer Maha Master Wassan of India, author of "Secrets of the Himalaya Mountain Masters" and "Ladder to Cosmic Consciousness" and discoverer of secret keys for opening the Fountain of Cosmic Vibration and Cosmic Ray; inventor of Cosmic Concentration, Blood Irrigation Button.

This master teacher of Raja Yoga teaching, well known in America for many years. Master Wassan is over a half century old. He will prove the power of Cosmic Ray by withstanding the pressure of 50 men against his solar plexus.

Come to see him. He will tell you if you are living or dying every day. Bring or send after your questions and he will read and answer right away.

Subject

Seeing, hearing, knowing, create success, everlasting youth, super health, super mind, and super-consciousness. Become a master healer, teacher, writer, scientist, or musician. Human psycho, color and vocational analysis. Also easy way to reduce or gain weight.

How to Use Yogi Wassan's "Cosmic Concentration and Blood Irrigation Button,"
which is the
"Chief Engineer" of the 17 Engines in the "Human Factory"

O, ANG SHANTEE

O, ANG SHANTEE

MY TEN STATES OF CONSCIOUSNESS

SLEEP NO MORE

SLEEP NO MORE

Yogi Wassan's Button is made to allow a certain amount of breath to pass through it, at a certain speed. A hole and tube of a different size and length will not work, for that is the secret of the button. By using something different, you cannot balance the amount of Carbonic Acid Gas, Oxygen or the sixteen (16) body salts.

Use the button for vitalizing the lungs, making the heart stronger, dissolving the impure blood clots in the body. It gives power over fatigued feeling by making the heart stronger, irrigating the blood through all the cells, tissues and 8 glands in the body. Wonderful for recharging the optic nerve and renewing the eyesight. Highly beneficial to the singer, for it stimulates the Thyroid Gland, and gives more power to the voice. In fact, magnetizes the entire body, giving it physical, mental and spiritual magnetic power. This means concentration on the "Breath of Life." Very wonderful for consumptives, feverish or feeble persons. I read in Sanscript, "that any incurable sickness can be cured, by applying and saturating with your own blood, from your own body, to your own body." Raja Yoga Science of Study uses this method of applying your own blood, from your own body, to your own body, by using Yogi Wassan's Cosmic Concentration and Blood Irrigation Button.

Any spot that is sick and sore, means that cells and tissues are dead or dying, turning to germs and pus. Yogi's button will bring the blood from other parts of the body, through cells, tissues, and blood vessels. This will flood these germs and kill them with the blood irrigation exercise. The exercise should be done twice a day, for it is wonderful for consumption, cancer and running sores.

You can think about this method and see if it is not correct. You know that when you hurt a spot on your body, by Nature and instinct you automatically moan and hold the injured part to control the pain, which helps to do it.

"How to Exercise With Cosmic Concentration and Blood Irrigation Button"

Lie flat on your back and relax the body as much as you can. Now put a pillow under your shoulder blades, leaving the head drop down and rest upon the Medulla Oblongata. Take the button and put the smaller disc into your mouth. Hold the tube gently between the teeth, while the larger disc remains on the outside of your mouth against the lips. Interlock the fingers of both hands, bring them over the head, placing them at the center of the top of your head. Let your elbows rest at the side of your body, throw your chest out as much as you can. Now inhale the breath gently through your nostrils in about three sniffs. Exhale the breath through the hole in the tube, keeping the lips very firm around it. Exhale very slowly and make the breath last as long as you can. Each time you exhale, pull your navel and abdomen inward and throw your chest out, at the same time stretch your legs. Begin this breathing exercise with five breaths. Increase one every day until you get 30 breaths. When you have reached the 30 breaths, stop increasing. Do these 30 breaths 2 times a day:

1st. In the morning before eating.

2nd. At night before you go to bed.

After five or six months of this practice, you can do it three times a day. After one year of this exercise, you can do it as many times as you wish to.

No words can express the many benefits derived by a person using this Button seriously and faithfully.

How to Use Breathing Button for Cosmic Concentration

Sit erect in a chair, have a mirror before you, keep

feet flat on the floor. Place back of hands on your knees, fold forefingers under the thumbs, let the other three fingers remain in a straight, extended position. Also throw the chest out. Begin breathing and make the breath last as long as you can. Look into the mirror and concentrate on the 7 colors. By and by, the "Breath of Life" and seven colors will flow through the hole in the Concentration Button.

Do this exercise one-half hour every other night for one year, then do it for one hour. After one year, "Light of Seven Colors" or "Light of the Cosmic Ray" will flow through the Button. This is the Cosmic Consciousness and Cosmic Ray Development.

When the frogs croak in India, we oftentimes see the light flow from their mouth like a sparkle of a diamond. This is known as "Cosmic Light" or "Christ Consciousness Light."

The physical, Spiritual and magnetic current flows from the within to the without, opening the 8 plexuses, which are known as the 8 doors to the holy temple. Hindus call them the 8 chakras. They are known in the Christian Bible as the "Holy Breath," "Breath of Life" and "Breath of God."

This breathing checks with the following passages of the Christian Bible:

"And the Lord God formed man of the dust of the ground, and breathed into his nostrils the breath of life, and man became a living soul." Gen. 2:27.

"Then said Jesus to them again, Peace be unto you; As my Father has sent me, even so send I you. And when He had said this, He breathed on them, and saith unto them, Receive ye the Holy Breath."—St. John 20:21-22.

This button can be used by a person of any age,

who wishes to rejuvenate the body, and keep a couple hundred years. Very few diets are connected with this. Do not eat or drink ice cream or ice water, or sour things. Do not crowd the stomach with too much of anything; stay a little hungry. Use the Liver and Stomach Engineer Recipes, which I call Nature's sulphur drink; eat anything else you have a craving for.

    O, ANG SHANTEE
    O, ANG SHANTEE
  MY TEN STATES OF CONSCIOUSNESS
     SLEEP NO MORE
     SLEEP NO MORE

Price List of Yogi Wassan's Books and Charts

YOGI WASSAN'S BOOK

	Non-Student	Student
"Secrets of Himalaya Mountain Masters and Ladder to Cosmic Consciousness	$25.00	$5.00
Blood Irrigation and Cosmic Concentration Button	5.00	*3.00

CHARTS

	Non-Student	Student
Chart of Universal Brain and Holy Mountain		
Chart of Door of Brahm; 8 Plexuses, Glands and Chakras		
Chart of Khechnee Mundra		
Chart of Ida, Pingala, Sushmuna or Water Shamadi		
Chart of Beeja Mantram, Devta, Devti and Chakras		

Chart for Opana Yama Breathing_____
Charts of 7 Holy Words and 10 States
   of Consciousness _____
Record of Holy Chant_____
Pictures of Yogi Wassan_____

After purchasing one button, the student price is only $2.00 for all consecutive buttons.

Your order for any of the above accepted now, or you can send for them when you are ready.

Yogi Wassan's Temple of Cosmic
General Delivery
Denver   -:-   Colorado

Summer school is open every year during June, July and August. For further information write to General Delivery, Denver, Colo.

Supplemental to Many Lessons in Soroda System Yoga Philosophy

BY

SUPER-AKASHA YOGI WASSAN

COMBINATION RECIPES—YOGI FOOD

Foods and Their Relation to Health

As mentioned in this Lesson, the Hindoo understanding of Chemicalization of the body by the foods taken in, is entirely different from a great many of the ideas holding forth in the Western world, but cases of serious illness and improper nutrition that have been handled successfully, and often with really very remarkable results, by the adoption and regular use of these Oriental ideas in the Western world, makes us desire to know more specifically what some of these combinations are, and how they may be used advantageously.

The human body is the most wonderful organization of life, the most wonderful mechanism that we can find. Its construction is most complicated, its constitution most subtle, and it has within itself the very essence of health and happiness, if proper materials are supplied.

According to Soroda System Yoga Philosophy, aside from accidents, injuries, and the like, there is no sickness in the human body unless there is "inharmony"—a lack of balance within the elements of the body—and according to this system, the several hundred or thousand named diseases may be boiled down to four (4) general phases, resulting from combinations that have produced too much heat, too much cold, too much fatness, or too much dryness (deficiency of fat)—with a still more general classification into two (2) general phases of body inharmony —too much "Acidity" or too much "Alkalinity."

This brings us up to the modern idea of natural methods of handling disease by many of the systems that are classified as "Nature Cures," the purpose of which is to subject the patient to a regimen of food, diet, exercise, etc., as nearly as possible simulating the original diet and habits of mankind, in sharp contrast to the modern modes of life that may, or may not, be responsible for the development within the individual of the particular phase of disease or abnormality evident. "Acidity and Alkalinity" are the two conditions usually most stressed in connection with these systems.

In this series of lessons on Soroda System Yoga Philosophy, the lessons on Breathing are very important in connection with the Diet and Recipes given, for, by proper vibration of the cells and tissues of the body, as taught in class-work, all functional activities of the body will be stimulated so the digestive system will be able to take care of practically any ordinary foods that may be eaten.

In this connection we might add that it is reasonable to suggest that the body be supplied with sufficient variety of all kinds of foods to supply it with the proper working materials, and that the better way to supply the "variety" is not to group a great many of them into one so-called "well-balanced" meal, but rather to let the variety come day after day, or meal after meal, with a simple menu at each meal, thereby simplifying the work of digestion, and avoiding inharmonious food combinations that can only be expected when a food that requires only a short time for digestion is eaten at the same meal with other foods that require a much longer period for digestion. Many charts and tables on this subject have been worked out by experimenting food-scientists, but for all practical purposes, as a general rule, the simple meal, with variations from time to time, instead of a general conglomeration at each meal, will be the wiser method to follow. Aside from that, each person who has a special problem will need to have that problem handled by an individual analysis as to his or her own particular needs.

It is not necessary at this time to go into any lengthy discussion or argument regarding Vegeterianism—a subject which has been debated the world over for a great many years, with all kinds of tests and experiments as to the comparative merits of a meat diet, or a non-meat diet. From the summary of all these, we may take one general principle that will be helpful: —

The kinds of vegetables chosen by meat eaters and non-meat eaters differ (and should differ) greatly—because a non-meat diet demands that the protein (muscle building) element, and the fat (fuel) element of the meat diet must be furnished by something else. The protein elements can be found in the legumes (peas, beans, lentils) and in nuts and cheese, etc., which two latter foods also furnish a good percentage of the oils or fats required. Otherwise, the fat element can be furnished by butter, vegetable oils, etc. A meat diet usually contains an excessive amount of protein and fat as compared to the actual needs of the body, so in a diet of that type, the vegetables used to supplement usually consist of carbohydrates (starches, etc.) to counterbalance this excess—with perhaps a leafy vegetable as an extra dish. For this reason, a vegetarian would not, and could not, be satisfied with the vegetables found on the table of a person using a meat diet, and vice versa.

With this variation in mind, it should not be a difficult matter to work out a meatless diet sufficiently diversified as to be both tasty and satisfying, if a person so desires, and the fact that this has been accomplished by whole nations should give encouragement to anyone who may, at first, look upon the matter as an almost impossible accomplishment.

To that end, the combination Recipes herein furnished will serve as a foundation sufficiently extensive that one need not worry about "what to cook," for even the most commoplace vegetables may be used in nourishing and tasty dishes at a low cost.

Combination Recipes

1. *How I Develop My Body*—I inhale, breathing through nostrils (with mouth closed), until lungs are

half filled; then swallow, which locks breath, and exhale through nostrils. Then hum, like a bee.

2. *How I Bathe My Eyes*—Every other night, before going to bed, I bathe the eyes (using two eyecups simultaneously) with the following solutions, in turn:

1st. One teaspoonful of table salt in one cup of water.

2nd. One teaspoonful of salt petre in one cup of water.

3rd. One teaspoonful of powdered alum in one cup of water.

4th. One cup of buttermilk.

Then, after washing the eyes, before going to bed I saturate a piece of cotton in the nutmeg and salt solution (made as directed), put on both eyes, under a bandage, and keep on all night.

2 tablespoonfuls of ground nutmeg.

2 tablespoonfuls of table sale.

1 pint of water. Boil together about five minutes. Let cool and strain, and keep in a bottle, ready for use.

The alternate night, when the eyes are not bathed, as above directed, the following should be used:

Candle Exercise

Place a lighted candle (blue) on a table in a darkened room, slightly higher than the level of the eyes when you are sitting before it. Hold eyelids open with forefinger and thumb, and look into the flame of the candle for five minutes, or until tears come. Do not wipe away this water from the eyes, but go to bed immediately. This strengthens the eyes. (In another Lesson, this practice is given, with directions for use, with small blue electric light bulb.)

3. *How to Make Home-made Spice*—Mix together two (2) ounces each of ground ginger and black pepper, and keep airtight in jar. Use this for seasoning food and making spice tea. For spice tea, boil one teaspoonful in a quart of water for five minutes. Sweeten with honey and add cream. Drink all you like.

4. *How I Make Home-made Candy*—Get two pounds of raisins (seeded or seedless) and eight (8) ounces of senna leaves. Mix well and grind through meat grinder. Roll a piece of the mixture the size of a marble, lightly in flour to make a smooth surface Let dry for two or three days, and keep in fruit jar in cool place. Eat one piece of this candy, followed by a glass of hot water, every other night forever.

5. *How I Prepare My Egg-Nog*—I put four (4) yolks of eggs in two (2) glasses of water and add a pinch of home-made spice (No. 3), sweetening with honey and stirring well. This may be taken two or three times daily, if desired. The yolk is pure, natural sulphur, and is a remedy for kidney, liver, bladder and bowels—and especially for the lungs and for purifying the blood.

6. *How I Make Almond Pudding and Almond Milk*—I take one (1) pound of shelled almonds, boil in three (3) quarts of water for five (5) minutes. Let stand in water overnight, then remove the brown hulls, and grind fine in meat grinder. I then take two (2) ounces of

(a) Tapioca, one (1) tablespoonful of graham flour, honey to taste, and one (1) quart of vegetable milk (more if necessary), cooking together until tapioca is clear.

(b) For almond milk, prepare almonds in the same way; then massage the pulp with tips of fingers in a quart of cold water. Strain through cheesecloth and sweeten with honey to taste. If too strong, reduce by massaging the pulp left from the first straining, in a little more water (cold) and add the weaker milk to the first quart.

(c) Vegetable milk can be made by taking one-quarter (¼) pound of celery, cut into inch pieces and grind through meat grinder two or three times. Strain the juice through cheesecloth and flavor with salt. Add this juice to almond milk and drink hot or cold, as preferred.

7. *How I Eat Olive Oil and Eggs for Purifying the Blood*—I take the yolk of six (6) eggs (no whites), one-quarter (¼) cup of olive oil, one-quarter (¼) cup of honey, and one-half (½) pint of almond milk. Beat all together well, cook in double boiler until thick, like gravy. Cook at night and let stand until morning. Then I eat all I like.

8. *How I Drink Almond Milk*—I put one-half (½) teaspoonful of home-made spices into one (1) quart of almond milk and sweeten with honey. Boil one or two mniutes. Let cool slightly and drink lukewarm. (Put honey and spices in before boiling.)

9. *What I Do Not Eat or Drink*—I do not eat fish, pork or beef, sour, sweet, ice cream or anything very cold; no foods that are too hot; no alcoholic drinks or cider. I never overcrowd my stomach or eat what does not agree with me.

10. *How I Eat Fruit*—All juicy fruit is ninety-five (95%) per cent. acid. I recommend that it should not be eaten by those who are under-weight, or have weak lungs, or weak kidneys, or acid blood. If taken, it should be cut up fine and sweetened with honey, which neutralizes the acid, as honey is Nature's sweetening, made from the perfume of flowers.

11. *How I Make Home-made Oil*—I mix together four (4) ounces of olive oil, one (1) ounce oil of cloves, one (1) ounce of oil of nutmeg. Stir together, mixing thoroughly, bottle and keep. Apply to the affected parts by palms of the hands once a week before going to bed. Use until well. Wash off in the morning with warm water. Do not use this if there are open sores.

12. *What I Do for Deafness and Buzzing in Ear*—I lie on my side and put in three (3) drops of home-made oil (No. 11) in out ear. Then I put finger in entrance to the ear and shake for one minute. Then I apply hot wet towel to ear and use hot water bag on ear to give heat. I continue this treatment while I remain lying upon my side for twenty or twenty-five minutes. The same night I treat the other, or opposite ear, whether affected or not. I con-continue this method until well. Use once a month, but not for children.

13. *How I Take a Bath the Year Round*—The first week I mix one pound (1 lb.) of saltpetre in a tub of lukewarm water and bathe in this for fifteen to twenty minutes at night. The second week I use one (1) pound of table salt in the bath in the same manner. The third week I use one (1) pound of epsom salts in the same manner.

Do not use No. 13 if there are open or running sores or any fever.

14. *How I Take a Hot Sitz Bath*—I take a bed sheet, wrap sheet around hips and between thighs, then sit in a tub of hot water, as hot as can be borne, with feet out of water, and water up to the waist in the tub. I sit for fifteen or twenty (15 or 20) minutes, then dry body and rub one tablespoonful home-made oil on abdomen, after which apply hot water

bottle when going to bed. This is a remedy for backache, lumbago, rupture, cramps (in women), falling of the uterus, leucorrhea, kidney trouble and high blood pressure. Continue this until well. Do not use this if you have any fever. Do not use during menstruation, or for children.

15. *How I Take a Cold Sitz Bath*—I fill a washtub with cold water, and one-half (½) pound of saltpetre, and sit with lower part of the body in the water, with feet out of tub. I take the water from the tub in both hands and rub over the stomach and abdomen. I take this bath fifteen to twenty-five (15 to 25) minutes before going to bed and do not take any hot water bottle to bed afterwards, but just keep between heavy covers. This is a remedy for the same trouble as No. 14, and should be taken alternately with it—the hot sitz bath one week and the cold sitz bath the next. Do not use if you have any fever.

16. *How I Take a Buttermilk Massage*—I take one (1) quart of buttermilk (or sour milk) for this massage. Take milk in palm of the hand and rub the entire body from the top of the head to the toes. I rub the scalp well with the tips of the fingers, giving a thorough massage. I do this before going to bed and take a warm shower bath the next morning, rinsing the body thoroughly. This is a remedy for insomnia, eczema, high blood pressure and all skin diseases. It beautifies the skin. Apply as needed, but not if there are open sores.

17. *How I Shampoo My Hair*—I wash my hair thoroughly and then apply shampoo, which I prepare by mixing four (4) tablespoonfuls of salt water with four (4) egg yolks. I massage this into the scalp thoroughly and leave for twenty minutes, after which I wash out with warm water and soap, rinsing

thoroughly. I use this the morning after the buttermilk massage.

18. *How I Take a Warm Bath*—I take a towel, put around neck, and pin like a soldier's cape. Then I take another towel, pin from the top of the forehead to the bridge of the nose, and back over the ears to the back of the head, wrapping around head several times, but leaving the top of the head bare. I then sit straight (like Buddha's statue) in the tub or on a stool or chair, under the shower. If there is no "shower" equipment handy this will serve instead: Dip water and pour on skull from an elevation of about six (6) inches. I take this bath for fifteen to twenty (15 to 20) minutes at night. This is a good method for relieving congestion in head and eyes, and is a remedy for head-catarrh—but should not be used if there are any open sores about the head or if there is any fever.

19. *What I Would Do if I Should Have a Hemorrhage or Diarrhea*—I would take one glass of cold water, and add one-fourth (¼) teaspoonful of natural henna leaves (powdered) and let it stand over night. The next morning (before breakfast) I would drink half of the water from the glass without shaking the settlings in the bottom of the glass. I would repeat this every morning until the trouble was relieved, and I would never use more than one-fourth (¼) of a teaspoonful of the powdered henna leaves to the glass of water, for henna leaves are poisonous. I do *not* use this treatment for hemorrhage from the lungs.

20. *How I Remove Wrinkles and Stay Young*—I take one-half (½) cup of sour milk, one (1) teaspoonful of rice flour, and one (1) pinch of borax; mix well, and then wash face with hot towel to open

pores, and apply this mixture to the face and neck. I leave this on until it becomes dry and hard, forming a white mask; then rub the face and neck with a cold, wet towel, dashing cold water on the face and drying thoroughly. Starch may be used instead of rice flour.

21. (a) *How I Make Chicken Soup*—I take one (1) chicken, weighing about two (2) pounds, clean well, taking out all fatty substance, chop fine, and grind through meat grinder, bone and all. I do not use the fatty substance in the soup. I then add the chicken to six (6) quarts of water, with one tablespoonful of home-made spices, and enough salt to taste. I then boil the mixture down to three (3) quarts; let cool and strain through cloth, leaving dry pulp, which I throw away. This may be sealed, hot, in fruit jars, and kept in a cool place. I heat soup before drinking it. This is a remedy for weak lungs and general debility, for those who cannot grasp the higher. If a person will drink a quart of this every day he need not grow old. Use Recipe "a" for general family purposes.

(b) Prepare chicken, same as indicated above, but add:—One (1) pound of onions, chopped fine, one (1) pound of celery, chopped fine, and one (1) pound of garlic, chopped, to the chicken and cook as directed. No. 21-B is for those who have consumption or any kind of tubercular trouble, and general weakness of a pronounced type.

22. *How I Reduce Weight*—I sleep on the mattress on the floor, commencing with one time the first week; three times the second week; four times the third week; five times the fourth week, and six times the fifth week. Then, having reduced as much as desired, I resume the normal bed sleeping.

23. *My Directions for Bathing and Swimming*—

Too much tub baths are not good. One or two a week should be sufficient, with a sponge bath daily. These baths should be lukewarm—never cold, in tub or shower. Cold baths stiffen the body, stop circulation, bruise sympathetic nerves, often resulting in pneumonia, consumption, paralysis, blindness and deafness. Bathing in cold water is permissible, however, in tanks, lakes or rivers, but not in ocean water, which may give disease. Don't bathe more than you can stand, but three times a week will be all right, if not suffering from consumption, heart trouble or running sores.

24. *Some Things You Should and Should Not Eat and Drink*—Drink one or two (1 or 2) quarts (or more) of warm goat's milk daily, or almond milk, or vegetable milk, sweetened with honey. Drink no cow's milk generally (except a little in tea or coffee) for it is feverish. Cheese is good, because it is cooked. The amount of water to drink will vary with the quantity of fluids taken otherwise. If sufficient fluid is taken into the body in this manner—drink water only when thirsty. Eat no raw vegetables, except — celery, lettuce, parsley, melons, watercress, spinach, onions, garlic, tomatoes or cucumbers (cutting one-half-inch off each end of the cucumber and rubbing ends together until milk comes out). Other vegetables should be cooked, fried in oil, steamed, boiled or roasted, or made in pie. All seed foods, root foods and cereals are good. Eat plenty of cracked wheat, cooked like mush or gruel, or baked into biscuits. Dried and baked fruit is good with honey, and a cupful of ripe olives daily is very necessary. Eat no unblanched almonds, no baked peanuts, but plenty of raw peanut butter is all right. Do not eat too much candy (except home-

made candy as directed in No. 4), no sour pickles, and instead of sugar use honey, a half-pound daily not being too much.

25. *How I Make Date Butter*—(a) I take one and one-half (1½) pounds of dates, stone them, and fry them in one-quarter (¼) pound of butter. Then put in one (1) pint of sweet milk and cook until creamy.

(b) *Date and Nut Butter*—One (1) pound of dates (stoned), one (1) pound of nuts, shelled and blanched. Grind together and use as a spread on whole wheat bread, or for sandwiches, if desired. This is very delicious and very nourishing.

26. *Hindoo Yogi Food for Keeping Young*—One (1) pint sweet milk, one-half (½) teacup shredded cocoanut, two tablespoonfuls of honey, one-half (½) cup of water, one (1) teaspoonful of Spanish saffron, and about five (5) dates. Bring to a boil and boil one minute. Drink lukewarm before going to bed, eating the cocoanut and dates. Take this three times a week for general rejuvenation.

27. (a) *How to Use Egg Yolks for Increasing Weight and Rejuvenation*—Put the yolk of one (1) egg in a glass of water, adding a little honey and mixed spices to taste, and drink every morning during the first week, before eating anything else. After taking this, drink the nectar or saliva. The second week, use two (2) yolks; the third week, use three (3) yolks; fourth week, four (4) yolks—increasing the amount of water a little, so the mixture will not be too rich. You may not like this at first, but later on you will. Also, you will enjoy the feeling of purification, for the yolk of egg is the purest sulphur, which cannot be bought in a drug store. This is a splendid remedy for liver troubles. The white of the

egg is heavy and clogs the liver, and, therefore, should not be used—so you can give the whites of the eggs to your neighbor to use for making Angel Food. After taking four (4) yolks daily, during the second month, the next month six (6) may be taken daily, the next month, seven (7) daily, and then eight (8) daily. I use a glass three and a half (3½) inches tall.

b. *How to Use Egg Yolks—Easy Way*—Take a bowl of any kind of soup, as prepared for a meal, and stir the egg-yolk into this when ready to eat. This is very palatable.

28. *Oranges and Lemons*—People in this country eat too many oranges and lemons, thinking they are good for the system, but my philosophy teaches that an acid as strong as lemon-juice kills the teeth and is bad for the stomach. People are constituted differently and therefore react differently to the eating of different kinds of fruit. If the fruit eaten turns to sugar, the person grows too fleshy; it is turns to acid, the person becomes too thin. If you desire to eat fruit, pour honey on it to neutralize the acid.

29. Do not eat *Chicken Soup* if you do not approve of meat. However, this is a remedy for consumption. There is no need to go to a different climate if you do not care to, and cannot well afford to do so. You can stay at home—rest, and live on this preparation. Many people here have consumption—no doubt due to the use of excessively cold drinks and foods. It is injurious to the lungs to take excessively cold foods, or to fan to cool off too quickly when overheated. Such methods produce a shock to the whole system. People perspire, and then go to the "fountain" for ice cream and iced drinks, which kill the roots of the teeth, deaden the brain and tonsils,

retard blood circulation, shock the kidneys so the urine becomes dark. Any teacher of Ancient Philosophy will tell you this. I do not believe in eating meat at all, but if you are ill and think you need meat, this is the preparation. You can get your weight back, and cure yourself.

30. *How to Use Watermelon*—(a) Take the meat out of watermelon, cutting not too close to the white part of the rind, and grind through meat grinder seed and all. Strain juice through cloth, and use the juice, mixing with a little honey, if desired. This is a wonderful vegetable and does not need to be cooked. It is fine for the liver, kidneys, bowels, and for the brain. My grandfather was a physician and used this for curing insanity.

(b) *Watermelon Syrup*—The juice of watermelon, as indicated in "a" may be cooked down with honey until a syrup is formed, which will keep like jelly. Ancient doctors used this for Brain Food, for increasing the power for remembering, this is fine for high blood-pressure, or low blood-pressure, as it equalizes the circulation.

This syrup can be mixed with cold water (not iced) for a *cooling drink* in summertime, or any time of the year.

31. *Cantaloupe Butter*—Slice ripe cantaloupes, peeling out the meat. Chop fine, or grind. Mix with butter and honey, and eat on bread. This can also be cooked with honey, like preserves.

32. *Pepper Cake—or Yogi Omelette*—Yolks of twelve (12) eggs, one (1) large green pepper (cleaned with stiff brush and trimmed outside, but leave seeds in), ground or chopped fine; one-quarter ($1/4$) teaspoonful of salt; one (1) teaspoonful black pepper. Mix in bowl, with mixer, like mayonnaise.

Then fry like hot cakes, on griddle greased with a little butter or olive or cooking oil. This quantity will make about ten cakes, like cookies. This is rejuvenation food. Eat it for retaining youth. May be eaten with butter and ketchup, if desired. It is better than beefsteak. Cream cheese may also be added to this recipe, if desired, one-quarter (¼) pound to above ingredients.

33. *Hamburger Steak* — One (1) pound of ground vegetables (one, two, or three different kinds —any kind, as radishes, tops, and all; onions, tops and all; or potatoes, spinach, with a bowl of cooked beans, peas, etc.), and one-half (½) cup oatmeal, one-half (½) teaspoonful salt (level); one (1) teaspoonful black pepper; two or three (2 or 3) egg yolks. Mix well, adding one or two (1 or 2) tablespoonfuls white flour, mixing well. If mixture adheres, all right; if not, add a little more flour. Then add two (2) tablespoonfuls cream or Carnation milk, mixing well, so as to be about consistency of mashed potatoes, and so will hold together when a portion is taken on tip of fingers. Drop on oiled griddle, in pieces the size of hamburger steak. Fry slowly until brown, turn and brown on other side. This cannot be distinguished from real hamburger, and is a good joke to serve this when company comes.

34. *Carrot Pudding*—Clean two or three (2 or 3) bunches of carrots, scrubbing with brush, but do not peel. Boil in water, in covered pan, until tender enough to mash like sweet potatoes. Mash and put in fry pan: one (1) pound mashed carrots, one (1) cup of water in which carrots were boiled; two (2) tablespoonfuls honey, one-half (½) cup cream, two or three (2 or 3) egg yolks, two or three (2 or 3) tablespoonfuls butter. Mix thoroughly and cook over

slow fire. This is laxative, and fine for the liver; especially good for gaining weight. Eat all you like.

35. *About Vegetables, Etc.*—Carrots contain iron and sulphur, with very little gas, and are good for people who are underweight. They may be eaten raw, but are better cooked.

Cucumbers and radishes have lots of gas.

Onions, garlic, celery, parsley, watercress, green peppers, horseradish, and tomatoes are without gas, and may be eaten raw. Tomatoes are neither a fruit or vegetable, and if taken raw, should be used with honey.

Raw cabbage has a great deal of gas. If boiled in water, the life is killed. Cut large pieces, and fry in butter or oil in a covered fry-pan, so steam will fall back and cook the vegetables.

Cook everything with lid on kettle, so the power from the steam will drop back into the food. All kinds of beans should be presoaked, and cooked slowly, with lid on kettle.

In India, milk is cooked over slow fire for twenty-four hours, and will make twice as much butter, per gallon, as if not cooked.

36. *Bread and Cereals*—It is not necessary to eat bread unless you so desire, but any kind of bread is good, although whole wheat or cracked wheat bread is better. Cook cracked wheat and eat like mush. This neither adds nor takes from weight, but is wonderful for power. Use honey and cream with cereals—no sugar.

37. *How to Use Fruit—Any Fruit*—Fry, or bake, or dry. Don't eat rhubarb any time, as it is acid. Strawberries may be taken with plenty of honey to neutralize the acid.

Honey neutralizes both acidity and alkalinity.

Maple sugar has too much whiskey in its chemical element, and will give heart-burn if too much is taken, for it is too rich.

38 (a) *Cactus Syrup*—In the South and West, the cactus plant is used for food, and is wonderful for many forms of sickness, including disorders of the kidneys and consumption. To make cactus syrup, take one (1) pound of barrel cactus meat, grind through meat grinder, and cook slowly for about one (1) hour in one (1) quart of water. Strain off juice, and add one cup of honey, cooking over slow fire until a syrup is formed. Mix a little of this syrup with water, and use instead of tea or coffee.

(b) *Cactus Candy*—One pound of barrel cactus meat, cut in pieces like dice. Cook in a syrup previously made of one (1) pound of honey, and one-quarter (¼) pound brown sugar. Cook until thoroughly done, and candied. Have the syrup very hot before adding the diced cactus. The brown or natural sugar makes a glazed surface, and will keep the candy moist inside.

39. *Tomato Drink*—Grind or chop fresh tomatoes. To one gallon of pulp thus prepared, add one quart water, cooking slowly for about one hour and strain. Then add two (2) quarts honey and cook slowly until a syrup is formed. A small quantity of this may be mixed with water, and used instead of tea or coffee. This is fine for liver.

40. *Green Pepper Syrup*—Grind or chop fine, (1) pound green pod peppers, leaving in the seeds, and cook slowly in one (1) quart of water. Strain off the juice, add one (1) pound of honey, and cook slowly until a syrup is formed. Mix a small quantity of this syrup with water, and drink as a tea.

This is fine for the liver, and for stimulating the sympathetic nervous system.

41. *Syrup Flavoring*—One (1) ounce each, ground black pepper, ginger, saffron, and shredded cocoanut, cooked together slowly, in one (1) pound of honey, until a syrup is formed, will give a nice flavoring for drinks, or may be eaten on bread, like preserves. This is good for the liver, and for stimulating sympathetic nervous system.

42. *Date Fruit Flavoring*—Cook together one (1) pound of dates seeded and ground, with one (1) pound of honey, until quite thick. Eat like preserves with bread, or use as a flavoring for drinks, by adding a small quantity to glass of water. Fine for sympathetic nerves.

43. (a) *Almond Flavoring* — Cook together, slowly, one pound almonds, previously blanched and ground fine, and one pound of honey, cooking down until quantity is about three-quarters ($3/4$) pound. Keep in jar, and use like preserves with bread, or add two tablespoonfuls to a glass of water for a refreshing drink. This is a food for rejuvenation of brain, body, and glands.

(b) Blanched almonds may be ground, and used for making pies—like apples in a double-crust pie, or mixed with the cream filling of a pie, as shredded cocoanut is used for cream pie.

44. *Yogi Food No. 1*—Yogi Wassan's Chicken— One (1) pound of Garbanza bean flour, seven (7) cups boiling water, four (4) cumeno seeds, crushed; one (1) teaspoon (heaping) of Yogi spice (recipe No. 3), and one (1) teaspoonful (level) curry powder; salt to taste. Add spices, salt, and crushed seeds to water; then add water to flour. Set this mush in double boiler and keep hot. Then prepare

the following: Fry four (4) cups chopped onions in about one-half (½) cup olive or cooking oil in a covered fry-pan. When onions are about half tender, add three or four (3 or 4) bunches of spinach or beet greens, thoroughly washed and dried, by dripping on a cloth, so there will be little or no water; then add two (2) bunches watercress, one-half (½) bunch parsley. Stir all these in with onions, and cook until tender. Then add the vegetables to the mush, and cook in double-boiler for half (½) or three-quarters (¾) of an hour. Let cool in a mold. Cut in slices, and fry brown in olive oil, like fried chicken.

45. *Yogi Food No. 2*—One (1) cupful Luk Tau (or Chinese beans) in six (6) cups of water. Bring to boil, and skim, then add one (1) level teaspoonful Yogi spices (No. 3) and two (2) buttons of garlic; one (1) cup of minced onions, and one-quarter (¼) cup olive oil. Cook until beans are tender and nearly all water is cooked out. Add a little olive oil. To prevent burning, *do not stir* the Luk Tau while it is cooking.

46. *Yogi Food Number 3*—Put an iron or aluminum kettle on fire, add two (2) pounds sweet butter, olive or vegetable oil or one (1) quart of Mazola; then: one (1) cup Fœnu Greek meal, two (2) cups flaxseed meal; one (1) cup shredded cocoanut, two (2) cups Garbanzo bean flour, one (1) cup Cream of Wheat, one (1) cup rice flour, or whole wheat flour. Cook until brown. Then add to the mixture the following: one-half (½) lb. blanched almonds, two (2) lbs. peanut butter, one-half (½) lb. English walnuts, broken in pieces; one-half (½) lb. pistachio nuts, one (1) pound seedless raisins, one (1) tablespoonful black pepper, one (1) tablespoonful ground

ginger. Keep stirring this mixture slowly, over a very slow fire, until the sugar or honey mixture is ready. To prepare honey or sugar mixture, take two (2) lbs. honey or brown sugar, or half-and-half, and eight (8) cups water. Cook until syrup will thread. Start this to cooking at same time the meal and nut mixture is being prepared, cooking over a slow fire. When the syrup threads, turn out fire under both mixtures, and add syrup to first mixture, stirring well, until everything is thoroughly mixed. Then turn into flat pans, press down like candy. Let cool and cut in squares, like cake, and put in airtight container. This will keep for six months. Eat one cup every morning, before any other food is taken. Eat with water, natural temperature (not iced) tea, goat or vegetable milk. The same quantity may be eaten once more during the day, if desired. Do not eat meat at the same time this food is being taken. This food will purify the blood and rejuvenate the body. It is also good for the liver.

47. *Hindu Curry Dishes*—Wash and cut in pieces, not too small, one (1) pound of cabbage, and turn over in a little hot olive or vegetable oil, in a covered fry-pan, adding a little minced onion and curry powder, with salt and pepper to taste; a little water may be added and the cooking continued, with pan covered tightly. While the cabbage is thus being steam-cooked, a pound of diced tomatoes may be browned in another pan, in cooking oil. When these are brown, add to the steaming cabbage, and also add one can of peas, letting all cook together thoroughly. When done, add one (1) dozen hard-boiled eggs, and serve hot. About one teaspoonful of curry powder is sufficient for two pounds of vegetables,

thus prepared, but this will have to be governed by the "taste" of those eating this dish.

As a variation of the above, all kinds of vegetables may be used in different combinations: Cabbage and lady fingers (or okra), with green onions, tops and all chopped small; or beet tops or spinach, radishes, tops and all, and potatoes—or radishes, tops and all ground, with green onions, tops and all ground, and Garbanza beans, previously soaked and boiled, and run through food grinder. Green pod peppers may also be added to taste, either the sweet or the hot pod pepper, as desired, to give an added flavor to any of these combinations. Also, the hard-boiled eggs may be included or omitted from the recipe, as desired.

By using such vegetable combinations as these, all food elements will be supplied to the body, and one will never need or desire to eat meat or flesh food.

48. *Onions*—(a) Everyone should eat plenty of onions—baked, fried, or stewed in the form of "creamed onions." (b) A soup may be made of one-quarter ($1/4$) lb. chopped onions (with one-quarter ($1/4$) lb. garlic added also, if desired), stewed in a little water until tender, after which add one pint of goats' milk and cook a few minutes, with salt and pepper to taste, and curry powder for seasoning, if desired. Drink the soup and eat the onion, like clam chowder. (c) For all kinds of colds, coughs, asthma, etc., plenty of onions should be eaten, raw or cooked. Raw onions, chopped and sweetened with honey, may be used in such cases. (d) 4 Raw onions, chopped and sweetened with honey, may also be used for strengthening or stimulating the vital forces.

49. *Shrimp and Onions*—One-half ($1/2$) lb. shrimp, fresh or dry, washed clean, to one-half ($1/2$)

lb. green or dry onions, chopped fine, and fried slowly in a little olive or cooking oil, simmering slowly for ten or fifteen (10 or 15) minutes with a little water if necessary. This is a food for stimulating and strengthening vital forces, for those who desire to include meat or fish in their diet.

50. *Other Foods for Strengthening Vital Forces* —(a) If meat is desired, eat plenty of chicken or bird meat. (b) Peanut butter and honey make a good food combination, with whole wheat bread. (c) Horseradish and honey may be used as a combination, with bread or with other foods (d) Banana tea, made from both fruit and peeling chopped fine, and boiled a few minutes, adding a pinch of black pepper. (e) Eggs with beer or malted milk; three eggs, one (1) glass any kind of beer or malted milk, a little lemon flavoring, but no ice. This is one drink, and a double portion may be used if desired, upon retiring.

Use recipes of No. 50 *only* when specified in individual analysis.

51. *For General Body Growth and Rejuvenation of Cells of Body*—Use cottonseed oil (Wesson or some good brand) for frying and cooking, in salad dressing, etc. Also for those who may desire, raw or unboiled fish oil may be used for seasoning green vegetables or other food, in proportion of two or three tablespoonfuls a day for each portion.

Special Recipes

52. *Areca Nut Powder Tea*—One (1) pint milk, one-half (½) teaspoonful (level or scant measure-

ment) Areca nut powder, and one (1) ounce of Sunmaid raisins. Boil five minutes, stirring thoroughly, and let cool. Drink the tea, and eat the raisins and all.

This recipe is to be used *only* when specified in individual analysis, for special condition.

53. *Hindoo Tooth Powder*—For relief and prevention of pyorrhea, toothache, decay, and germ encroachment, removal of tartar, for sore and bleeding gums, for preserving the enamel, and for making the teeth white and beautiful. Also for promoting even growth of teeth in children.

    1 ounce powdered French chalk,
    1 ounce Areca nut, powdered,
    ½ ounce powdered borax—thoroughly mixed.

Use three times daily, on tooth brush, with a little water to moisten, rubbing vigorously, morning, noon, and night. If not possible to use three times daily, use at least twice daily. This powder should preserve the teeth, beautiful and white, for one hundred years. Good teeth are powerful agents for the prevention of all diseases in the human body.

After the teeth are thoroughly cleaned by using this powder on the tooth-brush, a pinch of this powder may be used, with a little water, for a throat gargle, for cleansing around the tonsils. Do not smallow the liquid thus used. After using this gargle, the mouth may be rinsed with clear water.

This Lesson to be used by student of Yogi Wassan for his or her own personal use, *only*.

Curry Vegetable Cook Book
From India

OSAMAN SOUP

½ cooking apple—cut up
½ lb. rice
¼ teaspoon mixed spices
¼ teaspoon salt
1 tablespoon butter

¼ teaspoon cinnamon
½ stalk celery—cut up
¼ teaspoon turmeric
¼ teaspoon black pepper
¼ teaspoon sugar

Wash rice with cold water three times, then spread it on dry cloth. Boil two quarts of water, add rice; when it is almost cooked, strain it, save the rice water. Now put two tablespoons of butter in cooking pan, also two medium size onions sliced and chopped up and fry until light brown, then add chopped up celery and Turmeric, cinnamon, black pepper and ground mixed spices and stir well, then add rice water and let it boil for half an hour. Serve hot.

(Onion KANDA SOUP

1 radish
1 large onion
½ stalk celery
1 tablespoon butter
1 tablespoon pancake flour
¼ teaspoon turmeric

½ green pepper
½ carrot
½ bunch parsley
1 apple
¼ teaspoon salt and pepper
¼ teaspoon ground mixed spices

(All vegetables cut and chop up.) Put three tablespoons of butter or vegetables oil and fry onions almost brown, then add two tablespoons pancake flour and stir, add all vegetables and keep on stirring. Add pinch of salt, pepper, turmeric, cinnamon and mixed spices. Boil ½ hour and serve while hot.

GREEN VEGETABLE SOUP

1 good sized onion
1 cooking apple
½ head of lettuce
1 radish
1 oz. butter or veg. oil
¼ teaspoon turmeric
¼ teaspoon cinnamon

½ bunch parsley
½ stalk celery
½ green pepper
1 tablespoon pancake flour
¼ teaspoon salt and pepper
¼ teaspoon ground allspice
½ tablespoon sugar

Fry cut up onions in two ozs. of butter (be careful not to burn them) then add flour and all chopped up vegetables and stir them well until they get soft, then add pinch of salt and pepper, turmeric, cinnamon and mixed spices and stir well, then add two quarts of water together with chopped apples, green pepper and let boil for about half hour. Serve hot.

ALU SOUP

1 medium potato
½ oz. butter
½ green pepper
¼ teaspoon salt and pepper
¼ teaspoon cinnamon

1 medium onion
½ medium cooking apple
¼ teaspoon turmeric
¼ teaspoon mixed spices

Fry cut onions in one oz. butter until light brown, then add mashed potatoes, chopped apple, green pepper, salt, pepper, cinnamon, turmeric, ground spices and stir well until soft, then add three pints water and let boil ½ hour. Serve hot.

COBI SOUP

½ lb. cabbage
½ oz. butter
¼ teaspoon curry powder
¼ teaspoon turmeric
¼ teaspoon ground allspice
1 onion
½ green pepper
1 pint bottle buttermilk, salt and pepper and cinnamon
1 oz. pancake flour

Fry chopped onions and cabbage together until soft, then add flour, cut up green pepper, salt, pepper, turmeric, curry powder, cinnamon and spices; then add milk and boil one-half hour until desired thickness, and serve hot.

MUSHROOM SOUP

¼ lb. mushrooms
½ cooking apple
½ oz. butter
½ oz. pancake flour
¼ teaspoon salt
¼ teaspoon pepper
¼ teaspoon allspices
½ tablespoon tamirand syrup or juice of lemon, mixed with 1 teaspoon of molasses
1 medium sized onion
½ green pepper
½ hard boiled egg
¼ teaspoon turmeric
¼ teaspoon cinnamon

Cut up mushrooms in small pieces doing same with apple, green pepper and onions(keep onion separate). Fry onions in butter then add flour, allspice, salt, pepper, turmeric, cinnamon, stirring continuously. Add mushrooms, green pepper, apple, crushed egg and lemon juice and molasses or brown sugar. To this add two quarts of hot water, let this boil ½ hour. Stir well and serve while hot.

EGG SOUP

3 cut up boiled eggs
½ green pepper
½ oz. flour
½ oz. butter
¼ teaspoon turmeric
1 onion
1 apple
¼ teaspoon salt
¼ teaspoon pepper
¼ teaspoon allspices
¼ teaspoon cinnamon

Cut up very fine eggs, onions, apples and green pepper, separately. Fry onions, add eggs, flour and stir well; then add salt, pepper, allspice, turmeric, cinnamon and while stirring add green pepper, apples, one quart of hot water and let this boil one-half hour. If very thick soup is desired then add can of tomato or vegetable soup and boil until desired thickness. Serve while hot.

BUTTERMILK SOUP

1 pint buttermilk
½ stalk celery
½ green pepper
½ oz. butter
¼ teaspoon salt
¼ teaspoon pepper
¼ teaspoon allspices
1 onion
½ small head lettuce
1 oz. flour
½ sweet apple
¼ teaspoon turmeric
¼ teaspoon cinnamon

Heat together buttermilk, salt, turmeric and flour. Cut apple, lettuce and celery in small pieces. Fry cut up onions until brown, add celery, lettuce and apple; stirring briskly, then add allspices, pepper, turmeric, cinnamon and while stirring add cut up green pepper and buttermilk and boil one-half hour. Serve hot.

CELERY SOUP

½ stalk cup up celery
1 raw egg
½ green cut up pepper
1 onion
1 cooking apple
½ oz. flour

½ oz. butter
¼ teaspoon salt
¼ teaspoon pepper
¼ teaspoon allspice

½ cup milk
¼ teaspoon turmeric
¼ teaspoon cinnamon

Cut celery, onions, green pepper and cooking apple in very small pieces. Heat cup of milk and raw egg together, adding ½ teaspoon of sugar and keep warm. Fry cut up celery and onions until soft, add flour, apple, green pepper, salt, pepper, turmeric, allspices and cinnamon. Stir well and while doing so add heated milk and eggs; then 1 quart of hot water and let boil ½ hour, serve while hot.

YELLOW PEA SOUP

¼ lb. yellow peas
½ green pepper
½ oz. butter
½ oz. flour
¼ teaspoon salt
¼ teaspoon pepper

1 onion
1 cooking apple
¼ teaspoon turmeric
¼ teaspoon allspices
¼ teaspoon cinnamon

Soak peas over night in one quart of water. When preparing soup boil peas one hour in two quarts of water, strain and save water, crushing peas well. Fry onions, to this add flour, crushed peas, salt, pepper, allspices, turmeric, cinnamon, apples and green pepper, stir well and add the strained water and boil ½ hour. Serve while hot.

CAULIFLOWER SOUP

1 small sized head of cauliflower
½ green pepper
½ oz. butter
¼ teaspoon salt
¼ teaspoon pepper

1 onion
1 apple
¼ teaspoon allspices
¼ teaspoon turmeric

Boil cauliflower until it becomes soft, drain water off, and cut cauliflower in small pieces; then cut up green pepper, apples and onions in very fine pieces. Fry onions in butter, adding cauliflower, salt, pepper, turmeric, allspices, cinnamon and stir well. Then add chopped green pepper, apples and one quart of water. Boil ½ hour and serve hot.

LENTIL SOUP

¼ lb. yellow peas
½ green pepper
1 onion
¼ teaspoon salt
1 apple

1 oz. butter
¼ teaspoon turmeric
¼ teaspoon cinnamon
¼ teaspoon pepper
¼ teaspoon allspices

Soak rice, green or yellow peas over night. Strain water off; boil rice and peas one hour and strain again, saving this water. Crush rice and peas together with porcelain cup. Fry onions in butter, and add prepared lentils, stir well while adding flour. Stir continuously while adding cut up green pepper, apples, allspice, salt, turmeric, pepper, cinnamon and also the lentil water. Boil one-half hour, and serve hot.

RICES

PLAIN RICE

½ lb. rice
¼ teaspoon butter

½ teaspoon salt
½ quart hot water

Boil water and to this add salt. Wash rice three times with warm water, then spread on cloth to dry; when half dry rub it with ½ teaspoon butter, then add the boiling water and let it boil until almost soft, then strain rice through colander (save the rice water, which can be used in making soup). Pour cold water on the rice in the colander until almost cold. Put the rice in a pan and add a small amount of butter on the top. Put this in the oven for ten minutes. Serve hot.

SPICED RICE

½ lb. rice
½ teaspoon allspices
½ green pepper
1 pint hot water
1 onion
small amount cloves and cinnamon bark
¼ teaspoon turmeric
½ teaspoon salt

Wash rice three times in warm water, drain and let dry on cloth. Cut up onion and green pepper very fine; fry onions in butter, add cloves, cinnamon bark, green pepper, rice, turmeric and stir briskly. To this add the hot water and cook half hour or put in the oven and serve while hot.

BIRANJ RICE

½ lb. rice
½ tablespoon butter
1 pint hot water
¼ teaspoon turmeric
½ teaspoon salt
small amount of cloves and cinnamon bark

Wash rice with warm water three times, drain and spread on cloth to dry. Melt butter and add cloves, cinnamon bark, keep on fire until cloves swell, then add rice and stir well. To this add turmeric, and salt, stirring continuously, add water and boil ½ hour (be careful not to scorch at the bottom). It is best to put it in the oven when about cooked and keep there until done. When the water has completely disappeared, it is ready to serve.

BIRYANJ RICE

½ lb. rice
1 tablespoon butter
1 pint hot water
1 teaspoon salt
1 onion
¼ teaspoon turmeric

Wash rice and drain well, then spread on cloth to dry. Melt butter and add cut up onions; fry until brown and add raisins. When raisins begin to swell, add rice and stir well, then add salt, turmeric and water. Boil this one-half hour and put in oven until cooked. Serve while hot.

PULAV RICE

½ lb. rice
2 tablespoons butter
¼ teaspoon turmeric
¼ teaspoon salt
¼ cup raisins
1 onion
small amount cinnamon bark and cloves
few cardemon seeds with skins
¼ teaspoon pepper

Wash rice, drain and half dry on cloth. Cut onions in small pieces and fry in butter, when fried add cloves, cinnamon bark, whole cardamon seeds and raisins. When raisins swell, add half dried rice and while stirring add turmeric, salt, pepper and water. Cook until almost done, then put in oven and bake ten minutes. Serve hot.

SWEET RICE

½ lb. rice
1 pint hot water
¼ cup raisins
¼ teaspoon turmeric
¼ cup sugar
small amount cloves and cinnamon bark
¼ teaspoon salt
½ oz. butter

Wash rice, drain and half dry it on cloth; when half dry rub well with 1 teaspoon butter. Put the remaining butter in pan and melt; to this add cloves, cinnamon bark and raisins. When the raisins swell, add rice, turmeric, salt and hot water, stirring continuously. To this add the sugar and cook, when almost done put in oven for ten minutes. Serve hot.

POTATOE RICE

2 boiled potatoes
½ green pepper
small amount cloves and cinnamon bark
¼ teaspoon salt
1 onion
½ lb. rice
¼ teaspoon turmeric
¼ cup raisins
1 tablespoon butter

Boil potatoes for twenty minutes, then cut in halves. Wash rice with warm water, drain well and spread on cloth to dry. When half dry, rub with butter and cook in water with salt for fifteen minutes, drain through colander and pour cold water over rice until grains separate. Fry cut up onions with butter, adding raisins, cloves cinnamon bark, potatoes and rice. Stir this well and sprinkle with milk. Put in oven for ten minutes, after this it is ready to serve.

EGG RICE

2 boiled eggs
½ green pepper
small amount cloves and cinnamon bark
¼ teaspoon salt
1 onion
½ lb. rice
¼ teaspoon turmeric
¼ cup raisins

Wash rice with warm water, drain and spread on cloth to dry. When half dry rub with butter. Boil eggs for fifteen minutes and cut in halves, then cut up onions and green pepper very fine. Boil the rice in 1 quart of hot water, adding ½ teaspoon salt, for fifteen minutes, drain through colander and pour cold water over it for three minutes, or until grains separate. Fry cut up onions and when browned, add cloves, cinnamon bark, raisins, turmeric and salt. Stir well and add egg halves and rice. Stir carefully to mix the ingredients and sprinkle with milk. Put in oven for ten minutes.

CURRIED RICE

½ lb. rice
¼ teaspoon curry powder
¼ cup raisins
½ teaspoon salt
¼ teaspoon pepper
1 onion
¼ teaspoon turmeric
½ green pepper
1 pint hot water
1 tablespoon butter

Chop onions in small squares or cubes, doing same with green pepper. Wash rice with warm water, drain and dry on cloth until half dried. Fry cut up onions with butter, add raisins, rice, turmeric, curry powder, pepper, salt and green pepper. Stir well and add water, letting this cook and when it is almost done put in oven for ten minutes. Serve hot.

NUT RICE

½ lb. rice
¼ cup raisins
½ teaspoon turmeric
½ teaspoon salt
1 onion
¼ cup almonds
small amount cloves and cinnamon bark
½ green pepper

Boil almonds and cut in long thin slices. Chop onions and green pepper. Wash rice with warm water, drain and dry on cloth. Fry onions in 2 tablespoons butter, adding cloves, cinnamon bark and raisins. When raisins swell, add rice and turmeric. Stir well and add green pepper and almonds. To this one quart of hot water is added, which is cooked for fifteen minutes. Put in oven to finish cooking. Serve hot.

BOILED POTATOES

3 potatoes (medium)
¼ teaspoon cinnamon
¼ teaspoon salt
¼ teaspoon paprika
¼ oz. butter
¼ teaspoon pepper

Boil potatoes 30 minutes, and after removing from fire rub butter over them and put in oven for ten minutes. eRmove from oven and sprinkle with cinnamon and paprika. Put salt and pepper according to taste and serve hot.

CAULIFLOWER RICE

1 small sized head of cauliflower	1 onion
½ lb. rice	½ tablespoon butter
½ teaspoon salt	1 pint hote water

Wash rice with warm water, drain and spread on cloth to dry. When half dry, rub with one teaspoon of butter. Boil together one quart of water and salt, and when water is briskly boiling add rice, letting this cook until almost done; then drain through colander (save the rice water, this being used for soup), and pour cold water over rice. Put in pan and place in oven for ten minutes. Serve with butter on top.

POTATO ALU

3 potatoes (large)	½ onion
¼ teaspoon paprika	1 oz. butter
¼ teaspoon salt	¼ teaspoon turmeric
¼ teaspoon black pepper	¼ teaspoon cinnamon

Boil potatoes one hour, let them cool and cut in four parts. Fry cut up onions with butter until browned; then add potatoes (be careful to keep potatoes from being broken), turmeric and salt. Put in oven until brown and after taking it out, sprinkle with black pepper, paprika and cinnamon. Serve hot.

STEWED POTATOES

3 medium sized potatoes	½ large onion
½ oz. butter	½ green pepper
¼ teaspoon turmeric	¼ teaspoon cinnamon
¼ teaspoon salt	¼ teaspoon pepper
¼ teaspoon paprika	½ carrot

Peal and cut potatoes in four parts, then cut onions, green pepper and carrot in very small pieces. Fry onions in butter, adding potatoes, carrot and green pepper, also salt, pepper, turmeric and cinnamon. Stir this for two minutes then add 1 pint of hot water, letting this cook for half an hour or until potatoes and carrots are cooked. After removing from fire add paprika; stir well and serve.

GRAINED POTATOES

3 potatoes	¼ oz. butter
¼ Teaspoon paprika	¼ teaspoon salt
	pepper (according to taste)

Boil potatoes for 40 minutes or until well done. Then take each serving plate and put potatoes separately through a perforated potato masher, on each of the serving plates. After doing this add teaspoon of butter to the top of each, and then sprinkle paprika over it also. Put salt and pepper according to taste. Serve while hot and with vegetables.

MASHED POTATOES

3 potatoes	½ oz. butter
1 tablespoon cream	¼ teaspoon pepper
¼ teaspoon paprika	¼ teaspoon cinnamon
1 egg	½ teaspoon salt
1 onion	

Boil potatoes until well done, then peal and mash. To this add cream, salt, pepper and a beaten egg, then heat the ingredients until it gets light. Cut onions in square pieces and fry in butter; when they become soft and yellow mix with the mashed potatoes and sprinkle the cinnamon and paprika over top. Serve hot.

POTATO BALLS

2 potatoes
½ teaspoon salt
¼ teaspoon pepper
1 raw egg

½ tablespoon butter
1 tablespoon cream
¼ teaspoon cinnamon
¼ teaspoon paprika

Boil potatoes until well done, peel and mash. Beat together the raw egg and cream, adding the potatoes; and keep bating this until very light, then add the salt and pepper. While beating this together, make small round balls and roll in hot butter; after doing this put them in the oven until well browned. Sprinkle with cinnamon and paprika and serve while hot.

POTATO CUTLETS

2 potatoes
½ green pepper
½ oz. buckwheat flour
¼ teaspoon turmeric
¼ teaspoon pepper

1 oz. butter or its substitute
green onions
½ teaspoon salt
¼ teaspoon ground allspices
1 tablespoons milk

Boil potatoes for half hour or until well done, peel them and mash. Cut green onions and pepper in very small pieces, then add buckwheat flour and milk to the potatoes, and mix this well, adding the green pepper, onions, salt, pepper, turmeric and ground spices and after thoroughly mixing this, shape into oblong balls. Fry them brown and serve while hot.

POTATO CUTIE

2 potatoes
2 hard boiled eggs
¼ teaspoon cinnamon
¼ taspoon paprika
1 raw egg

½ oz. butter or - teaspoon
½ teaspoon salt
¼ teaspoon pepper
½ teaspoon shredded cocoanut
½ tablespoon cream

Boil potatoes until well done, peel and mash; then add the raw egg which has been beaten, also the cream, and beat this well. Now mash hard boiled eggs, add melted butter, cocanut and stir briskly. Take each potato and scrape the inside out, making a cup of each, then fill with mashed eggs, cocoanut until quite full. Heat butter and rub or put on the potatoes, then place in oven until light brown. Serve hot.

SLICED POTATOES

2 potatoes
¼ teaspoon salt
¼ teaspoon cinnamon

1 oz. butter or its substitute
¼ teaspoon pepper
¼ teaspoon paprika

After peeling potatoes, cut in halves, then cut the halves in thin slices or about ¼-inch in thickness; then soak in salt water for a short time, drain and dry the slices on a cloth. After doing this fry in butter and when fried, put in oven to brown for ten or fifteen minutes. After removing them from the oven, sprinkle with salt, pepper, cinnamon and paprika. Serve hot.

CHIPPED POTATOES

3 small potatoes
¼ teaspoon salt
¼ teaspoon cinnamon

1 oz. butter or substitute
¼ teaspoon pepper
¼ teaspoon paprika

After preparing potatoes, cut round chips about 1-8-inch thick, soak in one cupful of salt water for ten or fifteen minutes, drain and dry well. Fry in butter, and when fried, place in oven for about ten minutes or until brown. After removing, sprinkle with salt, pepper, cinnamon and paprika. Serve hot.

EGG POTATOES

3 potatoes
½ oz. butter
½ green pepper
1 onion
¼ teaspoon paprika
2 eggs
¼ teaspoon turmeric
¼ teaspoon pepper
¼ teaspoon salt

Prepare potatoes and cut in eight pieces, then boil for one-half hour. Boil eggs for fifteen minutes. Cut onions and green pepper in small pieces, also doing same with the eggs. Next fry onions in butter, adding turmeric, salt, pepper and potatoes; stir well and add eggs. Sprinkle green pepper over the top and put in oven for ten minutes. Serve hot.

BAKED POTATOES

3 potatoes
¼ teaspoon salt
¼ teaspoon paprika
½ oz. butter
¼ teaspoon pepper

Clean potatoes well and bake in oven for 30 to 40 minutes. When well done, put on serving plate, then cut in half, adding the butter, salt, pepper and paprika. Add the last according to taste.

BOILED SWEET POTATOES

3 sweet potatoes
¼ teaspoon pepper
¼ teaspoon paprika

Boil sweet potatoes for one-half hour, and when well done, peel and cut lengthwise. Then add the salt, cinnamon and paprika(add the last according to taste). Serve while hot and with other vegetables. (Butter can be added to the potatoes if so desired.)

BAKED SWEET POTATOES

3 sweet potatoes (medium)
¼ teaspoon salt
¼ teaspoon cinnamon
¼ teaspoon paprika
½ oz. butter
¼ teaspoon pepper

Clean the potatoes well and bake in oven for twenty minutes. When thoroughly baked, place on serving plate do not peel them), and cut in half. To this add butter, salt, pepper, paprika and cinnamon. Do this according to taste. Serve hot.

FRIED SWEET POTATOES

2 good sized sweet potatoes
¼ teaspoon salt
¼ teaspoon paprika
½ oz. butter
¼ teaspoon cinnamon

Boil and peel sweet potatoes; then cut lengthwise in four pieces. Next rub butter over potato well and put in oven until quite brown. After removing from oven, sprinkle with salt, cinnamon and paprika. Serve while hot and with other vegetables.

MASHED SWEET POTATOES

3 sweet potatoes
½ tablespoon butter
¼ teaspoon paprika
¼ cup cream or good milk
¼ teaspoon salt

After boiling and peeling potatoes, mash well, then add cream and salt. Beat this until very light, preferably with an egg beater. After mixing this thoroughly, put on plate and smooth out; then spread butter over the potatoes and put in oven for about five minutes or until the butter is absorbed. After removing from oven, put in serving dish and sprinkle with paprika.

POTATO CURRY

- 2 potatoes
- ½ apple
- ½ teaspoon sugar
- ¼ teaspoon turmeric
- ¼ teaspoon allspices
- ½ green pepper
- 1 onion
- ½ oz. butter
- ¼ teaspoon salt
- ¼ teaspoon pepper
- ¼ teaspoon curry powder
- 1 pint buttermilk

After preparing and cooking potatoes, mash until very fine. Then cut up onions, apple and green pepper in small pieces. Fry the onions in butter and when about fried add salt, pepper, turmeric, curry powder and allspices. Stir well, adding the mashed potatoes, apples and green peppers. Stir again and add buttermilk. Let this cook for 20 minutes and add sugar. Serve hot.

SPLIT PEAS CURRY

- ½ lb. split peas (green or yellow)
- ¼ oz. cloves
- ½ oz. butter
- ¼ teaspoon pepper
- ¼ teaspoon curry powder
- ¼ teaspoon allspices
- ¼ oz. cinnamon bark
- ½ teaspoon sugar
- ½ teaspoon salt
- ¼ teaspoon turmeric
- 1 apple

Soak peas over night and then crush. Cut onions in small pieces, then fry in butter, add cloves and cinnamon bark; then add crush split peas, salt, pepper, curry powder, turmeric and allspices. Cut up in small pieces, one cooking apple and add in the above mentioned. Then add one quart of hot water; stir well and let cook for one-half hour. Serve hot.

BUTTERMILK CURRY

- 1 pint buttermilk
- ½ sliced green banana (not ripe)
- 1 oz. pancake flour
- ¼ teaspoon turmeric
- ¼ teaspoon salt
- ½ oz. butter or substitute
- 1 onion
- ½ green pepper
- ¼ teaspoon curry powder
- ¼ teaspoon allspices
- ½ teaspoon sugar
- ½ apple (cut up)

Cut onions into small pieces, and then fry in butter. Then add pancake flour and stir well. When onions are fried, add cut up green pepper and apple, salt, sugar, turmeric, allspices and curry powder. Adding also 1 quart of buttermilk and stir well. Let this cook for about a half hour until gravy thickens. Serve hot.

EGG CURRY

- 3 eggs (hard boiled)
- ½ oz. pancake flour
- 1 cooking apple
- ¼ teaspoon allspices
- ¼ teaspoon paprika
- 1 onion
- ½ oz. butter
- ½ teaspoon salt
- ¼ teaspoon pepper
- ¼ teaspoon curry powder
- ¼ teaspoon turmeric

Boil eggs fifteen minutes, and after preparing them cut in small pieces. Cut onions and apples in small pieces. Then fry onions in butter and when about fried add pancake flour, salt, pepper, turmeric, allspices, curry powder and paprika. Stir good, adding apples and one quart of hot water. Cook this from twenty to thirty minutes or until it becomes thick. Serve hot.

CAULIFLOWER CURRY

½ head cauliflower
½ oz. butter
¼ teaspoon salt
¼ teaspoon pepper
¼ teaspoon curry powder

1 onion
½ apple (cooking)
¼ teaspoon, turmeric
¼ teaspoon, paprika
¼ teaspoon allspices

Boil cauliflower until well done, pour cold water over it to cool, and cut in small pieces. Then cut onions and apple into small pieces. Fry onions in butter and when about fried, add turmeric, pepper, salt, sugar, allspices, curry powder and while stirring briskly add the cauliflower and apple, also 1½ pints of hot water. Let this cook about twenty minutes, and after removing from stove, dash paprika over the top. Serve hot.

EGG PLANT CURRY

½ good sized egg plant
½ apple (cooking)
¼ teaspoon turmeric
¼ teaspoon paprika
¼ teaspoon allspices

1 onion
½ oz butter
¼ teaspoon salt
¼ teaspoon pepper
½ teaspoon curry powder

Cut egg plant in small pieces, doing the same with onions and apple. Then fry onions in butter and when about fried, add the egg plant and while stirring add salt, pepper, allspices, turmeric, curry powder and apple. Then add 1½ pints of hot water and let this cook from twenty to thirty minutes or until it becomes thick. After removing from stove, sprinkle with paprika. Serve hot.

NUT SALAD

1 small head lettuce
¼ lb. mixed nuts
¼ cup salad dressing
1 tomato
½ oz. shredded cocoanut

½ apple
½ oz. raisins
3 dates
½ tablespoon melted butter
2 figs

Slice each tomato separately into six slices. Dip lettuce leaf into vinegar. Cut apple into small pieces and cut dates and figs into four pieces. Then put lettuce on each plate and put three slices of tomatoes, adding mayonnaise on this, and in the center add the apple, mixed nuts, raisins, dates and figs, and spread with cocoanut.

CUCUMBER SALAD

½ cucumber
3 leaves lettuce
¼ cup mayonnaise
¼ teaspoon paprika
¼ teaspoon salt

½ tomato
½ green pepper
1 tablespoon cream
½ onion (cut up)

Cut tomatoes into six slices, then cut green pepper and cucumber into small pieces. Rub cucumber, green pepper, cut up onion, and lettuce leaves with vinegar. Add mayonnaise mixed with cream, to the above mentioned ingredients, stir good. Serve in separate plates on lettuce leaf with sliced tomato, and sprinkle with salt and paprika.

POTATO SALAD

1 teaspoon mazola oil	1 tablespoon cream
2 potatoes	½ onion
3 leaves lettuce	½ green pepper
¼ cup mayonnaise	¼ teaspoon pepper
½ oz. vinegar	¼ teaspoon paprika
1 green banana	¼ teaspoon Colman's mustard

Boil potatoes for fifteen to twenty minutes, then pour cold water over them, and peel and cut into eight pieces. Then cut onion, green pepper, green banana into small pieces. Add mustard, cream and oil to mayonnaise, and beat this well. Then add to this onion, green pepper and banana and potatoes, mixing this very good. Serve in separate plates and leaf of lettuce dipped in vinegar and sprinkle with salt and paprika.

EGG SALAD

1 small head lettuce	1 tomato
3 eggs (hard boiled)	¼ teaspoon pepper
¼ teaspoon salt	¼ teaspoon paprika
½ teaspoon butter	¼ cup mayonnaise
juice from ½ lemon	½ teaspoon ground cocoanut

Cut tomato into six slices, and cut eggs into two slices, removing the yolks from the whites. Mash the yolks, adding melted butter, salt, pepper, lemon juice and one heaping teaspoon of mayonnaise. Beat this well and fill the whites with this mixture, press well and round the top. Then serve on lettuce leaf dipped in vinegar, and 1 slice of tomato with mayonnaise. Put the egg on top of it and sprinkle with paprika and cocoanut.

TOMATO SALAD

2 tomatoes	1 bunch radishes
¼ cup mayonnaise	½ green pepper
1 tablespoon vinegar	½ teaspoon salt
3 leaves of lettuce	½ teaspoon paprika
few raisins	

Slice the tomatoes and cut radishes into ten slices, doing same with the green pepper. Rub radishes and green pepper with vinegar. Place sliced tomatoes on lettuce leaf dipped in vinegar, and add teaspoon of mayonnaise on tomatoes. Then add sliced radishes and green pepper on top, and sprinkle salt and paprika over it. Serve in separate plates. Place lettuce leaf on salad plates, then put three slices of tomato on top, forming a ring or triangle, after doing this fill the center with the radishes and green pepper. Put the mayonnaise on the tomatoes only. Sprinkle with a few raisins and paprika.

VEGETABLE SALAD

1 small head lettuce	¼ teaspoon paprika
½ onion	1 bunch radishes
½ stalk celery (chopped up)	1 green peppers
½ oz. vinegar	¼ cup salad dressing
juice of 1 lemon	½ teaspoon salt
¼ teaspoon cayenne pepper	½ tablespoon cream
	½ tablespoon salad oil or mazola oil.

Cut radishes and green pepper into small pieces, doing same with onion; also chop up celery very fine. Rub radishes, green pepper, onion and celery in vinegar, after doing this, add salt, lemon juice, and cayenne pepper. Then add salad, oil and cream in mayonnaise, and beat with egg beater. Mix the ingredients in this dressing and serve in separate plates on lettuce leaf dipped in vinegar. Sprinkle with paprika.

CABBAGE SALAD

1 small head cabbage	1 oz. Mazola oil
2 hard boiled eggs	¼ cup salad oil or mayonnaise
3 leaves of lettuce	½ oz. cream
½ onion	½ oz. vinegar
½ handful raisins	½ teaspoon salt
¼ teaspoon cayenne pepper	¼ teaspoon paprika

Cut cabbage into very thin shreds. Mash eggs. Then add cream, mazola oil into mayonnaise and beat this well. Cut onions into real small pieces, then rub lettuce leaf, onion and cabbage with vinegar, also rub it with this dressing. Then add cayenne pepper, eggs, salt and raisins and serve it on lettuce leaf.

EGGS—FRIED

3 eggs	1 onions (green)
½ tablespoon butter	½ green pepper
¼ teaspoon salt	¼ teaspoon pepper

Fry eggs separately, and on one side only. Cut green pepper and onions in small pieces. Fry the onions in butter and when about fried add the green pepper; then put this on top of the fried egg and sprinkle with salt and pepper. Serve hot.

BOILED EGGS

3 eggs	¼ teaspoon paprika
¼ teaspoon salt	¼ teaspoon pepper

Boil eggs for fifteen minutes and remove shells. Cut in four pieces and sprinkle with salt, pepper and paprika. Serve one egg to each individual. Serve hot and with green vegetables.

EGG OMELET

3 eggs	¼ cup cream
1 onion	½ teaspoon salt
½ oz. butter	¼ teaspoon turmeric
½ green pepper	¼ teaspoon pepper

Cut onions and green pepper in very small pieces. Beat eggs and to this add cream, turmeric and salt. Fry the onions in butter and when about fried add green pepper and remove from stove. Take three tablespoons of beaten eggs and pour into hot butter in pan; and when one side is half cooked; turn and put green pepper and fried onions over it; folding this in half. Put in oven for about five minutes and serve while hot. Before serving, dash with salt and pepper.

EGG KABAB

3 hard boiled eggs	½ oz. butter or substitute
¼ teaspoon cinnamon	¼ teaspoon pepper
¼ teaspoon salt	¼ teaspoon paprika

Boil eggs for fifteen minutes and after removing shells, take a tooth pick and pierce the eggs. After piercing the eggs good, fry in butter until a light brown (the idea of piercing the eggs is to let the butter soak in the eggs). After removing from the butter, dash with salt, pepper, cinnamon and paprika. Serve while hot.

EGG RAW

½ egg	¼ cup cream
two drops vanilla	1 teaspoon sugar

Beat egg well, gradually adding cream. Then add sugar and vanilla. Serve in small cup.

EGGNOGG

1 egg
½ tablespoon sugar
¼ oz. ground almonds
½ cup milk
1 drop vanilla
½ teaspoon nutmeg

Beat egg with egg beater, then add milk and stir well. Add sugar and vanilla, also almonds and dash with nutmeg. Serve cold with ice.

EGG PUDA

3 eggs
½ oz. butter
¼ teaspoon salt
¼ teaspoon allspices
1 onion
½ green pepper
¼ teaspoon pepper
¼ teaspoon turmeric

Cut onions and green pepper into very small pieces. Then beat eggs and add onions and green pepper, also adding salt, pepper, allspices and turmeric. Mix this very good. Put butter on frying skillet and drop four tablespoons of this mixture in butter; when one side is cooked turn on other side and let cook until light brown. Serve hot (doing same with the rest of the mixture).

SCRAMBLED EGGS

3 eggs
½ green pepper
¼ teaspoon salt
¼ teaspoon utrmeric
1 onion
½ oz. butter or substitute
¼ teaspoon pepper
¼ teaspoon allspices

Cut onions and green pepper into very small pieces. Beat eggs well and add to this onions and pepper. Then add salt, pepper, turmeric, allspices and mix this good. Put butter on skillet and pour the mixture in butter while stirring vigorously, and keep on stirring until all ingredients separates into small pieces, and when light brown remove from stove and serve hot.

(CRISPY CAKE) PAPAD

¼ lb. corn meal
3-4 cup of water
¼ teaspoon cayenne pepper
¼ lb. pancake flour
¼ teaspoon salt
1 teaspoon baking soda

Mix corn meal and pancake flour together. Put water into a pan and bring to a boiling point and when it begins to boil add salt, baking soda and cayenne pepper; then add little by little the mixture of flours while stirring and continue stirring until it becomes the form of thick dough. Remove from stove but keep in warm place, and take about 1 oz. of this dough and roll with rolling pin very thin and round on greased board, and let this dry. When all are rolled and dried, fry in grease or oil. Serve hot.

CHARAMIYA (HOT CAKE)

¼ cup pancake flour
¼ cup white flour
¼ cup cornmeal flour
¼ teaspoon turmeric
¼ lb. butter or oil
½ teaspoon salt
¼ teaspoon curry powder
¼ teaspoon pepper

Mix pancake, white and cornmeal flour together. Then add to this mixture melted butter and rub well together, or until it forms a cream, then add salt, pepper, turmeric and curry powder and enough water to make a very thick dough (thick enough to hold shape). Then take small parts, or little by little, and form in thin cakes, by rubbing with the hands, and about the size of a ginger cake. When all are rolled like this, fry in skillet with oil, also frying on both sides. Fry until light brown and serve hot.

VADA KABAB

¼ lb. butter or oil
¼ lb. black eye peas
¼ lb. pancake flour
¼ teaspoon baking soda
1 bunch green onions
½ teaspoon salt
¼ teaspoon pepper
¼ teaspoon allspices

Soak peas over night and boil for one-half hour, drain and crush well. Cut onions into very small pieces, and mix with the crushed peas. Then add pancake flour, salt, pepper, allspices, baking soda and mix well. Then sprinkle a small amount of water or just enough to make a very thick dough and then take small portions and roll into round balls about twice the size of olive, and when all are rolled, fry in oil or butter and serve hot.

BHAJI STRING BEANS

¼ pk. green beans or 1 can
1 green pepper
½ oz. butter
¼ teaspoon pepper
¼ teaspoon allspices
1 onion
½ cooking apple
½ teaspoon salt
¼ teaspoon turmeric
¼ teaspoon curry powder

If green string beans are used, remove strings and cut into three or four pieces (cut onions, green pepper and apple into small pieces), and boil the beans from thirty to forty minutes, drain and keep ready to use. Then fry onions in butter and when about fried, add salt, pepper, turmeric, allspices and curry powder, stirring well. Add beans, green pepper and apple; sprinkle 1 cup of hot water over this and let cook for fifteen minutes and serve hot.

ONIONS

3 medium sized onions
1 green pepper
½ teaspoon salt
¼ teaspoon turmeric
½ stalk celery
½ oz. butter
¼ teaspoon pepper
¼ teaspoon allspices

Cut onions, celery and green pepper into very fine pieces, mix them and fry in butter, doing so on a very low fire for about fifteen minutes, and when about fried add salt, pepper, turmeric and allspices. Serve hot.

CABBAGE

1 small head cabbage
½ green pepper
½ oz. butter
¼ teaspoon pepper
¼ teaspoon curry powder
1 onion
½ stalk celery
½ teaspoon salt
¼ teaspoon turmeric
¼ teaspoon allspices

Cut cabbage into long thin shreds and recut it into small pieces. Cut onions, green pepper and celery into small pieces. Fry onions in butter and add cabbage, green pepper and celery, let this cook for about fifteen to twenty minutes on slow fire (cover while cooking). When about cooked, add salt, pepper, turmeric, allspices and curry powder, stir good. Sprinkle little water over this and put in oven for ten minutes. Serve hot.

SPINACH

¼ pk. spinach
½ oz. butter
¼ teaspoon pepper
¼ teaspoon allspices
½ stalk celery
1 onion
1 green pepper
½ teaspoon salt
¼ teaspoon turmeric
¼ teaspoon curry powder

If fresh green spinach is used (wash and clean well). Cut onions, green peppers and celery into small pieces, mix together and fry in butter, for about fifteen to twenty minutes on low fire and when about fried add salt, pepper, turmeric, allspices and curry powder, stir this well. Put in oven for about ten minutes and remove from oven. Serve hot.

ONIONS AND CELERY (GREEN)

1 bunch green onions
1 green peppers
¼ teaspoon allspices
¼ teaspoon pepper
½ oz. butter

1 stalk celery
½ head lettuce
¼ teaspoon turmeric
½ teaspoon salt
¼ teaspoon cinnamon

Cut onions, celery, green pepper and lettuce into small pieces, mix together and fry in butter for about fifteen minutes and when about cooked add salt, pepper, turmeric, allspices and cinnamon. Stir well and serve hot.

(EGG PLANT) BHABTHA BHAJIE

½ egg plant
½ green pepper
¼ teaspoon pepper
¼ teaspoon turmeric

½ bunch green onions
½ teaspoon salt
¼ teaspoon allspices
¼ teaspoon curry powder

Put egg plant in oven after rubbing with butter or oil, and bake until the outside becomes wrinkled; remove from oven, peal and mash. Cut onion and green pepper very fine, and fry onion in butter, and when about fried add green pepper, salt, pepper, allspices, turmeric and curry powder stirring well. Then add egg plant and let this cook for five minutes. Serve hot.

SHAK. SOY BEANS

½ lb. beans soy
½ green apple
½ teaspoon salt
¼ teaspoon turmeric

1 onion
½ oz. butter
½ teaspoon pepper
¼ teaspoon allspices

Soak soy beans over night and boil for one-half hour, drain and dry. Cut onions and apple into small pieces, then fry onions in butter and when about fried, add salt, pepper, turmeric and allspices and stir briskly. Then add apple and beans while stirring, let this cook for five minutes. Serve hot.

SHAK'S NAVY BEANS

½ lb. navy beans
½ oz. butter
¼ teaspoon pepper
¼ teaspoon allspices

1 onion
½ green apple
½ teaspoon salt
¼ teaspoon turmeric

Soak navy beans over night and boil for one-half hour, drain and dry. Cut onions and apple into small pieces, fry onions in butter and when about fried, add pepper, salt, turmeric and allspices, stirring well. Also add apple and navy beans; and while stirring sprinkle small amount of water and let this cook for ten minutes and serve while hot.

LIMA BEANS

½ lb. lima beans
½ oz. butter
¼ teaspoon pepper
¼ teaspoon allspices

1 onion
½ green apple
½ teaspoon salt
¼ teaspoon turmeric

Soak lima beans over night and boil for one-half hour and drain. Cut onion and apple into small pieces and fry onions in butter and when about fried add salt, pepper, turmeric, allspices and stir briskly. And while stirring, add apple and lima beans, sprinkle with water and let cook for about ten minutes and serve hot.

KIDNEY BEANS

½ lb. kidney beans
½ green apple
½ teaspoon salt
¼ teaspoon turmeric
1 onion
½ oz. butter
¼ teaspoon pepper
¼ teaspoon allspices

Soak kidney beans in water over night and boil for half an hour and drain. Cut onions and green apple into small pieces and fry onions in butter and when about fried, add salt, pepper, turmeric and allspices and stir briskly, and while stirring add apple and beans. Sprinkle with water and let cook for ten minutes and serve hot.

HARD BOILED EGGS

3 eggs
1 green pepper
½ oz. butter
¼ teaspoon pepper
1 onion
½ teaspoon salt
¼ teaspoon turmeric
¼ teaspoon curry powder

Boil eggs for fifteen minutes, remove shells and cut into four pieces each. Cut onions and green pepper into very small pieces. Fry onion in butter and when about fried, add salt, pepper, turmeric, curry powder and allspices, stirring well. Then add green pepper and eggs while stirring and sprinkle with melted butter and put in oven for ten minutes. Serve hot.

CORN (GREEN)

6 corn
½ green pepper
½ oz. butter
¼ teaspoon pepper
¼ teaspoon allspices
1 onion
½ apple
½ teaspoon salt
¼ teaspoon turmeric
¼ teaspoon cinnamon
¼ teaspoon paprika
¼ teaspoon curry powder

If green corn is used, cut from cob first. Cut onion, apple, green pepper into very small pieces. Fry onion in butter and when about fried, add salt, pepper, turmeric, curry powder, allspices and stir well. Then add corn, apple and green pepper also adding cup of hot water and stir good. Let this cook for fifteen minutes and serve hot.

GREEN PEAS (FRESH)

¼ peck peas or can of peas
½ stalk celery
½ teaspoon salt
¼ teaspoon turmeric
1 onion
½ oz. butter
½ teaspoon pepper
¼ teaspoon allspices

If fresh peas are used boil for one-half hour first, drain and dry. Cut onions and celery into small pieces and then fry onions in butter and when about fried, add salt, pepper, turmeric, allspices, stirring well. Then add peas and celery, sprinkle little water over and stir briskly. Cook this for ten minutes and serve hot.

TOMATOES

3. medium sized tomatoes or 1 can
1 green pepper
½ teaspoon salt
¼ teaspoon turmeric
¼ teaspoon curry powder
½ oz. pancake flour
½ oz. butter
½ teaspoon pepper
¼ teaspoon allspices
1 onion

If fresh tomatoes are used cut them into eight pieces. Then cut onions and green pepper into small pieces. Fry onions in butter and when about fried add salt, pepper, turmeric, curry powder, pancake flour and allspices, stirring well. Then add tomatoes, green peppers and stir good. Sprinkle a small amount of water over it and let cook for ten minutes and serve hot.

ASPARAGUS

1 bunch asparagus
1 green pepper
½ oz. pancake flour
½ oz. butter
¼ teaspoon pepper

1 onion
½ teaspoon salt
¼ teaspoon turmeric
¼ teaspoon curry powder
¼ teaspoon pepper

If fresh asparagus is used, boil from twenty to thirty minutes before using, then cut in half. Cut onions, green pepper into small pieces. Fry onions in butter and when about fried add pancake flour, salt, pepper, turmeric, curry powder, allspices and stir good. Then add asparagus and green peppers and last add 1 cup of water and stir briskly. Let this cook for ten minutes and serve hot.

GREEN PEAS (SHEKS)

½ lb. dried peas
½ stalk celery
½ oz. butter
¼ teaspoon pepper
¼ teaspoon allspices

1 onion
½ teaspoon salt
¼ teaspoon turmeric
¼ teaspoon curry powder

Cut onion and green pepper into very small pieces, doing same with celery, and mix them. Soak peas over night in water, and boil them for half hour, drain and dry on cloth. Then fry in butter the mixture of onion, celery and green pepper and when about fried, add to this mixture salt, pepper, turmeric, allspices and curry powder, stirring this well. Then add peas, and let cook for about ten minutes. Sprinkle little water on top if too dry. Serve hot.

BLACK EYE PEAS

½ lb. black eye peas
1 onion
½ teaspoon salt
¼ teaspoon turmeric

½ teaspoon pepper
¼ teaspoon allspices
½ oz. butter
½ stalk celery

Cut onions and celery in small pieces. Soak peas over night, drain and dry on cloth. Then fry onions in butter and when about fried, add salt, pepper, turmeric, allspices, and stir well. And while stirring add peas and celery, mix good. Sprinkle very little water over it and let cook for about ten minutes and serve hot.

BASUDI PUDDING

1 quart milk
½ tablespoon rice flour
¼ teaspoon nutmeg

¼ cup sugar
½ oz. shelled almonds

Remove shells from almods by soaking them ten minutes in boiling water and after removing cut in long, thin slices. Boil milk one-half hour on slow fire, and add to this rice flour or substitute. Boil this until it becomes thick, and after it thickens add sugar. Mix this well and when the sugar is dissolved, remove from fire and add the almonds and nutmeg. Serve cold.

BANANA PUDDING

3 bananas
1 pint milk
½ teaspoon vanilla

¼ cup sugar
¼ lb. melted sweet butter
½ oz. shelled almonds

Crush bananas through potato masher, adding to this sugar and melted butter. Mix together well or beat with egg-beater, and after doing this add the vanilla. To this add the milk (do not pour but add in small portions) and continue stirring; while doing so add the shelled and sliced almonds. Mix the pudding very good and serve. Serve cold.

EGG PUDDING

2 eggs
½ tablespoon rice flour or substitute
¼ teaspoon nutmeg

1 pint milk
¼ cup sugar
1 teaspoon shredded cocoanut

Beat the eggs and to this add the milk. Before adding the milk to the eggs dissolve the sugar in it first. After mixing this well add rice flour, nutmeg and continue stirring. Put this in oven and when cooked and also brown, remove from oven and dash it with shredded cocoanut. Let this cool or do not serve until it becomes cold.

POTATO PUDDING

2 medium sized potatoes
¼ lb. butter
½ oz. almonds, shelled

¼ cup sugar
Handful of raisins

Boil potatoes from twenty to thirty minutes and after pealing, mash with potato masher. Fry onions in butter and when about fried add raisins. When the raisins start to swell add the sugar and stir well. Put this in oven for about ten minutes and after removing from oven add the shelled almonds, which have been cut in long, thin slices. Stir together very good and serve cold.

PLAIN RICE PUDDING

1 pint milk
¼ teaspoon nutmeg

½ cup rice
¼ teaspoon sugar

Wash rice very good, or three times; put the quart of water on fire and when it starts to boil, add rice, letting this cook, and when almost cooked add milk and sugar. Stir very good so that it will not stick to the bottom of pan. When the rice is cooked, or until it becomes thick, remove from fire and dash with nutmeg. Serve cold.

RICE PUDDING DELUSCE

½ handful rice
½ oz. shelled almonds
¼ teaspoon nutmeg

1 quart milk
¼ cup sugar
¼ teaspoon ground cardamon seed

Remove shells from almonds by soaking them in boiling water for ten minutes; then cut in thin, long slices. Wash rice well, drain and dry on cloth; and when about dried rub well with one teaspoon of butter. Cook rice in milk, stirring continuously. When the rice is almost cooked add sugar and keep stirring until it becomes thick, then add the almonds and mix this well. Remove from stove and let cool, or do not serve it until cold.

CAULIFLOWER

1 small head cauliflower
½ green pepper
½ oz. butter
¼ teaspoon pepper
¼ teaspoon allspices

1 onion
½ stalk celery
½ teaspoon salt
¼ teaspoon turmeric
¼ teaspoon curry powder

Boil cauliflower and after boiled cut into small pieces. Cut onions, green pepper and celery into small pieces. Then fry onions in butter, and when about fried, add salt, pepper, turmeric, allspices and curry powder, stirring well. Add cauliflower, green pepper and celery, also sprinkle little water over it, and let cook for about ten minutes. Serve hot.

EGG PLANT

½ egg plant
½ stalk celery
½ teaspoon salt
¼ teaspoon turmeric
¼ teaspoon curry powder

1 onion
1 green pepper
½ oz. butter
¼ teaspoon pepper
¼ teaspoon allspices

Cut onions, green pepper and celery into very small pieces. Then cut egg plant into sixteen pieces, or medium sized pieces. Fry onions in butter and when about fried add salt, pepper, turmeric, allspices and curry powder, stirring well. Then add egg plant, celery and green pepper and stir briskly. Add to this one-half cup of water and let cook for about fifteen minutes and serve hot.

KHAMAN DHOKLA (IMITATION MEAT)

½ head cabbage
¼ lb. pancake flour
¼ teaspoon baking soda
¼ teaspoon allspices
¼ teaspoon curry powder

¼ cup butter or oil
1 green pepper
1 onion
½ teaspoon salt
¼ teaspoon turmeric

Cut cabbage in long, thin slices and then cut in very small pieces, doing same with onions and green pepper. After mixing them together add pancake flour, salt, pepper, all spices, curry powder, baking soda, turmeric and stir until well mixed. To this add enough water to make a very thick dough (thick enough to hold its shape). After rubbing the baking pan with butter and dusting with baking soda, turn the dough into this to bake. When baked brown, cut in small pieces and serve.

DHAKLI (MUSH)

¼ lb. cornmeal
1 tablespoon butter
¼ teaspoon allspices
¼ teaspoon turmeric

½ bunch green onions
½ teaspoon salt
¼ teaspoon pepper
½ green pepper

Cut onions and pepper into very small pieces. Take one pint of boiling water, and to this add salt, turmeric and cornmeal; stir well and let cook until it becomes a thick dough. Turn this dough into a flat pan which has been rubbed well with butter; then press this dough in pan about the thickness of half of an inch. When this dough gets cold, cut in diamond-shaped pieces. Fry the onions in butter and when about fried add salt, pepper, allspices and the dough, also adding the green pepper. After mixing well together sprinkle a small amount of water over top. Before removing from fire stir this mixture very good and serve hot.

(SHIRA) RAB PUDDING

½ cup flour
¼ cup sugar
1 pint hot water

¼ lb. butter
½ tablespoon shredded cocoanut

Dissolve sugar in water and boil for five minutes; keep this in warm place until ready to use. Fry flour in butter and keep stirring until it becomes light brown, and add to the water, letting this cook until it gets thick. Keep stirring so that it will not stick to the bottom of the pan, and sir continuously until it gets thick. Remove from fire, put on separate plates and dash with cocoanut. Serve hot.

SHERA PUDDING

½ cup cornmeal
¼ cup sugar
Handful raisins
¼ lb. butter
1 teaspoon cocoanut
1 pt. hot water

Dissolve sugar in 1 pint of water and boil for five minutes, keeping this in a warm place until ready to use. Fry cornmeal in butter until browned, and while stirring add the raisins. When the raisins begin to swell add the hot water with the sugar and stir well. Let this cook until all water disappears; stir and put in oven for ten minutes. Put in separate plates and sprinkle with shredded cocoanut. Serve hot.

NOODLE PUDDING

½ box fine noodles
½ oz. shelled almonds
½ pt. hot water
¼ lb. butter (sweet)
¼ cup sugar
Handful of raisins

Cut noodles so that the pieces are about one inch long. Boil almonds for five minutes and remove the shells, then cut lengthwise in small, thin slices. Put the sugar in water and boil for about five minutes, then remove from stove and keep in warm place for further use. Fry the noodles in butter until browned, doing this on slow fire, and add raisins, and when they start to swell, add hot water with the sugar and stir vigorously. Let this cook until all water disappears, then add almonds and mix well. Put in oven for ten minutes, remove and serve hot.

HALVA PUDDING

½ cup cream of wheat
¼ lb. butter (sweet)
¼ cup sugar
½ oz. shelled almonds
Handful of raisins
½ pt. hot water

Put sugar in the water and boil for about ten minutes or until it boils down so that there is only about ¼ pint left; remove and keep in warm place. Remove shells from almonds by putting them in hot water for five minutes; after doing this cut in thin slices. Fry cream of wheat in butter and when browned add raisins and still well; then add the hot sugared water, stirring briskly. Let this cook until all water disappears, then add almonds, stirring good, and after doing this put in oven for ten minutes. Serve hot.

SAMOSAN FRITTERS

1 onion (green)
¼ lb. oil or butter
¼ teaspoon allspices
½ green pepper
2 potatoes
¼ lb. flour
½ teaspoon salt

Make a thick dough of flour, and roll with rolling pin into very thin layer, or about 1-16 of an inch thick, doing this on a greased board, sprinkled with flour. Cut this into strips about the size of two inches by four inches. Boil potatoes and after peeling, mash with potato masher. Cut green onion and pepper into small pieces; fry onion in butter and when about fried add potatoes and green pepper, stirring well; also adding salt and allspices; mix well and remove from fire. Put about one tablespoon of this mixture on the strip of dough, which has been previously cut into strips, and fold in closed triangles. Fry in hot butter or oil and when light brown remove and serve hot.

DHEBRAN COOKIE

¼ lb. flour
¼ lb. butter or oil
1 tablespoon molasses
½ tablespoon salt

Rub flour with one tablespoon cream or milk, butter and molasses, adding enough water to make a thick dough. Then make six even portions of this dough and roll each into a round cake; when finished, fry in butter on both sides until it becomes brown. This can be served either hot or cold, with tea or coffee.

ONION BHAJIYAN (FRITTERS)

1 onion
¼ teaspoon allspices
¼ teaspoon turmeric
¼ teaspoon baking soda
¼ lb. butter or oil
¼ lb. cornmeal
¼ lb. pancake flour
½ teaspoon salt

Cut onion into thick slices, about ¼ inch in thickness. Mix corn and pancake flour. Dissolve salt in one cup of water, adding the mixture of flour, also turmeric, baking soda and allspices, and finally add enough water to make a soft dough, like pancake dough. Then dip each slice of onion in this dough and fry in butter or oil until well browned. Serve hot.

POTATO BHAJIYAN (FRITTERS

¼ lb. butter or oil
¼ teaspoon allspices
¼ teaspoon turmeric
¼ teaspoon salt
1 potato
¼ lb. cornmeal
¼ lb. pancake flour
¼ teaspoon baking soda

Cut potatoes into slices about ¼ inch in thickness. Dissolve salt in one cup of water, adding the mixture of flours, also turmeric, baking soda and allspices, and then add enough water to make thick dough, similar to pancake dough. Dip the potato slices in the mixture and fry in butter, doing this separately with each potato slice, frying until both sides become light brown. Serve hot.

ROTALY BREAD

½ lb. white flour
½ teaspoon salt
2 oz. butter

Dissolve salt in one cup of water and add to this the flour. Also add enough water to make very thick dough, thick enough to hold its shape. Work the dough for at least ten or fifteen minutes, then take two ounces at a time, roll with rolling pin and put in oven for ten minutes, doing same with the remaining dough; remove from oven and add one tablespoon of butter to each of this roty. Serve while hot.

BHAKHARI

½ lb. white flour
½ teaspoon salt
2 oz. butter

Dissolve salt in one cup of water and add to this the flour, which has been rubbed with one tablespoon of butter; then add enough water to make a thick dough, thick enough to hold its shape, and work this dough for about ten minutes. Divide in four parts, roll each part with rolling pin into thin round cakes and about one-fourth of an inch in thickness and six inches in diameter. Now put one tablespoon of butter in skillet, then put cake in butter; when the cake becomes brown, turn on other side and as it gets brown, remove, and do the same with the remaining cakes. When all are cooked, rub with butter and serve hot.

PURI (THE FLUFFY WALLS)

½ lb. white flour
¼ lb. butter
¼ teaspoon salt
¼ teaspoon baking soda

Dissolve salt in water as in previous recipes and rub flour with butter, adding to this baking soda. And to this add the salt water mentioned above, and if necessary add enough water to make a thick, hard dough to hold its shape. Divide in sixteen parts and round with hand, roll with rolling pin one-eighth of an inch in thickness and three to four inches in diameter and let this dry. When all are rolled, start frying in butter, and whey they puff or get light turn on other side, and when both sides get brown remove from skillet, doing same with the rest of the puris. Serve hot.

MONWALA ROTALA (THICK, CRISP BREAD)

¼ lb. white flour
1 tablespoon butter
¼ teaspoon salt
¼ teaspoon baking soda

Rub flour with butter and dissolve salt in cup of water. Add enough of this water to the flour to make a tough dough, thick enough to hold its shape. Work this dough for about ten minutes, then roll all of the dough with the rolling pin in round cake form, about one-fourth of an inch in thickness and about six inches in diameter. Put in oven and bake until both sides become brown, and when browned remove from oven and rub with one tablespoon of butter. Serve hot.

ROTY

¼ lb. cornmeal
¼ lb. white flour
½ teaspoon salt
2 tablespoons butter

Dissolve salt in one cup of water and add to this the mixture of flours. Also add enough water to make a very thick dough, or thick enough to hold its shape. Work the dough for at least ten to fifteen minutes. Divide this dough into eight parts and roll thin, one-eighth of an inch, and six inches in diameter. Put this in oven and cook for 15 minutes, remove from oven and rub with tablespoon of butter while hot, also doing same with the rest of the dough and rubbing each with butter. Serve while hot.

BHAKHARI ROTALA

¼ lb. white flour
¼ lb. cornmeal
2 tablespoons butter
½ teaspoon salt
¼ teaspoon baking soda

Dissolve salt in cup of water and add to this the mixture of flour, which has been rubbed with two tablespoons of butter, and then add baking soda, also enough water to make a thick dough, or thick enough to hold its shape. Work this dough for about ten to fifteen minutes, then divide into four parts, rolling each part into thin round cake about one-fourth inch thick and six inches in diameter. Put in oven and let cook until it becomes brown on both sides, and when all are done rub each with tablespoon of butter and serve while hot.

DAHINTHARA (DELICIOUS COOKIES)

¼ lb. white flour
½ lb. pancake flour
¼ cup milk
¼ lb. butter
¼ teaspoon baking soda
¼ teaspoon salt

Rub flour with two tablespoons of melted butter, then add one-half cup of condensed milk or cream; also rub pancake flour with two tablespoons of butter and mix both flours together, stirring well. Add to this the salt and baking soda, then add enough water to make a thick dough, or thick enough to hold its shape. Divide the dough into sixteen small, round, flat cakes, rolled and pressed with hand. Fry them in butter on both sides and when brown take from fire and serve hot.

KHARI PURI

½ lb. white flour
¼ teaspoon baking soda
¼ lb. butter
½ teaspoon salt

Rub flour with two tablespoons of butter, then dissolve salt and baking soda in one-half cup of water, adding this to the flour, and mix well. To this add enough water to form a hard, thick dough, or thick enough to hold its shape. Work this dough for about ten to fifteen minutes, then roll this on a greased board which has been sprinkled with flour, in a very thin layer, about 1-16 of an inch in thickness. When all are rolled, cut in long, thin strips and then recut into one-half inch wide and one inch long strips, and fry in butter, and when browned remove from fire and serve hot.

EGGPLANT BHAJIYAN

½ thin eggplant
½ teaspoon salt
¼ teaspoon baking soda
¼ teaspoon allspices
¼ lb. cornmeal
¼ lb. pancake flour
¼ lb. oil or butter
¼ teaspoon turmeric

Cut eggplant into thin slices, about one-eighth of an inch in thickness. Dissolve salt in one cup of water, adding the mixture of flours, also turmeric, baking soda and allspices, and finally add enough water to make a dough similar to pancake dough, then dip each slice in dough and fry on both sides in butter or oil until brown. Serve hot.

GREEN PEPPER (FRITTERS)

1 large green pepper
¼ lb. cornmeal
¼ lb. pancake flour
¼ lb. butter or oil
½ teaspoon salt
¼ teaspoon allspices
¼ teaspoon baking soda
¼ teaspoon turmeric

Cut green peppers into four long slices. Dissolve salt in one cup of water, adding the mixture of flours, also turmeric, baking soda, allspices, then add enough water to make thick dough, similar to pancake dough, and dip slices of pepper in dough and fry in butter until they become light brown. Serve hot.

BANANA FRITTERS

2 oz. pancake flour
2 oz. cornmeal
¼ lb. butter or oil
¼ teaspoon turmeric
1 green banana (not ripe)
½ teaspoon salt
½ teaspoon baking soda
½ teaspoon allspices

Dissolve baking soda and allspices in one cup of water, then add the mixture of flours and mix good. Also add enough water to make it thick, like pancake dough. Then cut banana into eight long pieces, dip and smear with this dough and fry until it becomes a light brown, doing same with each slice of banana. Serve hot.

SWEET POTATO FRITTERS

½ sweet potato
¼ lb. butter or oil
¼ teaspoon turmeric
¼ teaspoon baking soda
2 oz. corn flour
2 oz. pancake flour
¼ teaspoon allspices
½ teaspoon salt

Mix both flours together, dissolving salt in one cup of water, and add mixture of flours, also add to this turmeric, baking soda and mix well. Add to this enough water to make it thick, like pancake dough. Then cut sweet potato into thin slices, or about one-eighth of an inch in thickness, and dip separately in dough and dry until light brown. Serve hot.

COFFEE

1 heaping tablespoon coffee
½ cup cream
3 cups of water
sugar

Soak coffee in one-half cup of water. Put six cups of water into coffee pot to boil, and when water is almost at the boiling point add the soaked coffee to the water. Let this percolate about ten to fifteen minutes. Remove from fire and serve hot. Add enough cream and sugar to suit individual taste.

COFFEE PUNCH

1 heaping tablespoon coffee
½ lemon
3 cups of water
sugar
pieces of ice

Make coffee as described above. Let this cool and then add lemon juice and one-half cup of sugar. Mix this very good and serve in six glasses, adding to this pieces of ice in each glass. Serve with slices of lemon.

TEA

1 heaping tablespoon tea
¼ cup sugar
3 cups water
¼ cup cream

Boil water, and when it begins to boil add tea. Remove and cover the pot. Let this set for fifteen minutes before serving. Stir and serve with cream and sugar.

ICED TEA

1 tablespoon tea
¼ cup sugar
3 cups water
½ lemon
pieces of ice

Prepare tea as described above and when ready, cool; then add sugar and serve in individual glasses. Add to each glass slice of lemon and pieces of ice and serve.

SWEET MILK DRINK

1 raw egg
1 pint milk
3 drops vanilla
⅛ teaspoon turmeric
⅛ cup sugar
pieces ice

Dissolve sugar in milk and add raw egg and beat together with eggbeater. Then add turmeric and vanilla, beating good. Serve in individual glasses with pieces of ice.

PASTRIES

LADU (SWEET BALLS)

½ lb. white flour
¾ lb. sugar
½ cup milk
¼ lb. sweet butter (unsalted)
¼ teaspoon salt

Dissolve salt in little water and add to the flour. Then rub the flour with two tablespoons of butter and add enough milk to make a thick dough or thick enough to hold its shape. Knead the dough for ten to fifteen minutes, then roll into two cakes, about one-fourth of an inch in thickness and six inches in diameter. Rub butter on both sides of cakes and put in oven and bake until it becomes brown. When browned remove from oven, let cool and crush into powder form, then add melted butter and sugar and roll into round balls. Serve cold.

MALPUWA (THIN SWEET CAKE)

¼ lb. wheat flour
¼ lb. pancake flour
¼ teaspoon baking soda
½ lb. butter (sweet)
¼ lb. sugar

Mix both flours together, then add sugar and baking soda mixing thoroughly. To this add enough water to make a thin dough, similar to pancake dough. Put butter in skillet and pour one cupful of dough in this and let fry in butter on both sides until brown and when browned remove and also do same with the remaining dough. When all are done, serve either hot or cold.

JALEBI (SWEET DAINTY)

¼ lb. white flour
½ lb. sugar
¼ teaspoon baking soda
¼ lb. butter

Mix baking soda with flour and add enough water to make a dough, similar to pancake dough. Then make syrup from the mixture of sugar and water. Take an empty clean can and make a hole in the bottom about 5-16 of an inch in diameter. Fill can about one-fourth full with this dough, keeping finger on the hole in the can; then put butter in frying pan and when about to boil remove finger from the hole and with a twist of the hand make a couple circles, making a cake like doughnuts in the hot butter, and fry brown. When browned, lift from butter and dip in hot syrup, which has been previously made. Remove from syrup and serve either hot or cold.

PURAN POLI (SWEET PEA PIE)

½ lb. yellow peas
½ lb. butter
¼ teaspoon baking soda
¼ lb. white flour
¼ lb. sugar
¼ teaspoon salt

Soak peas over night boil for one-half hour with one-half teaspoon of baking soda, and when boiled until soft remove from fire; drain water. Crush the peas well with cup and to this add the sugar, mixing well. Take white flour and add butter and rub well; then add enough water to make a thick dough, or thick enough to hold its shape; take a small portion of dough and form into a shell with the thumb and in the hollow of the shell add the mixture of the peas and sugar. Close the shell from the top and press into small cake with hand, then roll with rolling pin from four to five inches in diameter and about one-fourth inch in thickness. Being careful not to let the mixture come out of the shell, fry in butter, and when fried brown on both sides serve hot. Serving lots of butter on top.

SUKHADI PAK (HINDU FUDGE)

½ lb. whole wheat flour
¼ lb. butter
¼ cup milk
½ lb. molasses
½ tablespoon shredded cocoanut

Rub the flour with milk and after rubbing well fry flour in butter, and when browned add molasses, and let this cook for fifteen minutes, stirring continuously, being careful that it doesn't stick. Then pour this into flat pan and pat down; let cool and cut in two-inch square pieces. Ready to serve.

MAGAJ (DAINTY BALLS)

¼ lb. white flour
¼ lb. pastry flour
½ lb. sugar
⅛ cup milk
½ lb. butter

Mix the flours and rub with butter, rubbing well. Fry the flour in butter, continuously stirring, and when browned add sugar; stir and mix well. Let this cool a little and take small portions and round into small balls. Serve cold.

JAMBU (CREAMED BALLS)

¼ lb. white flour
¼ lb. butter
½ cup milk
¼ lb. sugar
½ teaspoon baking soda

Mix flour and baking soda together, then add enough cream to make a thick dough, or thick enough to hold its shape. Then take small portions, round them in small balls with hand and fry in butter. When browned dip in syrup, that is, sugar and water boiled together until it forms a syrup. Serve either hot or cold.

SAUCES

BANANA SAUCES

½ banana
pinch salt
½ glass buttermilk
¼ teaspoon mustard (Colman's)

Chop banana in very small pieces; add to this buttermilk and beat well with egg-beater and after mixing them good, add salt and Colman's powdered mustard and beat well. When mixed good it is ready to serve.

SPICED SAUCE

½ teaspoon cayenne pepper
½ teaspoon black pepper
½ teaspoon allspices
½ teaspoon paprika
½ teaspoon cinnamon
1 tablespoon butter
juice from ½ lemon

Mix Cayenne pepper, salt, paprika, cinnamon, pepper and allspices together, then add to this lemon juice and mix good. Melt butter and when melted pour in dish and add the mixture while stirring. After stirring good it is ready to serve.

FRIED GREEN PEPPERS

3 green peppers
½ teaspoon salt
1½ tablespoons butter
½ teaspoon pepper

Split peppers on one side and insert the mixture of salt and black pepper. Then put butter in frying pan and when melted put peppers in the butter to fry. Turn them on all sides and when they become soft and browned on different spots, remove from stove. Serve hot.

STUFFED GREEN PEPPERS

3 green peppers
1 onion
¼ teaspoon turmeric
¼ teaspoon pepper
½ cup mashed potatoes
¼ lb. butter
¼ lb. curry powder
¼ teaspoon paprika

Cut onions in very small pieces and fry in butter and when about fried add salt, pepper, turmeric and curry powder. Stir good, then add mashed potatoes and continue stirring until everything is very well mixed. Then split green peppers on one side and fill with the mixture made as above. Fry them in butter and when fried good remove from fire and serve hot.

CHILI SAUCE

1 tomato
pinch salt
¼ teaspoon cayenne pepper
½ teaspoon paprika
¼ teaspoon turmeric

Crush tomatoes, and when crushed add salt, pepper, paprika and cayenne pepper and beat it good; then add turmeric and beat it again, and when thoroughly mixed remove the loose tomato skin from the sauce and it is ready to serve.

GREEN PEPPER CHATNI

1 green pepper
bunch parsley
½ teaspoon paprika
½ lemon
¼ teaspoon cayenne pepper
pinch salt

Crush green peppers, also removing seeds before crushing. Cut up parsley in very small pieces, then add the green peppers and crush together well. When crushed, add to this salt, pepper, paprika and cayenne pepper. Mix this well and when mixed add juice from one-half lemon and mix good.

SOUR MILK AND RED PEPPER CHATNI

1 teaspoon butter
½ teaspoon paprika
½ teaspoon salt
¼ teaspoon cayenne pepper
½ pt. sour milk or buttermilk

Mix salt, pepper, paprika and cayenne pepper in plate and when well mixed add to this melted butter and while stirring good add buttermilk and take from stove. Serve hot.

CHATNIES—APPLE

½ apple (sour)
¼ teaspoon cayenne pepper
pinch salt
½ green pepper
½ teaspoon paprika
juice from ½ lemon

Peel and crush apple, also green pepper, and when crushed add salt, pepper, Cayenne pepper and paprika, mixing this good with egg-beater, then add juice of half lemon. Mix this good again and it is ready to serve.

GRAPE CHATNI

¼ lb. grapes
¼ teaspoon red pepper
juice from half lemon
½ green pepper
½ teaspoon paprika

Crush seedless grapes and green peppers, and when crushed add to this salt, pepper, paprika and Cayenne pepper. Mix this good with egg-beater; when mixed add to this the lemon juice and beat good. Serve.

COCOA

1 tablespoon cocoa
¼ cup cream
½ cup sugar
1 pint milk

Mix cocoa in one-half cup of water and when it becomes in a paste form thin down by continuously adding hot water. Boil in pint of hot water for about fifteen minutes, then add quart of milk, adding to this sugar. Serve in individual cups. Serve hot.

CHOCOLATE PUNCH

1 tablespoon cocoa
¼ cup cream
½ cup sugar
pieces of ice
1 pint milk

Prepare cocoa as described above by boiling in milk, and after removing from fire, cool. And when it becomes cold add one-half cup cream and serve in individual glasses with pieces of ice. Serve cold.

Different Fruits, Nuts and Spices

Fruits

Apples
Apricots
Cantaloup
Watermelon
Pomegranate
Banana
Pears
Peaches
Lemons
Oranges
Tangerine
Plums
Pineapple
Grapefruit
Grapes
Mango
Honeydew
Pumpkin
Raspberry
Gooseberry
Huckleberry
Blackberry
Cherries

Spices

Pepper (black)
Pepper (white)
Pepper (Cayenne)
Paprika
Turmeric
Cinnamon
Cardamon
Curry powder
Cinnamon bark
Cloves
Allspices
Mixed spices

Mixed Nuts & Dried Fruits

Almonds
Dates
Hickory nuts
Cocoanut
Pistachio
Walnuts
Raisins
Salt
Sugar
Honey
Molasses
Milk (sweet)
Milk (sour)
Buttermilk

Time Required for Cooking Vegetables

Vegetables	Time
Artichoke	30 to 45 minutes
Asparagus	20 to 30 minutes
String beans	30 to 1 hour
Lima beans	45 to 1 hour
Kidney beans	50 to 1 hour
Soy beans	50 to 1 hour
Navy beans	50 to 1 hour
Green peas (dried)	55 to 1 hour
Black Eye peas	50 to 1 hour
Split peas or other lentils	55 to 1¼ hours
Beets (young and green)	30 to 45 minutes
Sprouts	15 to 30 minutes
Cabbage	30 to 45 minutes
Carrots	15 to 45 minutes
Cauliflower	25 to 45 minutes
Celery	20 to 30 minutes
Corn (on the cob)	10 to 30 minutes
Dandelion	30 to 40 minutes
Eggplant	30 to 40 minutes
Onions	15 to 30 minutes
Parsnips	30 to 45 minutes
Green peas (fresh)	15 to 30 minutes
Potatoes (sweet or white)	20 to 45 minutes
Spinach	15 to 30 minutes
Squash (fresh)	20 to 35 minutes
Tomatoes	15 to 30 minutes
Turnips	20 to 30 minutes
Rice	
Macaroni	15 to 45 minutes
Kail	20 to 30 minutes
Lettuce	15 to 20 minutes
Parsley	
Peppers (fry)	10 minutes
Radishes	
Cucumber	

Contents

Yogi Wassan Plans Hindu Yoga Yug	10
Chart of Holy Chant—Soroda System	10
Ladder of Development	12
Ida, Pingala, Sushmuna	12
100 Secret Keys of the Soroda System of Yoga Philosophy	14
Secret Keys of Ancient Wisdom	14
How to Recharge and Vibrate Everything	14
How to Chant Holy Word for Spirituality	16
How to Chant Yoga Secret Mantram for Everything	16
How to Chant for Mental and Spiritual Power	18
How to Chant Mentally with Soundless Sound	18
Secret Keys for Opening the Door of Knowledge, Fountain of Cosmic Vibration and Cosmic Rays, Elevating You From the Ignorant State of Consciousness to the Cosmic State of Consciousness	18
How I Get the Occult Power for Recharging the Optic Nerve	22
Occult Concentration No. 3	28
Occult Concentration No. 4—Sun Practice	28
Occult Concentration No. 5	30
Occult Concentration No. 6	30
Occult Concentration No. 7	30
How I Bathe My Eyes	32
How I Massage the Body	34
How I Make Home-made Candy	34
Star Chart No. 3—Showing Proper Method for Concentration for Opening the Third Eye and Developing the Sixth Sense	36
Star Chart No. 3—For Making the Eyes Strong for One Hundred Years Without Glasses	42
Chart of Soroda System—Rishi and Devo Shamadi	48
As We Start on Our Journey	52
Basic Truths of Soroda System Yoga Philosophy	54
Padam—Asana—Uprightness of Power	60
Padam Asana or Posture	62
Straightening the Spine	64
Benefits of Rajana Asana	66
Mantra Yoga	68
The Seven Holy Words	74
Using the Mantra Yoga	76
Yogi Method of Teaching	78
The Robe	80
Shrine for Concentration and Meditation	82
Padam Asana	84
Modified Padam Asana	84
What Padam Concentration Really Is	84
That Ye May Know Yourselves	88
The Three Great Vibratory Forces of the Atma	94
Emotive Energy—Love	96

Life or Creative Energy	96
You Are God of Your Body Universe	98
Exercise for Awakening Consciousness of the Body Universe	100
The Tongue	106
The Humming Breath	108
Chant for Strengthening Eyes, Improving Hearing, and Relieving Catarrh	112
Hoong, Yang, Yang, Yang Chant for Power	112
Physical Exercises—On Rising in Morning—for Relaxation	114
Care of Mouth	116
Food	120
Diet Must Be Adapted to Individual Needs According to an Individual Analysis of Each Person	120
Water	124
Regulation of Eliminative Processes	126
Home-made Laxative Food Candy	130
The Seven Mantrams	130
Pranayama—Control of Prana	132
The Slow Breath—Storing Personal Magnetism	132
Physical Benefits	134
Proportions of Various Parts of the Body	136
Early Morning Exercise	138
Baths, Body Massage and Scalp Massage	140
Ida, Pingla and Sukhmuna—for Personal Magnetism	142
The Science of Magnetic Breath	142
Key for Opening These Nadi	146
Invisible Vibration for Concentration of All Forces to Resist Attack or Make Grand Assault for Business Success	152
The Magnetic Tones	152
The Power Tone	158
Practice for Developing the Three Tones	160
How to Make the Ether Tube—for Occult and Mental Telepathy, Physical-Clairaudience, and Thought Transference	162
Definite Instructions for Forming the Ether Tube	164
Charging the Body with Atmic Energy	170
Intensifying Dynamic Activity of Mind Emotive Force or Creative Centers—at Will	172
Invisible Vibration	174
Dynamic Emotive (Attractive) Power	176
Charging the Love-Brain for Telepathic Love Transference	178
Advanced Practice	182
Dynamic Creative Power—Stowing Life-Prana	182
Charging the Body for Creative Effort	184
Opening the Solar Plexus	186
Grunting Breath	188
Invisible Chanting	190
Etheric Vibration	190
Balance or Poise of the Body	192
Exercise for Developing Poise or Balance	194

Advanced Exercise—Vibrating Mind Brain	194
Shoes—a Factor in Bodily Poise	196
Spiritual Breath—for Telepathic Development	198
Advanced Exercise—Humming Breath for Clairaudience	198
Exercises for Improving Eyesight and Hearing	202
Exercises for Developing Occult Power	202
The Hero Posture	204
Strengthening the Eyes	208
Massage for Relaxing Neck Muscles	214
Eye Exercise to Be Taken Without Chart	216
General Exercise for Quickening the Activity of the Brain Centers of Motion, Color, Sound, and Direction	218
Color	220
Exercise for Improving the Hearing	222
Strengthening the Eyes	224
First Concentration Exercise for Clairvoyance and Clairaudience	224
Second Concentration Exercise for Developing Clairaudience, etc.	226
Exercise with Blue Light for Vibrating Retina of Eye and for Strengthening Eye Muscles	228
Vitalizing Eye-Muscles and Brain Centers by Rotary Exercise and Spiritual Breath—Without Light	228
Exercise for the Muscles of the Eyes with "Black Star" Chart	230
"Levitation Exercise" for Developing Occult Power	232
Advanced Course—Soroda-Yoga Philosophy	236
Postures	240
Qualities Developed	250
Chakras—Kala and Sahansrara	262
Mudras	266
Yogis Automatic Devine Healing and Self Healing Called Mantram Yoga in Sanscript	274
Exercise for Awakening Consciousness of the Body Universe	274
Yogis Auto-suggestion Mantram	280
How I Chant Holy Word for Cosmic Vibration	280
Maha Atma Bramvidya Brahm Giyan, Vigiyan, Jeven Mukti	282
Rajah Yoga System of Munee and Rishee Philosophy	282
Tattwa Pirkirtee—Pirkirtee Purusha—Manish Avratara	282
Chant Chart	287
Practical Breathing for Health	288
Secret Key for the Yoga Philosophy, Ida, Pingla, Sukhmuna	288
Mahan Wack of the Four Vedas of the Sanscript, Reg Veda, Pragiya, Nama, Nad Barum	296
Vojar Veda, Ahang Burum Usmee	296
Shaman Veda, Tat Twang Masee	296
Atherban Veda, Aing Atma Buram	298
Ida, Pingla, Sukhmuna	300
Suake Breathing—Cat Breathing	304
Dog Breathing—Frog and Leach Breathing	306
Vibration Chart	312
The Optic Nerve	314

The Ear	318
The Adenoids	320
The Mouth, Throat, Tonsils and Teeth	326
The Thyroid Gland	328
The Liver	330
The Stomach	332
The Heart and Blood Purifier	336
All over the Body	342
Eight Glands and Plexuses	344
How to Use Yogi Wassin's Cosmic Concentration and Blood Irrigation Button	351
Price List Yogi Wassin's Books and Charts	355
Foods and Their Relation to Health	356
Combination Recipes	359
How I Develop My Body	359
How I Bathe My Eyes	360
Candle Exercise	360
How to Make Home-made Spice	361
How I Make Home-made Candy	361
How I Prepare my Egg-Nog	361
How I Make Almond Pudding and Almond Milk	361
How I Eat Olive Oil and Eggs for Purifying the Blood	362
How I Drink Almond Milk	362
What I Do Not Eat or Drink	362
How I Eat Fruit	362
How I Make Home-made Oil	363
What I Do for Deafness and Buzzing in Ear	363
How I Take a Bath the Year Round	363
How I Take a Cold Sitz Bath	364
How I Take a Buttermilk Massage	364
How I Shampoo My Hair	364
How I Take a Warm Bath	365
What I Would Do if I Should Have a Hemorrhage or Diarrhea	365
How I Remove Wrinkles and Stay Young	365
How I Make Chicken Soup	366
How I Reduce Weight	366
My Directions for Bathing and Swimming	366
Some Things You Should and Should Not Eat and Drink	367
How I Make Date Butter	368
Date and Nut Butter	368
Hindoo Yogi Food for Keeping Young	368
How to Use Egg Yolks for Increasing Weight and Rejuvenation	368
How to Use Egg Yolks—Easy Way	369
Oranges and Lemons	369
Do Not Eat Chicken Soup	369
How to Use Watermelon	370
Watermelon Syrup	370
Cantaloupe Butter	370
Peppe Cake or Yogi Omelette	370

Hamburger Steak	371
Carrot Pudding	371
About Vegetables, etc.	372
Bread and Cereals	372
How to Use Fruit—Any Fruit	372
Cactus Syrup	373
Cactus Candy	373
Tomato Drink	373
Green Pepper Syrup	373
Syrup Flavoring	374
Date Fruit Flavoring	374
Almond Flavoring	374
Yogi Food No. 1	374
Yogi Food No. 2	375
Yogi Food No. 3	375
Hindu Curry Dishes	376
Onions	377
Shrimp and Onions	377
Other Foods for Strengthening Vital Forces	378
For General Body Growth and Rejuvenation of Cells of Body	378
Special Recipes	378
Areca Nut Powder Tea	378
Hindoo Tooth Powder	379
Curry Vegetable Cook Book	380

CPSIA information can be obtained
at www.ICGtesting.com
Printed in the USA
BVOW09s2327280118
506482BV00001B/199/P

9 781162 570563